Fighting Back

Fighting Back

Winning the War against Terrorism

Edited by
Neil C. Livingstone
Terrell E. Arnold

Lexington Books
D.C. Heath and Company/Lexington, Massachusetts/Toronto

363.32
F 471

Credits for photographs and cartoons following p. 144:

All photographs used with the permission of AP/Wide World Photos.
Flag cartoon © 1984 San Diego Union. Reprinted by permission of Copley News Service.
Terrorist/Diplomat cartoon reprinted by permission of John Treves, Albuquerque Journal, © 1984.
Bullseye cartoon reprinted by permission of Clyde Wells, The Augusta Chronicle.
Shoot Back cartoon © 1985 Tribune Media Services. Reprinted by permission.

Library of Congress Cataloging-in-Publication Data
Main entry under title:

Fighting back.

   Bibliography: p.
   Includes index.
   1. Terrorism—Addresses, essays, lectures. 2. Terrorism—Addresses, essays, lectures. I. Livingstone, Neil C. II. Arnold, Terrell E.
   HV6431.F54   1985   363.3'2   85-18084
   ISBN 0-669-10808-1
   ISBN 0-669-11139-2 (pbk.)

Published simultaneously in Canada
Printed in the United States of America
Casebound International Standard Book Number: 0-669-10808-1
Paperbound International Standard Book Number: 0-669-11139-2
Library of Congress Catalog Card Number: 85-18084

The paper used in this publication meets the minimum requirements of American National Standard for Information Sciences—Permanence of Paper for Printed Library Materials, ANSI Z39.48-1984. ∞™

To our wives, Susan and Yvonne,
who were indispensable to this study
by being indispensable to us.

Contents

Foreword   ix
Robert C. McFarlane

1. Democracy under Attack   1
    Neil C. Livingstone and *Terrell E. Arnold*

2. The Rise of State-Sponsored Terrorism   11
    Neil C. Livingstone and *Terrell E. Arnold*

3. Terrorist Violence: Its Mechanics and Countermeasures   25
    Christine C. Ketcham and *Harvey J. McGeorge II*

4. Vehicle Bombs: Death on Wheels   35
    Beth A. Salamanca

5. Organized to Combat Terrorism   49
    William R. Farrell

6. Target America: The Undeclared War   59
    James Berry Motley

7. The War of Words: Can Diplomacy Be Effective?   85
    Robert M. Sayre

8. Executive Protection: Living Long in a Dangerous World   95
    Harvey J. McGeorge II and *Charles F. Vance*

9. Proactive Responses to Terrorism: Reprisals, Preemption, and Retribution   109
    Neil C. Livingstone

10. Covert Responses: The Moral Dilemma   133
Guy B. Roberts

11. The Legal Case for Using Force   145
Victoria Toensing

12. Using the Law to Combat Terrorism   157
Harry H. Almond, Jr.

13. Rewriting the Rules of Engagement   175
Terrell E. Arnold

14. Moral Response to Terrorism   191
James Tunstead Burtchaell

15. Terrorism and the Media Revolution   213
W. D. Livingstone

16. Fighting Back   229
Terrell E. Arnold and *Neil C. Livingstone*

Afterword   249
Neil C. Livingstone and *Terrell E. Arnold*

Index   253

About the Editors and Contributors   265

Foreword

Robert C. McFarlane

A cts of terrorism, calculated political crimes against people, have emerged as the chosen instrument for a new and vicious pattern of international bargaining. Violent acts have become the easy option for groups that feel otherwise they will not be heard, and for states that lack the power, wisdom, or patience to pursue their causes through peaceful give and take. That pattern is a trap that locks a country like Lebanon into a repetitive, self-feeding cycle of violence, and visits on cities of the West a plague of terrorist crimes, committed mostly by traveling terrorists against people of other countries.

As we recently were reminded by the hijacking of TWA Flight 847, the possible responses to an act of terrorism may not be swift, or simple, or satisfying. When the 847 case was resolved, we were all grateful that our people were free. We were frustrated, though, because no forthright rejoinder to the cold-blooded murder of one American and the confinement of thirty-nine others seemed ready to hand. What we really learned in this seventeen-day ordeal was that reason or logic carried little weight in the charged atmosphere of violence, stress, and excitement created by a terrorist attack.

In national security terms, terrorist attacks place leadership in a quandry. The nation is not in any immediate sense threatened. Attacks are short; they do not occur on a battlefield or in enemy territory; they are likely instead to occur on a city street of a friendly country. The adversary usually remains hidden and undeclared until after the attack.

It is difficult to focus the immense resources of a strategic power on this kind of target. But the attacks must concern us. The casualties and the human distress caused by such acts are a worry well beyond their numbers. We cannot forget. Yet, for a large, open democratic society with global responsibilities, the answers do not come easily.

This book identifies and discusses the important issues we must address

---

Mr. McFarlane is assistant to the president for national security affairs.

in winning the fight against terrorism. It does not prescribe remedies or get caught up in pushing pet formulas. One of the most compelling thoughts in the whole book is a quotation from Count von Moltke, who said: "Strategy is a system of makeshifts." That sense of difficulty with designing an integrated response is uniquely apt for the case of terrorism.

Our government is working to respond effectively to terrorism in all the policy areas discussed by the authors. We cannot attack the problem with any hope of success on only one front, and we cannot go it alone. The many different lines of action outlined in the last chapter must all be pursued. So, too, must others, like arranging a peace in the Middle East and persuading the Soviet Union and its allies to stop using support for low-level violence as an instrument of warfare against the West.

We can win the war against terrorism, but as this book makes clear, there are no shortcuts. In seeking to win, we must protect our values, institutions, friendships, and alliances, and we must help those with legitimate grievances to find ways of achieving just ends without resort to terrorism. This book helps to express those needs and to map many of the ways we might serve them; I strongly urge everyone who is interested in trying to understand and solve this problem to read it.

1
Democracy under Attack

Neil C. Livingstone
Terrell E. Arnold

While the continental United States has been spared much of the terrorism epidemic in the rest of the world in recent years, U.S. citizens (diplomats, business executives, and military personnel) and property increasingly have been targeted by foreign terrorists. Even more ominous, some nations have discovered that terrorism represents a cheap and effective method of warfare against more powerful adversaries whose arsenals and weapons are of little comfort against small bands of marauding proxy forces armed with the latest technologies, imagination, and stealth. Today international terrorists and their patrons are, in effect, at war with the United States, and it is only a matter of time before they decide to carry the war to U.S. shores.

In recent months leftist terrorist groups in Europe have coalesced into a new anti-NATO (North Atlantic Treaty Organization), anti-U.S. alliance, what Italian Defense Minister Giovanni Spadolini has described as a kind of "terrorist multinational . . . capable of striking throughout Europe."[1] Anchored around elements of West Germany's Red Army Faction, France's Action Directe, and Belgium's Communist Fighting Cells, the movement is believed to have linkage to Greek, Italian, Portugese, Spanish, and other terrorists. It also enjoys the support of patron states like Libya. On February 25, 1985, for example, an official publication of Libya's Revolutionary Committees, *Al Zahf Al Akhadar*, said that Libya should support, train, and arm West German and Irish terrorists in retaliation against Western countries that harbor anti-Qaddafi "terrorists."[2] A few days later, Libya's strongman, Colonel Maummar Qaddafi, spoke by satellite to a Black Muslim convention in Chicago and pledged that Libya was ready to give black separatists arms so that they could create their own "sovereign state in America."[3] He also called on blacks in the U.S. military to desert and form the backbone of an army of liberation.

Iran has threatened to strike at targets in the continental United States and has been linked to terrorist attacks on the U.S. embassies in Beirut and Kuwait and the blast that leveled the U.S. Marine headquarters in Beirut with the loss of 241 American lives. At one point, Iranian leaders were quoted as saying that 1,000 suicide bombers poised to strike were in the United States.

Similarly, Palestinian terrorist leader Abu Nidal claimed that 1985 would see a wave of terrorist attacks against the United States. "You will see in the course of this year we are going to mount operations against the Americans," Nidal reportedly told a French journalist, "and the billions of dollars their forces have will be insufficient to protect them."[4]

Palestinian and European terrorist groups established contact with their U.S. counterparts and supporters during the 1970s, and those links are said to be considerably stronger today. Foreign threats, however, are not the only problem. In addition to the forty or more foreign terrorist groups operating on U.S. territory, there are dozens of domestic terrorist groups, private armies, and religious cults capable of carrying out violent designs against their enemies and the U.S. government. Puerto Rican separatists like the Armed Forces of Puerto Rican National Liberation (FALN) and Macheteros continue to wage an unrelenting terrorist campaign in the United States and on the island of Puerto Rico. A particularly vicious group, the FALN is fond of combining explosives with butane canisters, creating crude fuel air bombs. A group identifying itself as the Armed Resistance Unit claimed responsibility for the bombing of the U.S. Capitol building in 1983 and may be the same as the so-called Guerrilla Resistance Movement that bombed the Officers' Club at the Washington Naval Yard. Both groups have announced their solidarity with leftists battling the U.S.-backed regime in El Salvador. Other leftist threats include those posed by environmental and antinuclear radicals, heavily armed black criminal groups that attempt to recruit a sympathetic following by papering over their crimes with Marxist sloganeering, and a small number of the foreign students studying in the United States who are actually members of terrorist organizations or under the control of foreign intelligence services. In this connection, two Libyan students were indicted in 1984 after attempting to purchase three .45-caliber pistols with silencers from an undercover FBI agent posing as an illicit arms dealer.

The threat is not only from the Left. A host of rightist groups and organizations, each with its own agenda, well armed, and actively engaged in paramilitary training, have been linked to terrorist incidents or possess the capability to engage in acts of terrorism. These include the Jewish Defense League, the Legion of Zion Army, the United Jewish Underground, the Ku Klux Klan, the American Nazi Party, fanatical antiabortionists, the Posse Comitatus, the Aryan Brotherhood, and a whole panoply of survivalist cults.

Welcome to World War III

Many observers believe that World War III has already begun. It is a protracted conflict composed of thousands of nameless engagements and hit-and-run attacks by terrorists and other state-sponsored proxy forces, their targets most often the liberal democracies of the West and their allies in the developing world. Although it is strategic warfare on the cheap, its stakes are no less significant or meaningful to the United States and the other nations of the West than a direct clash between the two superpowers. Indeed, the cumulative impact of low-intensity violence in the world today has the power to rewrite the geopolitical map of the globe, to deny the West access to vital straits and raw materials, and ultimately to isolate and transform the liberal democracies of the West into embattled garrison states fighting for their survival.

During 1984 there were over 650 international terrorist incidents, and more than 70 percent of them were violent bombings and armed attacks. Almost 88 percent of these attacks occurred in Western European, Middle Eastern, and Latin American areas of critical foreign policy importance to the United States. Two out of every five attacks took place in Western Europe, chiefly against close NATO allies of the United States or against facilities essential to the alliance. Forty percent of the victims of such terrorist attacks were diplomats, other government officials, and military personnel. The trend is on the rise. After hitting a plateau of around 500 attacks per year during the period from 1979 to 1982, attacks rose slightly in number, but sharply in casualties, in 1983. In 1984, the number of attacks climbed by 30 percent.

Behind this trend is the involvement of states in assisting, sponsoring, and actively engaging in terrorist attacks. In 1984, three governments alone—Iran, Libya, and Syria—accounted for almost one hundred acts of terrorism. All of the spectacular attacks against the United States in 1983 were state sponsored, the product of groups supported by Iran and Syria. Indeed, an increasing number of terrorist attacks are occurring in countries remote from the terrorists' countries of origin.

Today the streets of the world's great cities, its airport tarmacs, and military bases are being turned into battlefields as small bands of terrorists and lone assassins seek to achieve political goals through assaults on people and places with symbolic value. Their targets are often the wellsprings of political and economic power in Western societies. Their victims, however, are usually ordinary people whose death, injury, or agony as a hostage or kidnap victim serves the calculated purpose of drawing attention to the terrorist's cause, with the incumbent intimidation value this implies. Terrorists hope to force change: political, economic, social, and religious. The principal tools they employ are violence and intense news media coverage. They are practicing an old kind of warfare made new by modern weapons, targets, and tactics and modern notions about how to influence human behavior.

New Landscape of Terrorist Warfare

Modern terrorism poses grave new challenges to the United States and the other industrial democracies. Nearly all of the terrorist attacks witnessed in recent years fall below the thresholds of conventional warfare and the conditions normally requisite to declaring the existence of a state of war between two or more belligerents. Yet governments are duty bound to protect and defend their citizens, property, and national interests, and therefore new policies must be developed and new instruments created to meet the expanding terrorist threat, a threat that is constantly changing, complicating the task of policymakers.

In 1980, for example, law enforcement agents raided a safe house in Paris and discovered a secret laboratory that had been used to produce deadly botulinal toxin. The house had been rented by members of the German Red Army Faction terrorist group. Shortly after, another faction safe house, this one located in West Germany, was discovered. Inside authorities found several hundred kilograms of organophosphorus compounds that they speculated were being accumulated as part of the terrorist group's drive to create a chemical-biological warfare capability. Both incidents are part of an emerging pattern whereby terrorists are seeking to scale ever greater heights of terror and perhaps even build a weapon of mass destruction.

Virtually every terrorist group in the world today—and the count exceeds a hundred major groups operating on the international scene—has access to sophisticated weapons, explosives, and training, courtesy of a host of patron states and terrorist movements that regard terrorism as a cost-effective and successful strategy for achieving their objectives. The United States and the other industrial democracies are particularly vulnerable to this kind of warfare. Their economies and social fabric are dependent on dozens of critical nodes and networks such as water, power, sanitation, transportation, and communications. Our complex postindustrial societies are at the mercy of terrorists who know how the system works and where to strike. In New York City, for example, terrorists have been attempting to drop a commuter train tunnel under one of the rivers abutting Manhattan on a crowded rush-hour train. One can only imagine the staggering loss of life that likely would accompany such a disaster.

Terrorism can be expected to become more serious in the years ahead, with a growing impact on the foreign policies of the United States and the other industrial democracies. In this connection, there can be little debate over the fact that the United States pulled its marines out of Lebanon chiefly as a result of the terrorist attacks it sustained in 1983. It was, moreover, a terrorist incident—the seizure and captivity for 444 days of the U.S. hostages in Iran—that contributed, more than any other single factor, to public disillusionment with the presidency of Jimmy Carter and his administration's defeat at the polls. President Reagan survived a succession of terrorist-related disasters in the Middle East in 1983 and 1984, but had the president not enjoyed such great personal popularity, the bombing of the marine barracks in Beirut might well have jeopardized his reelection prospects.

The impact of terrorism is perhaps nowhere more dramatic than on modern diplomacy and the U.S. diplomatic presence abroad. U.S. embassies and other government facilities overseas require ever more extensive and costly security measures, and in some high threat environments, the total number of security personnel exceeds the number of diplomats and working staff. Embassies have increasingly come to resemble bunkers, dispensing with the graceful architecture of the past. In some countries, U.S. embassies have been reduced in size or shut down altogether when it was deemed impossible to protect them any longer.

Terrorism is changing the way we all live. Because of the terrorist threat, public buildings in the United States are becoming increasingly inaccessible, and security precautions are making elected officials ever more isolated from the public. Moreover, Americans traveling anywhere in the world may be at risk simply because they carry a U.S. passport. Corporations are being forced to expend huge sums of money to protect their executives, assets, and facilities from the threat of terrorism. One of every four international terrorist attacks in 1984 was against business, and not surprisingly one of the by-products of this violence has been the growth of an enormous private security industry, which some critics argue is a dangerous development and one that potentially threatens to erode personal privacy and individual liberties.

Terrorism is being used to undermine U.S. allies and to chip away at the Western alliance. Some allies, like Turkey, have responded to an internal terrorist threat with harsh tactics and countermeasures and thereby earned the wrath of the organized political Left and various human rights advocates in Western Europe and the United States. Democracy survives in Turkey only because its terrorist problem was successfully, if at times brutally, suppressed; however, the methods employed by the Turkish government certainly complicate that nation's relations with its allies. France has been forced to reexamine its long-standing tradition of political asylum as a result of growing terrorism directed against both French targets and foreigners residing within its borders. Every major nation in Europe is afflicted with some kind of potentially destabilizing terrorist outbreak.

Terrorism will not disappear. Small, weak states have discovered that it can greatly increase their political clout, and plagued as they are by resource shortages, they are not likely to abandon terrorism as a political and military tool. Larger, stronger states, by contrast, have discovered that terrorist proxies can help them achieve their national objectives without the risk attendant to other forms of warfare and without the protracted delays characteristic of the bargaining table. The United States and the other Western democracies, by contrast, have been less than successful in devising methods to combat terrorism that are effective but do not compromise their basic values and institutions.

Search for Answers

On May 12, 1985, the *Washington Post* revealed that President Reagan had approved covert training and support of several antiterrorist units tasked with collecting intelligence and preempting terrorists before they could carry out new attacks on U.S. facilities in the Middle East.[5] One of the units, composed of Lebanese and other non-Americans, subsequently acted entirely on its own in carrying out a vehicle bombing intended to kill Hesbollah (Party of God) leader Mohammed Hussein Fadlallah. Hesbollah terrorists were clearly implicated in the 1983 bombings of the U.S. Marine barracks and the U.S. embassy in Beirut, and Fadlallah himself reportedly not only helped plan the attacks but blessed the suicide bomber who drove the bomb-laden yellow Mercedes truck into the lobby of the marine barracks. The attack on Fadlallah failed, while killing a number of his bodyguards; more than eighty people who lived near Fadlallah in the Beirut suburb were killed, and some two hundred were injured.

The effort to assassinate Fadlallah was foolishly conceived and executed and can only be condemned, but disclosure by the *Washington Post* of the training programs being implemented to assist Lebanese authorities deal with terrorism not only endangered the lives of several Americans still being held hostage in Lebanon (or Iran) but may well lead to a new round of terrorist strikes against U.S. targets in the Middle East and Europe. Moreover, since the Central Intelligence Agency (CIA) and the administration had already taken steps to correct the situation and ensure that it would not happen again, the decision by the *Washington Post* to print the story served no useful purpose and could not have been justified as a constructive effort to halt a self-defeating program or policy. The only conclusion that can be drawn is that the *Post* continues to be more concerned with dwelling on U.S. failures and inadequacies rather than the problems and threats that were the source of concern in the first place.

Predictably, those in the media and the Congress who would have the United States respond to the growing international terrorist threat with what amounts to defensive measures, or less, gloated with self-satisfaction and a sense of moralistic vindication over the administration's embarrassment. The events in Beirut seemed to be confirmation, too, of the worse fears of many at the CIA who viewed any effort to engage in covert operations against terrorists as a sure formula for disaster, a regression to the 1970s when the agency was vilified for its involvement in such activities abroad. "The intelligence community comes back into the headlines, and into the public pillory. American agents abroad do become subject to retaliation. A major asset of foreign policy is thus weakened, if not rendered inoperative. The loss incurred almost always dwarfs the wrong that was to be righted."[6]

Supporters of strong action against terrorism, on the other hand, were disturbed by the ineptitude of the Lebanese team that planned and carried out the attack on Fadlallah, but they did not view the Beirut incident as a repudiation of the wisdom of taking aggressive actions to combat terrorism. The real lesson of the Beirut incident, contended advocates of a tough counterterrorism policy, was the critical need to impose appropriate controls on any program undertaken. More important, they continued, errors and failures should not deter the United States from resolving to hit back at terrorists, and hit back hard.

The controversy over the Beirut incident underscored how complicated and controversial is the development and implementation of any national policy designed to address the problem of international terrorism. Some view it as a no-win issue where any action taken will be seen as too extreme in some quarters and inadequate in others. Moreover, there is widespread public confusion as to what constitutes terrorism, and the decision-making processes of the Western democracies are increasingly vulnerable to terrorist propaganda designed to elicit sympathy and support and to fuel the already contentious debate over what are morally and legally acceptable responses to terrorism on the part of victimized governments. The debate today has been turned upside down, with more time spent agonizing over what are acceptable responses to terrorism than over the threat of terrorism itself. If one examines the popular media, it is easy to get the impression that the real threat comes from the governments grappling with the complex threat posed by terrorism rather than from the terrorists.

One consequence of the rising tide of terrorism and other forms of low-intensity violence directed against the industrial democracies has been a perceivable attrition of self-confidence on the part of Western governments and a lack of certitude with respect to the superiority of Western values to those embraced by terrorists and their patrons. This has produced a paralysis of action in many quarters and a deep soul searching on the part of policymakers over the efficacy of force in combating terrorism, doubts that do not plague U.S. adversaries.

Added to such considerations are a variety of legal and institutional impediments that, by contrast to the situation in totalitarian and authoritarian states, makes it difficult for the liberal democracies of the West to respond effectively, in many cases, to terrorist outrages. As Jean-François Revel has written:

> A democracy cannot employ one citizen out of five in the police, cannot close its borders, restrict travel inside the country, deport part of a city's population if necessary, keep an eye on every hotel, every building, every apartment on every floor, spend hours scrupulously searching travelers' cars and luggage—*all* travelers'. If the democracies could borrow these totalitarian tricks, they would soon enough liquidate terrorism at home and intercept

aid coming to it from abroad. Nor can they consider the kind of state counterterrorism used in Argentina against the *guerrilleros* and their supposed
accomplices, many of whom were innocent.[7]

The openness of Western societies permits terrorists to cross national frontiers and move about freely without fear of arbitrary arrest or detention. The
rule of law is fundamental to all liberal democracies, and extensive restraints
are placed on the activities of police and security forces. Suspected terrorists
are entitled to careful protection of their civil liberties and accorded due process of law, and the state is prohibited from acting capriciously in bringing
them to justice. This is the paradox of democracy: the very qualities that
make democracies so vulnerable to terrorists are the same qualities that make
them superior to other systems and so worth preserving; however, this does
not mean that the liberal democracies cannot develop effective measures, defensive and offensive, to fight back against terrorism.

Fighting Back

Terrorism has presented many new challenges to policymakers. The answers
to this menace are not simple or obvious, and they are rarely neat and clean
from a moral or legal standpoint. If there is any one certainty, it is that there
is no single ideal strategy for addressing terrorism. In many respects, every
terrorist incident is unique and calls for a solution or response tailor-made to
the particular events, actors, and interests involved.

This is not to say, however, that no generalizations concerning how the
West should respond to terrorism are possible. Quite the contrary. It is the
premise of this book that the United States and the other western democracies
have for too long taken a reactive posture with respect to terrorism and that
the time has come for new, bolder, and more aggressive strategies. As Colonel
Harry G. Summers Jr., has written, "Carrying the war to the enemy and the
destruction of his armed forces and his will to fight through the strategic
offensive is the classic way wars are fought and won."[8] Today the West finds
itself at war with international terrorism, and the lessons of conventional
combat are applicable to low-intensity warfare just as they are in the context
of large-scale warfare. It is time, in short, to carry the war to the terrorists.

The alternatives are poor. Although the necessity of good physical security is readily admitted, hiding behind a shield of security guards, thick walls,
and hardened cars and waiting for the terrorist enemy to strike is a bad policy
doomed to failure. Similarly, withdrawing in the face of a terrorist challenge
or capitulating to their demands is also rejected as an untenable and self-
destructive policy.

Taking the war to the terrorists, however, is much easier said than done.

Taking the war to the terrorists in Lebanon, for example, would automatically invoke the interests of a half-dozen or more countries. Indeed, there would be few disinterested bystanders. But while terrorism is truly a multinational problem, no really appropriate international forum exists to address the issue. The United Nations is, for the most part, useless in combating terrorism. Although the United Nations has produced several useful agreements addressing such problems as the protection of diplomats, aircraft hijacking, and hostage taking, it was able to do so only because the interests of virtually all U.N. member states were involved. But on the larger question of punishing terrorists and sanctioning nations for using and sponsoring terrorist attacks, the United Nations has been silent. It should be recalled that a majority of the U.N. membership was more interested in condemning Israel than Uganda in the aftermath of the daring raid on Entebbe. Moreover, the lukewarm condemnation of North Korea for its 1983 attack on the leadership of South Korea at the Martyrs' Mausoleum in Burma is clear testimony of the U.N.'s ambivalent attitude toward international terrorism.

Although other multilateral efforts on the part of concerned governments to devise strategies for dealing with terrorism are welcome, there are practical limits as to what can be achieved. The most effective cooperation to date has been accomplished in the context of the Economic Summit Seven through such actions as the Bonn Declaration on aircraft hijacking and the Vienna Declaration on the protection of diplomats. Nevertheless, if recent meetings are any gauge, no accord on hard issues such as the use of force is likely, particularly as it would address questions regarding the deployment, use, and support of forces engaged in counterterrorist operations.

There is recognition, therefore, that national governments will, for the most part, have to devise their own strategies for controlling and suppressing terrorism. Every concerned nation will surely pay careful attention to the successes and failures of other nations, but what works in one context may not always be translatable to another place and context. What Israel finds acceptable, for example, in combating terrorism may not be acceptable to the United States, particularly inasmuch as the continental United States has been relatively free of terrorism. In this connection, the nature of the threat environment will always configure the limits of what is possible and what is acceptable to policymakers, who must be sensitive to legal, moral, practical, and public relations considerations. What is an unacceptable response today to terrorism may be acceptable tomorrow in the wake of some terrorist-produced catastrophe.

The threat to the United States has never been greater, even if—for the time being at least—it is chiefly international and aimed largely at its diplomatic missions, military facilities, and far-flung corporate interests. Moreover, the day may not be far away when foreign terrorists strike at the very heart of civilization in the United States, and the nation must not be found unprepared. This book explores the issues that must be considered in responding to the threat posed by international terrorism and is dedicated to policymakers who must grapple with this challenge and find answers that do not undermine the U.S. Constitution, U.S. values, or U.S. national security.

Notes

1. Giovanni Spadolini, quoted in "New Generation of Violence," *Time*, February 11, 1985.

2. "Libya: Terrorists are 'Noble,'" AP Videotex, February 18, 1985.

3. "Desert Military, Blacks Urged," *Washington Post*, February 25, 1985.

4. "Palestinian Extremist Leader Is Alive, a Paris Journal Says," *New York Times*, February 22, 1985. For a report on the status of Abu Nidal, see also "Middle East: The Abu Nidal 'Resurrection,'" *Defense and Foreign Affairs Daily*, March 13, 1985.

5. "Anti-Terrorism Plan Rescinder after Unauthorized Bombing," *Washington Post*, May 12, 1985.

6. Joseph Kraft, "The CIA in Trouble," *Washington Post*, May 16, 1985.

7. Jean-François Revel, *How Democracies Perish* (Garden City, N.Y.: Doubleday, 1983), p. 211.

8. Harry G. Summers, Jr., *On Strategy* (Novato, Calif.: Presidio Press, 1983), p. 187.

2
The Rise of State-Sponsored Terrorism

Neil C. Livingstone
Terrell E. Arnold

On October 9, 1983, the Aung San, or Martyrs' Mausoleum, in Rangoon, Burma, was devastated by an explosion that destroyed the shrine and claimed the lives of twenty-one South Korean and Burmese dignitaries and officials and injured forty-eight others. Four of the Korean victims were cabinet ministers, including the deputy prime minister and the minister of foreign affairs. The primary target of the attack, South Korean President Chun Doo Hwan, survived only because his motorcade was running slightly late.

Burma, shocked that such an attack had occurred on its territory, mobilized immediately to discover the identities of the perpetrators and to bring them to justice. After nearly a month-long investigation based in large part on examination of physical evidence and the interrogation of two men captured shortly after the blast, a Burmese tribunal ruled that the attack had been carried out by members of a special North Korean commando unit.

The technical evidence and the statements of the captured North Korean officers left little question that the Poyngyang government had directly and deliberately plotted to kill the president of South Korea. In addition to the testimony of the two captured suspects, the physical evidence was conclusive. A pair of Claymore antipersonnel mines, designed to be detonated by radio signal, had been secreted in the roof of the mausoleum; however, one of the devices failed to explode, and components of the system, plus parts of a dud incendiary bomb, were found to be of a type identified in other North Korean terrorist attacks. Survival kits carried by the suspects, moreover, bore a strong similarity to those commonly in the possession of North Korean agents infiltrating into South Korea.

What made the incident in Rangoon unique was not so much the viciousness of the act and the high positions held by its victims but the fact that a direct link had been established between the commission of a terrorist crime and a national government. In recent years, it has been almost impossible to discover the proverbial smoking gun in such incidents and to authenticate the involvement of a small but growing number of nations in the spread of international terrorism, both by their support of terrorist groups and by the use of terrorism to further their national interests. Most often the evidence of direct state participation in terrorist crimes is only circumstantial and therefore easily hidden or denied by the sponsoring state. The Western media, moreover, are often quick to deride claims of state sponsorship, despite established patterns of support for terrorism on the part of sponsoring states. "The South Koreans offered no proof to support their accusations against North Korea," wrote the *Washington Post* in the aftermath of the Rangoon attack, dismissing Seoul's allegations almost out of hand. "But they historically have accused the Communist north of terrorist plots to destabilize their noncommunist system ever since the Korean Peninsula was divided following World War II."[1]

Terrorism has been used in warfare a number of times in history. Nevertheless, the rise of systematic state-sponsored terrorism is a relatively new phenomenon and represents a serious and growing danger to the United States and the other Western and Allied nations that are most often its victims. Terrorist attacks in 1983 and 1984 took the highest annual toll of lives and property on record. More U.S. lives were lost in 1983 alone to international terrorism than in the previous fifteen years combined. And with rare exception, the often spectacular attacks during 1983 and 1984 were carried out by groups that were state supported.

Evolution of State Sponsorship

Prior to 1970, most terrorist groups were self-sufficient, autonomous, homegrown organizations with local agendas and little outside support. In his study of 335 terrorist groups between 1961 and 1970, Ted Robert Gurr could find only nineteen that received significant outside aid in the form of safe havens, training, arms, or other materiel assistance.[2] By the early 1970s, authorities began to notice a significant shift in terrorist groups involving growing cooperation among fraternal revolutionary organizations, including the exchange of arms, ideology, tactics, intelligence, and other logistic support. Terrorist summits brought diverse groups closer together, creating a kind of loosely knit terrorist mafia with established linkages and subversive centers.[3] Even more disquieting was the apparent support being given to various terrorist movements by nations like the Soviet Union and its East European allies, Cuba, Libya, South Yemen, Syria, and Iraq. Although there is no evidence that the Soviets orchestrated and directed each terrorist act from Moscow, it is a well-established fact that the Soviet Union provided much of the infrastructure of world terrorism, ranging from terrorist training camps within its own borders to the export of arms and other materiel to terrorist groups, much of it channeled through surrogates like the Palestine Liberation

Organization (PLO), Syria, and Libya. According to Roberta Goren, the Soviet Union consciously backed terrorist groups in the Middle East as part of its power drive into the region. The PLO was to emerge as the "fulcrum of the Soviet Union's strategic approach" and "the initiator of the terrorist recrudescense which was to plague Western democratic societies from the late 1960s on, and the central coordinator of logistical and material support to a vast network of terrorist groups worldwide."[4] According to Ray Cline and Yonah Alexander, the PLO serves as the primary conduit for Soviet arms transfers to other revolutionary terrorist movements.[5]

The Soviet Union has found the present pattern of terrorism to be a cost-effective and low-risk policy for disrupting the West and challenging the United States for control of key populations, vital straits, raw materials, strategic minerals, and markets. Soviet support of Turkish terrorists, for example, is an attempt to destabilize the eastern flank of the North Atlantic Treaty Organization (NATO) and has created a lingering human rights problem for the government in Ankara that serves to isolate Turkey from its allies even today. Moscow similarly aids the Irish Republican Army (IRA), the Italian Red Brigades, and the German Red Army Faction as a way of compelling NATO member states to devote resources to the control and suppression of internal violence that otherwise might go to bolstering their external defense capabilities. Soviet Foreign Minister Andre Gromyko reportedly offered the Spanish government of Prime Minister Felipe Gonzalez a deal whereby Moscow would end its support of The Basque Homeland and Liberty Movement (ETA) in exchange for Spain's agreement not to join NATO. When the Spanish rejected the Soviet blackmail, in retaliation Moscow stepped up its clandestine shipments of arms to ETA.

While the United States and other nations of the West benefit from a stable, well-ordered international environment, the Soviet Union sees advantages in global turmoil and upheaval. The Soviet Union also "gains considerable psychological benefits in a conflict environment that tends to push pluralist states to compromise, accommodation, or outright appeasement."[6]

Direct links to many terrorist groups, especially those in Western Europe, are maintained by the Soviet KGB, Cuba's DGI, and various East European intelligence services. Soviet operatives manipulated numerous terrorist movements, aiding compliant elements, to succeed over more moderate and less ideological rivals. In the 1960s and early 1970s, terrorists began going abroad to acquire their weapons and training, but most often they returned home to use their new skills and hardware. Their attacks were still directed largely at their own leaders and at supporters of the home government. Foreigners were generally secondary targets. By the mid-1970s, however, for many terrorists foreign countries had become the preferred battleground and foreign citizens and facilities the targets of choice. As a result of this shift, international terrorists no longer merely assisted home-grown terrorists in their parochial struggles but made common cause and collaborated across international boundaries. Both terrorists and their causes grew ever more distant from their original enemies and grievances.

Indeed, by the mid-1970s international terrorism had become highly cooperative, with little regard to geographical or political boundaries. By contrast to earlier years, few revolutionary terrorist groups were any longer self-sufficient. In the words of Walter Laqueur, terrorism had come to resemble the workings of a multinational corporation: "An operation would be planned in West Germany by Palestine Arabs, executed in Israel by terrorists recruited in Japan with weapons acquired in Italy but manufactured in Russia, supplied by an Algerian diplomat, and financed with Libyan money."[7]

For the most part, the patron states of international terrorism still preferred to remain in the background, ever opportunistic, content to add fuel to the terrorist brushfires around the globe, but rarely managing their terrorist proxies and surrogates in any direct or consistent fashion. Control still rested with the leadership of the individual terrorist groups, although they were clearly subject to manipulation and suggestion from their patron states. A new and even more disquieting trend began to emerge in the late 1970s as a small but growing number of nations began to adopt the methods and tactics of terrorists for their own national purposes. No longer satisfied merely to aid and abet terrorist movements, nations like Iran and Libya came to view terrorism as an effective method of conducting war by other means against more powerful adversaries whose nuclear and conventional arsenals, together with their military rules and doctrines, were illsuited to respond effectively to the new threat. Indeed, smaller, weaker states discovered that terrorism is a force multiplier that greatly augments the effectiveness and clout of their military and intelligence establishments, enabling them to substitute stealth and blackmail for direct confrontation and superior force. As these states see it, the force-multiplying impact of terrorism is a political and military equalizer of immense potential significance to their roles in local and regional affairs.

State as Terrorist

Americans were shocked into awareness of the shifting character of international terrorism on November 4, 1979, when Iranian militants, with the complicity of the revolutionary government of the Ayatollah Khomeini, seized the U.S. embassy in Tehran and took its diplomatic personnel hostage. The crisis continued for 444 days before the final fifty-two hostages were released. Resolution came quickly on January 20, 1981, during the inauguration of Ronald Reagan, presumably because the Iranian government feared that the new administration would be under public pressure to resolve the matter swiftly, by force if necessary. The Iranians undoubtedly also felt that they could secure better terms from the outgoing Carter administration than the incoming Reagan team. To add to its humiliation, the United States, in exchange for the hostages, agreed to revoke all trade sanctions against Iran, to freeze the deposed shah's assets in the United States, to transfer frozen Iranian assets out of the country, to withdraw the U.S. case against Iran pending before the World Court, and to prohibit all claims against Iran filed by the hostages and to transfer U.S. claims and legal undertakings arising out of the incident to an international arbital tribunal.[8] While the United States resolved the hostage crisis with only limited bloodshed (in connection with the aborted rescue operation), the crisis nevertheless represented a clear victory for state-sponsored terrorism. Although it is generally accepted that international agreements are void if they are the result of duress or coercion, the United States chose not to renounce the accords, implemented by means of executive orders and Treasury regulations.

Having proved the value of terrorism as a tool in the hostage crisis, during the years that followed Iran came to employ terrorists either under direct control or responsive to the Iranian government in repeated attacks against the United States and other Western nations. According to Central Intelligence (CIA) director William Casey, "more blood has been shed by Iranian terrorists than any other," including more than fifty incidents in 1983, and sixty-six, according to preliminary State Department data, in 1984.[9] Terrorists operate out of Iranian embassies and student centers in Europe and elsewhere, and Tehran provides direct political, financial, and military support to elements of the Islamic Jihad, or "holy war," and constituent or related groups such as the Islamic Amal and Hesbollah (Party of God). The Iranian government also maintains close ties with the exiled Iraqi Shiite opposition party Al Dawa (Islamic Call), which has a base in Tehran and conducts and sanctions terrorism as a means of realizing its political objectives.

Iran has carried out its most violent and deadly terrorist attacks in Lebanon and Kuwait. Vehicle bombs heavily damaged the U.S. embassy in Beirut in April 1983 and the embassy annex in September 1984. In October 1983, vehicle bombs destroyed both the U.S. Marine barracks and the headquarters of the French Multinational Force (MNF) in Beirut. Another bomb damaged the French MNF headquarters in December 1983. The Iranian-sponsored Islamic Jihad claimed credit for all these attacks, and Iranian complicity has been confirmed by U.S. intelligence sources. Indeed, it has been reported that the money that financed the truck bombings of the U.S. and French military headquarters in Beirut originated in Tehran and was passed to the terrorists by Iran's ambassador to Syria, Ali Akbar Mohtashami, described as a key figure in Middle Eastern terrorism.[10] In December 1983, Iraqi dissidents from Al Dawa carried out six bomb attacks in Kuwait City, including a truck bomb assault on the U.S. embassy. There is evidence that the attacks were planned in Iran with the assistance of Syrian military officers and that the explosives and firearms used in the operation were smuggled from Iran into Kuwait.[11] It has been confirmed, moreover, that the actual signal to launch the attacks also emanated from Iran.

Aircraft hijackings since 1983 also provide clear evidence of Iranian support for international terrorism. After a hijacked Air France flight landed in Tehran in early September 1983, Iranian authorities gave the incident several hours of media play and then terminated the hijacking without a struggle and let the hijackers go. Evidence gathered in Vienna by Austrian authorities indicated that the hijackers stayed in the Iranian embassy until just before the hijacking took place. When a Kuwait Airlines flight was hijacked to Tehran in October 1984, Iranian sympathy for the terrorists was immediately apparent. Moreover, U.S. eavesdropping on the conversations between the terrorists on board the hostage aircraft and the Tehran control tower leaves little doubt that the Iranian government provided support and comfort to the terrorists. Despite the fact that several opportunities arose to storm the plane and rescue the hostages, such as when cleaning crews and photographers were permitted on board, the Iranian government declined to take action. The hijackers demanded the release of the Iraqi Shiite dissidents who had been imprisoned in Kuwait following the December 1983 bomb attacks in Kuwait City. With the hijacked airliner on the ground in Tehran, Iran put heavy pressure on Kuwait to meet the hijacker's demands, and by failing to interfere with the murder of two U.S. citizens and the torture of two others on board the aircraft, Iran hoped to influence the United States to increase the pressure on Kuwait. However, when it became apparent that neither the Kuwaitis nor the U.S. government intended to give in and as Iran's involvement in the incident became increasingly visible because of world media coverage, Iranian authorities resolved the incident and took the hijackers into custody. To date, the Iranian government has made no attempt to prosecute the hijackers for their crimes, and it can be expected that they will probably be permitted to slip away quietly in the near future, if it has not already happened.

Iran has also masterminded a number of politically motivated kidnappings. In July 1982, the acting president of the American University in Beirut, David Dodge, disappeared in Beirut. His release was effected a year later with Syrian assistance. Although his captors never identified themselves, there is evidence that he was drugged and transported to Iran where he spent a large part of his captivity. Beginning in early 1984, a series of other kidnappings occurred in Beirut. The first was a U.S. embassy political officer, William Buckley, followed shortly after by the Cable News Network bureau chief, Jeremy Levin (who escaped from his captors in February 1985), American University of Beirut professor Frank Regier (who was later found and released by Amal Shia militia in Beirut), and Presbyterian minister Benjamin Weir. A new wave of kidnappings took place beginning in December 1984 with the seizure of the Reverend Lawrence Jenco, a Catholic priest, and continuing with the abduction of several other Americans. The Islamic Jihad has taken credit for most of the kidnappings, but the actual perpetrators are members of the Hesbollah subgroup. In either case, Iran is the principal sponsor.

The pattern of Iranian-backed attacks against U.S. and other targets in the Middle East and elsewhere is clear and is part of an ongoing effort by the Khomeini regime to internationalize its revolution.[12] The radical clergy at the helm of the Iranian government believe that both Western and Eastern (Soviet) values and institutions are corrupt. They believe that many Middle Eastern governments are Islamic in name only and as instruments of either the United States or the Soviet Union must be undermined and replaced with authentic Islamic regimes.[13] Moreover, there is an element of revenge in the bloody Beirut bombings for U.S. support of the late shah. In addition, Iran uses terrorism as a device to influence the course of the Iran-Iraq war and to undermine the regime of Iraqi president Saddam Hussein and it hopes, install a Shiite government in Baghdad more sympathetic to Iran. In this connection, the 1983 bombings in Kuwait were designed to jolt Kuwait out of its support for Iraq in the war. The attacks against the French MNF headquarters in Beirut in October and again in December 1983; the bombings of French offices in Karachi, Pakistan; several attacks carried out in France by the Carlos Apparat, operating under the name of the Armed Arab Struggle; and the 1983 hijacking of the Air France flight to Tehran can all be seen as attempts to stop France from supplying weapons to the Iraqis. Thus, it can be anticipated that Iran will continue to represent a real threat to U.S. interests and those of other countries in the Middle East for some time to come. There is no sign that the mullahs are ready to abandon terrorism as an instrument to achieve their national purposes. Iran is less a nation today in many respects than an organized mob, and until the revolutionary impulses begin to abate and Thermidore sets in, the potential for a direct U.S.-Iranian clash remains very high.

After Iran, Libya—reminiscent of the pirate state it once was—is the other nation that has most openly and directly employed terrorism as a form of warfare against its adversaries. In 1984, there were approximately twenty-six acts of Libyan-sponsored terrorism. Libya's terrorism, like that of Iran, grows out of the personality of its leadership. Libya's erratic leader, Colonel Muammar Qaddafi, began using terrorism almost immediately on assuming power in 1969. A man of violent extremes, Qaddafi sought to break Libyan society out of its traditional Oriental monarchist mold, personified in the reign of King Idris, whom Qaddafi ousted. Qaddafi sees himself as the logical successor to the mantle of pan-Arabism once worn by Egypt's Gamal Abdel Nasser, and he believes that he can provide leadership to the many diverse Muslim communities around the world, particularly those in north and sub-Saharan Africa. As such, he is the benefactor of numerous Muslim revolutionary movements, including the Polisario Liberation Front in the former Spanish Sahara and the Moro National Liberation Front in the Philippines.

Not only does Qaddafi openly and publicly indicate his support for various terrorist groups, but Libya operates a number of terrorist training camps, which over the years have provided training and weapons to members of more than forty terrorist organizations. In addition, Libyan diplomatic facilities are often used as safe houses to provide refuge to fugitive terrorists, Libyan diplomats have been implicated in the commission of terrorist acts, and Libyan diplomatic pouches have been utilized to smuggle weapons and explosives across national frontiers. After the murder of a British policewoman outside the Libyan People's Bureau in London in June 1984, large quantities of weapons were found inside the building, and it is suspected that the bureau was being used as a base for mounting operations against anti-Qaddafi dissidents living in the United Kingdom and Western Europe. Because of such activities, the United States closed down the Libyan People's Bureau in Washington in 1981 and has not permitted it to reopen. There is strong evidence that the Libyan mission to the United Nations now serves the same function, and a series of arrests of Libyan agents by the Federal Bureau of Investigation in May 1985 suggested that Qaddafi was in the process of mounting a major antidissident campaign inside the United States.

During 1982 and part of 1983, Libya's support for international terrorism seemed to wane, but a rapid escalation in Libyan-sponsored incidents was observed around mid-1983, and the trend has yet to abate. A Libyan-backed group is credited with trying to disrupt the Haj, the holy pilgrimage of Muslims to Mecca, in 1983, and with trying to assassinate the leader of Chad's government that same year. Libyan agents are believed to be behind the explosion of a bomb in the baggage room of Kinshasa airport in Zaire, plots to attack the U.S. and French embassies in Ndjamena, Chad, the bombing of a French jet on the ground in Ndjamena, certain efforts to assassinate or unseat Yasir Arafat from his position as chairman of the PLO and the bombing of Arab nightclubs in London and Manchester frequented by Libyan dissidents.

By contrast to the use of terrorism by Iran and Libya, Syrian-sponsored terrorism appears to be a good deal more institutional than personal. It is dispassionately linked to calculated objectives, especially the projection of power into strife-torn Lebanon. The Syrian use of terrorism involves a strange and disturbing partnership with Iran. In Syrian-controlled areas of Lebanon's Bekaa Valley, Iran's Revolutionary Guard maintains a military contingent, including training facilities for terrorists. Revolutionary Guard personnel move regularly back and forth between these facilities and Tehran, and Iranian movements through Damascus International Airport appear to receive only cursory monitoring by Syrian authorities.

The Syrian-Iran arrangement in support of terrorism is symbiotic for a number of reasons. Iran is desirous of allies, and in the Arab world today they are not easily found inasmuch as the Ayatollah's particular brand of fundamentalism is at least as frightening to many Arabs as the threat of Marxism. Khomeini also wants the support of Shiite fundamentalists outside Iran because he views them as an instrument for the spread of his teachings and as a fifth column to overthrow anti-Shiite regimes. From the Syrian perspective, Assad needs assistance managing the fragmented Muslim communities of Lebanon, and Iran is helpful in working with the Shiites, specifically in keeping them from mounting terrorist operations against targets in Syria. The anti-U.S. activities of the Islamic Jihad, moreover, have been a convenient method of exerting pressure against U.S. policies in Lebanon with relatively little risk to Damascus.

The kidnapping of David Dodge appears to have been successful because the Iranians were able to operate freely in Syrian-controlled territory. Iran's direct support and management, moreover, of the Islamic Jihad is greatly facilitated by the ability to operate virtually unimpeded inside Lebanon, and it is believed that the bombings of the U.S. embassy in Beirut and of the U.S. Marine barracks, as well as the French Multinational Force headquarters, were mounted with Iranian support from within areas of Lebanon under Syrian control. Such evidence is buttressed by the fact that Jeremy Levin, after escaping, fell immediately into the hands of the Syrian Army, indicating that Hesbollah has been holding its American and other captives practically under the nose of the Syrian Army in the Bekaa Valley.

Syria uses terrorism most directly in efforts to coerce the leadership of the PLO to keep PLO policies from deviating from Syrian objectives in Lebanon. In this connection, sometime between 1982 and 1983 Syria appears to have reached an understanding with Abu Nidal, leader of the notorious terrorist organization Black June, to carry out terrorist operations against moderate Arab and Palestinian leaders. Until Saddam Hussein expelled the group in 1983, Black June had been operating primarily out of Baghdad, although it was also based in Damascus. Whatever the terms of the arrangement between Assad and Abu Nidal, shortly after Black June's headquarters was consolidated in Damascus, and in the past eighteen months the organization has carried out numerous operations at the behest of Syria. The Abu Nidal group assassinated a PLO observer to an international conference of socialists in Portugal, carried out seven bomb attacks against a variety of targets in Amman, Jordan, and is credited with a number of attacks against

Jordanian diplomats abroad. An on-board bomb that downed a Gulf Air flight between Karachi and Abu Dhabi may also have been the work of Abu Nidal's Black June.

While Syrian-sponsored terrorism has been largely confined to the Middle East, Western authorities believe that a liaison office established in 1983 by the Syrian Defense Ministry in Athens actually is a front to mask support for various terrorist activities in Western Europe. If true, this represents an alarming escalation of Syrian potential to sponsor terrorism in Western Europe.

Several other governments appear to have made calculated decisions to aid and support international terrorism. Among these is Nicaragua. There have been numerous confirmed sightings of Basque ETA terrorists in Nicaragua in recent years, suggesting that the Sandinista government may be planning on using the ETA as a terrorist instrument in Central America. One ETA member, for example, was arrested in San José, Costa Rica, in conjunction with an assassination attempt on the life of Contra leader Eden Pastora. In addition to ETA terrorists, Nicaragua is known to be a sanctuary for members of the PLO, the Montoneros (Argentina), the Baader-Meinhof Gang (West Germany), and as many as forty-four members of the Italian Red Brigades. Nicaragua maintains close ties with Cuba, the Soviet Union, Libya, and Iran and is a major recipient of Soviet and Libyan aid. In view of these developments and the fact that U.S. Navy Lieutenant Commander Albert Schaufelberger was assassinated in El Salvador in May 1983 by a member of the Farabundo Marti National Liberation Front, a group that regularly receives support from Managua, Nicaragua should be added to the State Department's list of state sponsors of terrorism.

In this connection, since the passage of the Fenwick amendment to the Export Administration Act, the secretary of state has designated six states under the act for engaging in a pattern of support for acts of terrorism. These states currently are Iran, Libya, Syria, the People's Democratic Republic of Yemen, and Cuba. Iraq was removed from the list in 1982 as its relationship with the United States improved, leading State Department officials to conclude that there was an opportunity to work directly with Baghdad to persuade that government to withdraw its support from two terrorist groups of particular concern to the United States: Black June (Abu Nidal) and May 15 (Abu Ibrahim). Both groups had been given safe haven and financial support by Iraq's government, as well as having been provided the opportunity to support their activities by engaging in lucrative business deals originating in Baghdad. Iraq cut off support to both groups in 1983.

The State Department list of state supporters of terrorism is notable not only for those listed but those not. Absent is Nicaragua despite its support for the terrorist activities of antigovernment rebels in El Salvador, Honduras, and Costa Rica. Missing also are the governments of North Korea, which carried out the attack against the cabinet of South Korea at the Martyrs' Mausoleum in Rangoon, and the Soviet Union and many of its Warsaw Pact allies. Bulgaria, East Germany, and Czechoslovakia qualify for inclusion on the State Department list by virtue of their arms transfers to terrorist movements and training camps operated on their territory. They also supply vital intelligence to terrorist groups, including information critical to striking at NATO-related targets in Western Europe. Bulgaria has been implicated in the attempted assassination of Pope John Paul II and in the murders of Bulgarian opposition figures in the West.

In many respects, the hardest omission to understand is the Soviet Union. A vast reservoir of information links Moscow to terrorist groups and activities around the globe. And although the Soviet leadership does not exert direct control over the operational aspects of various international terrorist groups, there is little question that many of those groups would be forced to curtail or end their activities if the Soviet Union withdrew its support. From the Soviet point of view, the use of surrogates and international terrorist proxies is probably preferable to a centrally controlled and directed network since other governments and movements take the heat for specific acts of terrorism while the Soviet leadership is able to deny any role in sponsoring terrorism.

Perhaps the clearest evidence of Soviet involvement in international terrorism is contained in the pattern of its relations with terrorism-sponsoring states. At least ten states are direct sponsors and patrons of international terrorism, and only one of them, Iran, is outside the Soviet orbit. The Soviet Union is well aware of the extent of Libyan, Syrian, Yemeni, Cuban, Nicaraguan, North Korean, and Warsaw pact involvement in activities that aid and abet international terrorism. As a consequence, Soviet support of international terrorism presents an especially difficult and possibly even intractable problem for the West.

Growing Threat

From the alarming increase in the number and magnitude of state-sponsored attacks in 1983—1984, it is apparent that the leading state sponsors of terrorism clearly view it as a successful and effective method of advancing their national aims and objectives. Moreover, the pattern of recent incidents yields the inescapable conclusion that terrorism can be an even more successful instrument in the service of states than individuals and groups. Practically all of the media spectaculars growing out of recent terrorist incidents have paid far more attention to the question of state sponsorship than to the actual terrorist groups involved, who have been forced into the background. The 1984 Kuwait Airline hijacking, for example, degenerated into an international debate over the culpability of Iran and questions relating to the Iranian handling of the incident. The identities of the hijackers and their motivations received relatively little attention.

The political consequences of the 1983 bombings in Lebanon directed at U.S. targets should make it evident to the perpetrators of the attacks and their state sponsors that terrorism works and is capable of directly influencing American policy. Notwithstanding its public hard-line stance of no concessions to terrorists, the United States clearly acted in concert with the goals of the terrorists following the 1983 bombings in Lebanon and the 1985 hijacking of TWA flight 847.

To a degree, in the wake of the April 1983 bombing of the U.S. embassy in Beirut, the U.S. leadership was entrapped by its own logic. The April attack led to an intensive reappraisal of security measures at the embassy and reinforced the feeling within the administration that it was correct in supporting the introduction of a U.S. Marine contingent as part of the multinational peacekeeping force (MNF) in Lebanon. Despite strong support for the MNF by the Gemayel regime, there was little enthusiasm for it from other factions, a fact reinforced by the rising number of attacks on the force mounted in the weeks following the embassy bombing. The devastating vehicle bomb attack on October 23, 1983, on the marine barracks was the means finally chosen by Iran, Syria, and their agent, the Islamic Jihad, to demonstrate their opposition to the U.S. military presence in Lebanon and also to demonstrate their conviction that the marine presence was not directly negotiable.

The attack must have succeeded beyond the wildest dreams of its perpetrators, for its timing was excellent. Public debate in the United States was already intense due to press and congressional concerns over creeping involvement of U.S. Marines in combat situations. Sporadic shelling and small arms attacks on the marines from Muslim-held positions overlooking Beirut and the airport were slowly, out of necessity, drawing the marines into a combat posture, whether or not the United States intended for that to happen. Doubts over the American role in Lebanon were aggravated by the bombardment of radical Shiite and other Muslim encampments on the slopes of the Chouf Mountains. The impact of the October 23 bombing was effectively to close debate in the United States on U.S. military involvement in Lebanon. Whether or not it was desirable on policy grounds to keep them there, the marines had to come home. U.S. power and prestige in the Middle East suffered a major setback; the terrorists and their sponsoring states had won again.

The United States has been particularly handicapped in its dealings with Syria and Iran because the lives of U.S. hostages probably being held in Syrian-controlled areas of Lebanon are at stake. While appreciating that Syrian leadership is certainly knowing and probably culpable with Iran in sponsoring the various kidnappings, the United States has been forced to conduct its relations with Damascus in such a way a to keep the door open for Syrian assistance in securing the eventual release of the hostages. For the United States, the fate of the hostages must be weighed in any decision to take direct action in Lebanon or against Iran.

Conclusion

A profound change has occurred in recent years in the nature of warfare, witnessing a situation arise in which, by every traditional measure of international conflict, two or more nations can be found to be in a state of belligerency without any of them acknowledging the fact. Such a state of belligerency exists today between the United States and both Libya and Iran. Libya, Iran, and at least a half-dozen other nations are conducting hostilities by means of various terrorist proxies and surrogates against the United States and its citizens, property, and national interests. As but one measure of the intensity of this warfare, the number of U.S. servicemen killed in one terrible instant in the bombing of the U.S. Marine headquarters in Beirut is equal to two-thirds the entire number of casualties from hostile action suffered by the United States during the Spanish-American War.

The United States and the other Western democracies must acknowledge that a state of war exists between them and certain terrorism-sponsoring nations. Only by acknowledging the enormity of the problem and the indisputable nature of the attacks already suffered can steps be taken to combat it. The United States and the other countries bearing the brunt of terrorist attacks sponsored by nations such as Iran and Libya are clearly justified in waging defensive war against them.

Notes

1. "Blast Kills Top Aides to South Korean President," *Washington Post,* October 10, 1983.

2. Ted Robert Gurr, "Some Characteristics of Contemporary Political Terrorism" (unpublished manuscript), March 1976, p. 21.

3. See Shlomi Elad and Ariel Merari, *The Soviet Bloc and World Terrorism,* Paper No. 26 (Tel Aviv, Israel: Tel Aviv University/Jaffee Center for Strategic Studies, 1984), pp. 40–41.

4. Roberta Goren, *The Soviet Union and Terrorism,* ed. Jillian Becker (London: George Allen & Unwin, 1984), p.106.

5. Ray S. Cline and Yonah Alexander, *Terrorism: The Soviet Connection* (New York: Crane, Russak, 1984), p. 63.

6. Ibid., p. 77.

7. Walter Laqueur, *Guerrilla: A Historical and Critical Study* (Boston: Little, Brown, 1976), p. 324.

8. See "Agreement on the Release of the American Hostages," *Department of State Bulletin* (February 1981): 1–22. See also Stuart S. Malawer, "Rewarding Terrorism: The U.S.-Iranian Hostage Accords," *International Security Review* (Winter 1981–1982): 477–496.

9. William J. Casey, remarks to the International Security Studies Program/ Fourteenth Annual Conference, Fletcher School of Law and Diplomacy, Medford, Mass., April 17, 1985.

10. "Beirut Bombing: Mysterious Death Warriors Traced to Syria, Iran," *Washington Post*, February 1, 1984.

11. "Message from Iran Triggered Bombing Sprees in Kuwait," *Washington Post*, February 3, 1984.

12. Marvin Zonis, "Seminar on the Psychological Roots of Shiite Muslim Terrorism," (unpublished manuscript, March 1, 1984).

13. Ibid.

3
Terrorist Violence:
Its Mechanics and Countermeasures

Christine C. Ketcham
Harvey J. McGeorge II

V iolence has been, and in the future will be, perpetrated by an almost limitless number of means; rarely has a lack of necessary technology been a significant factor in limiting any outbursts of terrorist violence. In this chapter, we propose to outline the mechanics of terrorist violence today and perhaps tomorrow and to offer some thoughts on its countermeasures. Through a wider dissemination of this knowledge, we hope to stimulate an understanding of the magnitude of the threat facing the United States. The mechanics of violence can, for ease of study, be divided into seven categories. These categories are listed in their usual order of appearance in previous and presumably future conflicts:

Mechanical devices.

Small arms.

Incendiaries.

Explosives.

Standoff weapons.

Chemical, biological, and toxin agents.

Nuclear Devices.

Mechanical Devices

Mechanical devices can be classified as passive or active in nature. The passive device is one that does not require any direct confronting action on the part of the user for its employment. A good example is the ubiquitous caltrop. Originally used a thousand or more years ago, caltrops were small, spiked, chestnut-like nettles that were scattered on the roads and fields in advance of oncoming enemy troops dependent on horse-drawn transport. Moving these devices out of the way slowed the enemy's advance or caused him to lose his primary transportation.

Modern metal caltrops, shaped to resemble their namesake, the spiny star thistle, are used to puncture tires on automobiles, trucks, and other conveyances with pneumatic tires. Caltrops surfaced again recently during the ongoing coal mine strike in Kentucky and West Virginia. In this particular altercation, union sympathizers on several occasions pounded hundreds of nails into roads traveled by trucks carrying coal from nonunion mines. When only a few inches of nail remain above the surface, a large pair of bull cutters is used to clip off the heads of the nails, leaving a sharp point. As the trucks roll over this bed of nails, its tires are shredded, forcing the truck to halt while the tires are changed. The extra cost to the coal company and the truckers of hundreds of dollars per load of coal ensures that the price of the nonunion coal becomes noncompetitive. This is economic terrorism. Although the union sympathizers have not directly attacked the coal company, they have taken an action that by exerting economic pressure, forces capitulation to their demands.

A slight variation on this technique used by the same group is the use of two or three nails bent in an approximate U-shape and welded together. The heads of the nails are clipped off, so no matter how they land when thrown on the road, at least one point will be sticking up. This technique allows quick emplacement of a mechanical barrier to these trucks and is equally as effective as pounding the nails into the roadway. Either technique requires as a countermeasure a car moving along in front of the trucks to inspect the road and spot where these devices have been emplaced. People have to get out and sweep the road clear or with a large hammer pound the nails all the way into the road. Sweeping and pounding are time-consuming and not conducive to an efficient operation.

An ice pick is a particularly good example of an active mechanical device. Law enforcement personnel and other threatened individuals presume that bullet-resistant vests and other garments made from Kevlar cloth afford some measure of protection against handgun ammunition and other types of instruments, including knives and swords. What is not generally recognized is that an ice pick will usually penetrate these garments with ease.

The amount of energy developed by the velocity and force of the thrust of the ice pick is distributed over the very small cross-section of the ice pick tip. Although the velocity may not be significant, the energy density is very high and therefore often sufficient to overcome the resistance of the otherwise projectile-resistant vest. The only practical means of defeating an ice pick is to have a hard surface material on the outside of the vest sufficient to blunt the force of the ice pick. Since the ice pick cannot be thrust at a very high velocity, the hard surface material does not have to be particularly thick or heavy. The shock plate that some bullet-resistant garment manufacturers include in the front of their vest is desirable for this reason.

Small Arms

Small arms, particularly submachine guns, have long been the badge of the urban guerrilla or terrorist. The greatest emerging threat from small arms is not from the weapons themselves but from the significant proliferation of increased performance ammunition. This special ammunition falls in two general categories: ammunition meant to be armor piercing and ammunition meant to have a rapid energy transfer rate or shock value.

In the armor-piercing category, KTW (Teflon-coated) bullets have been available since the mid-1960s and enjoyed a brief spurt of popularity. They have faded from prominence, although they remain available, generally only to police departments. In some locations they are obtainable through over-the-counter sale to anyone who can afford the price of between one and two dollars per round.

Following the trail of the KTW came the French Arcane round. Simpler in construction though made of lathe-turned copper bar stock, the Arcane rounds were almost as effective as KTW and much less expensive to produce. There was never a large enough market in the United States to enable production to be undertaken here, but a number of lots of this ammunition were imported. Just a few years ago, one lot of 700 rounds imported by or on behalf of the U.S. government was reported as lost and is presumed to be in the hands of terrorist or other crime factions.

A more recent introduction is the black steel projectile. Representing a lower level of technology than either KTW or Arcane, black steel projectiles are nevertheless effective at piercing bullet-resistant garments, have no sporting value, and are attractive only to criminal.

One legitimate type of sporting cartridge that has significant terrorist potential is the sabotted round typified by the Remington Accelerator series. The accelerator rounds, with their subcaliber projectile and plastic skirt or sabot, develop high velocities when fired from normal sporting rifles. Typically these velocities exceed 4,000 feet per second, and at that velocity, these projectiles (which are normal soft-point-jacketed hunting projectiles) can penetrate light armor at short distances. The military has been so impressed with the accelerator concept that they have developed their own version, termed a SLAP round, for use as a light armor penetrator. SLAP rounds have a hard steel or tungsten core in lieu of a soft, pointed projectile and achieve approximately the same 4,000 feet per second velocity levels. They are devastating on armor. Without question, they can penetrate typical armored cars.

The rapid energy transfer projectiles that are of interest include the French THV round and the American Glaser Safety Slug. The THV represents a bridge between the armor-piercing and high energy transfer projectiles because its very high muzzle velocity (approximately 2,000 feet per second or more in almost every handgun caliber) yields a high degree of penetration in several kinds of armor material. Because of their extremely light weight (sometimes as little as a third the normal bullet weight), they tend to slow down rapidly in a body. This rapid slowdown and consequent loss of energy results in a tremendous shock to the body, causing a devastating wound, which can be lethal.

The Glaser Safety Slugs have been around for a number of years and attract occasional interest. They, like the THV, develop high velocity but differ in that they are the absolute opposite as far as armor penetration goes. They have no proclivity to penetrate armor and lack the propensity to ricochet typical of armor-piercing projectiles. When striking flesh, however, they exhibit a higher energy transfer rate than any other conventional or known unconventional design projectiles. Their ability to wreak havoc in a body is unsurpassed; no one struck between the groin and the nose is likely to survive the impact. The design of the projectile, which incorporates hundreds of small lead balls, makes the wound from a Glaser Safety Slug especially difficult to treat.

Currently there is no ready countermeasure to enhanced performance ammunition. Both armor-piercing and high energy transfer rounds are readily produced in underground workshops. A small lathe and common reloading tools are all that is required to turn out ammunition that will defeat virtually any practical bullet-resistant vest.

Because manufacturing these deadly rounds is so easy, legislation alone cannot prevent their illicit use. Protection will depend on a dramatic increase in the effectiveness of the bullet-resistant materials fabricated for police and for use by threatened individuals.

Explosives

The major threat from explosives as a terrorist weapon today in the United States comes from car bombs. A car bomb typically consists of a fairly large amount (up to 1,000 pounds) of bulk high explosive or a smaller amount of high explosives in combination with a number of pressurized cylinders of flammable gas, such as propane or butane. These explosives are detonated by a timing device or a radio control device or by a wire run from the parked vehicle to a safe vantage point from which the adversary can observe the action around the bomb and detonate it by signal over the wire.

Vehicle bombs are used for several purposes. The primary example is the attack on a specific individual who is traveling a known route and will pass a parked car concealing a large bomb. Alternatively, both the bomb car and the target car can be in motion. The bomb vehicle would either approach from a side street and ram into the intended target vehicle prior to detonating the bomb, overtake the victim from the rear, or approach them head on. The emir of Kuwait was attacked by a mobile vehicle bomb in early 1985.

A third use of the device is as a means to attack buildings. Explosives can cause a tremendous amount of damage to a building when they are detonated close enough to the building. This was clearly demonstrated in the attacks on the marine corps compound in Beirut and on the U.S. embassies in Kuwait and Beirut. Similar attacks have taken place in the United States starting in the early 1970s with the attack on the University of Wisconsin and much more recently with numerous attacks on defense contractors involved in the Pershing II and cruise missile production. When car bombs are used in this manner, they are either driven into the building prior to detonation or driven as close as possible to the building and then detonated. Since it takes only a dozen or so pounds per square inch (PSI) of dynamic pressure to topple virtually any common structural material and a typical car bomb produces a shock wave on detonation that may hit a building with several hundred PSI of dynamic force, it is clear that car bombs are a very effective means for terrorists to accomplish goals in a spectacular manner.

The countermeasure to a car bomb is to eliminate the ability of the vehicle to gain close access to its target. In the case of a moving target, this is fairly difficult and requires a moving box motorcade formation around the target vehicle, which is generally not practical; however, it is the only effective measure. If the target is a building, the bomb vehicle must be prevented from approaching close to the building. This can be accomplished in a number of ways.

Incendiaries

The use of incendiaries by terrorists has not increased much in recent years. The only significant advance in technology has been in the area of barrier penetration. A number of devices have recently surfaced and are presumably available to terrorists that allow rapid penetration through virtually any imaginable type of barrier, including barriers used to protect strategic weapons and other important materials. These hand-held incendiary devices generate a tremendous amount of heat (reportedly in excess of 4,400 degrees Fahrenheit) and in a matter of seconds will penetrate through steel doors up to an inch or more in thickness. Using this type of device, a terrorist group could penetrate a bunker, steal, modify or destroy the contents, and escape in less than the average response time of the armed force responsible for protecting the facility.

Standoff Weapons

Standoff weapons such as truck-mounted mortars, shoulder-fired antitank rockets, and suitcase-sized wire-guided missiles have emerged as the new technology of terrorism. The mortar systems perfected by the Irish Republican Army typically consist of large steel open-ended cylinders embedded in sand in the back of a dump truck. Often up to a dozen cylinders are found in each truck. In each cylinder, there is a propelling charge at the bottom, either black powder or some homemade propellant mixture, along with the mortar bomb itself. These mortars can weigh from a few pounds apiece for a 60 mm diameter system up to 40 pounds or more for the 250 mm behemoths that have been used most recently. These mortar systems are aimed by maneuvering the truck so that it is pointed at its intended target and is a certain distance from it. When the truck is in the right position, the mortar bombs are triggered. They are fired either one after another or all at once from the back of the truck, and the truck is then driven hastily away. This type of attack has proved to be a difficult technique to develop a countermeasure for when employed in an urban environment.

Although shoulder-fired antitank rockets have been available to terrorists for a decade or more, they have been used only sporadically in the United States. Recently, however, probably because of the availability of these rockets through the Cuban government, more and more have been discovered in the United States. Recently a shoulder-fired antitank weapon of Chinese or Soviet origin was discovered on the property of a Pacific Northwest utility company. Reportedly the company had received a threat that its oil storage tank would be attacked with such a weapon. Officials dismissed the threat as being unlikely, presuming the unavailability of these weapons. This dismissal was noted by the adversaries, who then chose to reinforce their threat by leaving one of the launchers propped against a fence as a clear indication that they certainly did have the hardware required to carry out their threat.

The common RPG-2 and RPG-7 shoulder-fired antitank rockets typically have a range of at least several hundred meters and on impact (at any range) will penetrate 10 inches or more of steel armor. Thus, virtually anything that they hit will be perforated. The countermeasures to these antitank rockets involve either erecting a wire fabric fence some distance from the surface of the target to cause the rocket to detonate before it reaches the target or erecting a false exterior or interior wall placed at least several inches away from the prior existing wall to minimize the penetrating qualities of the high-velocity jet formed by the explosion of the rocket warhead. Either countermeasure involves a considerable construction expense and, in the case of the wire fabric, considerable loss in aesthetic quality of the protected building.

The suitcase-size wire-guided missiles are similar in effect to the shoulder-fired antitank rockets except that they are slightly less convenient to employ. This is, however, offset by a significantly increased range (1,000 yards or more) combined with greatly enhanced penetration due to their larger diameter warhead. The latest missiles in this category reportedly penetrate 20 inches of steel armor and approximately 60 inches of concrete. The defenses against these missiles would be similar to those outlined for the shoulder-fired antitank rockets.

Chemical, Biological, and Toxin Agents

The use of poison gas or, more properly, chemical, biological, and toxin agents, is one of the greatest terrorist threats facing the United States. It was once thought that these agents were too complex for use by terrorists or that terrorists would avoid their use due to a fundamental abhorrence of their effects and fear of retribution, but this is no longer the case.

In the last several years, there have been several documented cases where terrorists or those that might harbor terrorist inciinations have, within the United States, sought to procure or have procured lethal toxins such as ricin, botulinal toxin, and tetanus toxin. Each of these toxins is several times more toxic than standard nerve gases held in the U.S. arsenal.

A terrorist or would-be terrorist could acquire these lethal agents from three likely sources. The first is purchase or theft of toxic gases used for industrial purposes, such as hydrogen cyanide, carbonyl chloride (commonly known as phosgene), arsine, or nickel carbonyl. All of these are commercially readily available. A second source for toxic agents is leftover war materials, principally from World War II. When the Allied forces withdrew from North Africa, they left hundreds, if not thousands, of tons of toxic chemicals in a variety of loaded munitions. These munitions remained untouched in the desert ammunition dumps for years. More recently, these dumps have been the source of chemical agents used by several different warring factions. Egypt used them in their attacks on the Yemen. The Iraqis used them against the Kurds and then against the Iranians. The third alternative source is patron states. The Soviets, and presumably the Libyans and Cubans, are known to maintain stocks of chemical agents, and the Soviets have given these agents to their surrogates for use.

Appropriate or likely targets for these agents fall into the classic categories of people, plants and animals, and material. It is more useful, however, to think of the targets in terms of economic or political value. The Tylenol scare of 1982 is an example of an economic target. In that instance, an as yet unidentified person or persons contaminated a small number of Tylenol capsules with a substance that killed the people who took the tablets. It was not a large-scale operation; few people were directly affected. But it brought a major pharmaceutical house virtually to its knees. It attracted major headlines and caused that company to lose a tremendous percentage of its market share, which only recently has it begun to regain. Thus, with a very small amount of toxic or effective agent, one individual was able to cause many millions of dollars worth of business interruption.

The use of a genetically modified bacterium to infect members of a specific ethnic group with a lethal disease would exemplify a politically devastating attack. It is feasible to devise such an agent and equally possible to disseminate it. The effects of such an attack, particularly if it were done serially in various places around the United States, would be immense. The executive branch of the government would come under immediate and intense media and congressional pressure to find and stop the perpetrators of such a hideous event, as well as to find an antidote for whatever was being disseminated. Due to the potential complexity of such a genetically engineered bug, it could take a long time to isolate the problem and to devise a suitable antidote. While the research was underway, an administration could fall to the pressures that would surely result from such an attack.

Nuclear Devices

What about nuclear terrorism? The subversive has several possible scenarios to act out. First is the construction of a functioning fission-type nuclear device. Alternatively, a terrorist could seek to contaminate a city with nuclear waste material by blowing a few hundred pounds of it up in the air from atop a tall building and allowing the wind to let it drift over the city. Finally, a terrorist group could seize and cause the meltdown of or other damage to a nuclear power facility.

Although these scenarios are theoretically possible, only the second one, the dissemination of nuclear waste material as a particulate cloud, is feasible. Designing and constructing a working nuclear weapon is difficult; were this not so, undoubtedly many more countries would be members of the nuclear club. Seizing and causing the destruction of a nuclear power plant would require in most cases at least a small army, as well as a significant amount of technological knowledge. An inside operation might be able to wreck havoc, but significant protections are in place in U.S. nuclear power facilities to guard against such a seizure.

Dispersal of nuclear waste material as an aerosol is thus the most likely initial step in nuclear terrorism. Nuclear waste materials continue to accumulate, high explosives are commonplace, and little in the way of technology is required to ascend a tall building and pile the nuclear trash on a box of explosives. The detonation of a simple dispersal device such as this would likely result in a significant area with severe radioactive (alpha) contamination, requiring both an evacuation of the populace and a massive clean-up operation. The costs associated with this type of incident would be in the millions of dollars.

How does the United States prevent such an occurrence? First, it must cut off the domestic source for waste material by moving rapidly toward development of secure, long-term storage sites. Then it must sharpen its ability to spot the illicit movement of nuclear materials to prevent introduction from abroad. Last, it needs to ensure that its response forces, principally within the Federal Bureau of Investigation and the Department of Energy's Nuclear Emergency Search Team, are kept at a high enough state of readiness to ensure a timely and effective interdiction capability.

Summary

The mechanics of terrorism, like the machinery of war, will continue to escalate in sophistication and destructive power as opposing defensive systems counter the techniques currently in vogue. Terrorists have shown little hesitation to adopt whatever technology is required to accomplish their desired goals. As the scope of these goals is increased or the level of violence is driven higher by a need to impress their patrons, terrorists will turn to the various technologies of mass destruction to accomplish these goals. This evolution is unlikely to be rapid, but it is inexorable and will culminate as the trigger to general war.

4

Vehicle Bombs:
Death on Wheels

Beth A. Salamanca

T he car bomb has been, and will continue to be, a popular terrorist attack method for a number of reasons. First, the use of a car bomb is a relatively easy technique; the construction of the bomb requires comparatively little technical know-how and can be accomplished using readily available information and materials. Second, the car bomb can be placed, concealed, and detonated with no hazard to the bomber. He or she can be positioned safely a great distance away yet be assured the device will explode as planned with precision accuracy. Third, because a vehicle can hold a large quantity of explosives, the resulting detonation creates mass casualties, effectively produces the desired psychological effect, and draws immediate media attention.

Vehicle bombs are explosive devices placed on or in vehicles for the purpose of causing death, injury, or property destruction. Traditionally the types of vehicles used to house explosive devices have been cars, vans, and trucks. With the recent surge in terrorist activity, the devices have also been placed on buses and railroad cars to obtain greater casualty rates and thus greater media attention.

The car bomb tactics and methods used to date include the following:

The use of an explosive device placed on or in a car to kill one or more occupants.

The use of a vehicle to transport and conceal an explosive device for delivery to the target.

The use of a vehicle to conceal a launching system for projected munitions.

The use of a vehicle as the primary container of the bomb when large quantities of explosive are employed.

The use of multiple bombs when a number of devices are employed in a coordinated bombing effort.

The use of well-concealed, booby-trapped devices to entrap law enforcement officers and bomb disposal experts.

Although all of these methods are still in use, the trend is toward terrorist employment of large explosive quantities and the placement of multiple devices, for the continued purpose of obtaining large numbers of casualties.

Construction of Car Bombs

All bombs, whether car bombs or other types of explosive devices, generally consist of a number of basic elements whose configuration may vary depending on the use and application. Their configuration, methods of configuration, and fusing mechanisms are limited only by the imagination of the bomber. The design of a car bomb or any other type of bomb can be extremely complex. Because the inner contents of a bomb are usually not visible, it cannot be ascertained how a particular device operates without expert interpretation using sophisticated tools and equipment; even then, it is difficult. (The types of bombs described here are simple in nature and discussed only to provide a general understanding of explosive devices and how they have been used. Readers should not conclude that all bombs work in only one way because the types of bombing methods and tactics are virtually limitless.)

Generally bombs contain an initiating explosive (such as a blasting cap), a main explosive charge, a power source, and a switch or series of switches. Blasting caps can be set off electrically or by use of a burning fuse. Blasting caps, though relatively small in size and destructive capability (an explosive amount comparable to the volume of a pencil eraser), produce the intense explosive forces required to ignite the less sensitive, larger, more powerful explosive charge such as TNT or plastic explosive. The larger charge or main charge produces the greatest destructive force and is what is generally referred to when bomb quantities are described. An electrical power source (battery) is required to set off an electrically fused bomb; a heat power source is necessary to initiate a burning-type fuse. A switch is required to turn the bomb on or cause it to detonate when desired. The types of switches available for use in explosive devices are limitless. Virtually anything that turns something on or off could be used to cause a bomb to explode. In some instances, a number of switches have been employed in a single device to make dismantling it difficult or impossible. Booby-traps are actually bomb switching mechanisms placed strategically to entrap the victim. These components generally constitute the basic elements of explosive devices and are also the basic components of vehicle bombs.

As with all other explosive devices, car bombs can be activated by numerous means. Methods used to date include time-delay (using clocks, timers, burning time fuse, or chemical delays), remote control (using walkie-talkies, model airplane controls, or paging systems), mechanical actions such as a pressure switch triggered when the victim sits down, and electrical-mechanical actions such as opening doors, turning ignition keys, opening glove compartments, and turning on lights.

Use of the Car Bomb to Kill Occupants

Historically, car bombs first consisted of small explosive devices placed on or in the vehicle, usually for the purpose of killing the occupants; the car served merely as another location in which murders could be carried out. Motivations for these bombings were similar to those of other murders, such as revenge, financial gain, anger, or suicide.

These early devices consisted of approximately 2 to 5 pounds (a few sticks of dynamite) of explosives placed where they would have the greatest killing effect on the intended target. Explosive devices have been placed on the firewall separating the passenger compartment from the engine, on the gas line, in the wheelwells, under headrests, in visors, under dashboards, and under seats. Small quantities of explosives, ¼ to ½ pound or less, produce devastating effects when placed effectively.

Al Capone and his henchmen were notorious for using bombs to persuade rivals, politicians, and law enforcement officers to do their bidding, and one of the earliest car bomb incidents dates back to the prohibition era. In that instance, a small dynamite bomb was attached to the firewall forward of the dashboard and wired to the electrical system of a car belonging to a Department of Justice agent. The agent noticed his hood latches were unfastened, suspected something was amiss, and detected the otherwise concealed device before turning the ignition key and activating the bomb.

Organized crime has continued to use car bombs and other bombing techniques to achieve coercion. Extortion, insurance fraud, punishment of informers, and the elimination of rivals are common motives. In one incident, a car bomb was used to murder a government witness to a Chicago gambling case. The 1975 bombing resulted in the death of Louis Bombacino as he unknowingly attempted to drive the bomb vehicle.

Hundreds of accounts illustrate the use of car bombs as a means to settle domestic quarrels. A North Carolina incident involved an attempted murder of the bomber's wife in the case of the "baby food bomber." Two explosive devices contained in baby food jars were wired to the ignition system and placed under the driver's seat. The jars were filled with bullet propellant and

M-80 firecrackers and were to have exploded when the ignition key was turned. The bombs were discovered and subsequently dismantled when the bomber, too impatient to await his wife's departure, removed them and carried them into the house to make good his threats to kill her.

Strategic location of the device and how well it is concealed are two factors that affect the relative success of a bombing attack. Often placement of the device depends on the bomber's accessibility to the vehicle. An unattended vehicle left unlocked and unobserved for a lengthy period of time would allow ready access to a bomber intent on wiring a bomb to the ignition system or concealing the device within the passenger compartment or under the frame. In this situation, both the bomber and the bomb would go undetected. Locking car doors and parking the car in a well-lighted, heavily trafficked, or often frequented location minimize the time available to the bomber to place the device. Thus, choices for bomb location would be reduced to those places where quick and easy placement could be accomplished: on firewalls, in tailpipes, and under gas tanks. In these instances, placement can be achieved in seconds, but the concealment of the device is minimal.

One of the most elementary ways of finding these devices, should one be traveling in a country where car bombs are regularly employed (Western Germany and other North Atlantic Treaty Organization countries), is a visual search. In wheelwells, under gas tanks, and in tailpipes are common hiding spots for bombs and devices can easily be detected by checking the car briefly before entering it. Diplomats traveling to high-threat posts are instructed to check their vehicles on a regular basis if the car has been left in an unsecured area. This can be done by standing at a distance of 15 feet or so and walking around the car, visually checking the area around and under it for suspicious items. Wires, bits of electrical tape, or other bomb components signal the potential existence of a bomb. Once it has been ascertained that no device is under the vehicle, the doors, hood, trunk, gas tank, and windows should be checked for signs of tampering. Tool marks or other signs that attempts have been made to force entry into the car serve as clues to a bomber's intentions. Before the driver opens the car, the interior should be checked for packages or other out-of-place items protruding from under seats, dashboards, or other locations within the passenger compartment. Only after this check can one have some assurance that a bomb has not been placed on or in the car. Drivers should always lock the doors of an unattended vehicle and obtain a locking gas cap.

An attempted assassination of a U.S. diplomat in Paris was thwarted when a simple search was conducted. A passerby noticed a package placed under the diplomat's car and reported the sighting to police officers and bomb disposal experts. The bomb squad arrived to check the suspect item and attempted to neutralize it. A detonation occurred that killed the bomb expert, illustrating the hazards of dealing with explosive devices. If a bomb is discovered, no attempt should be made to move or disturb the device in any way. The area should be evacuated and expert assistance immediately sought.

The successful assassination of Orlando Letelier illustrates the role that accessibility of the vehicle plays in whether a bombing can be carried out. Letelier, former Chilean ambassador to the United States, was the victim of a political assassination that took place at Sheridan Circle, Washington, D. C., September 21, 1976. A remotely controlled bomb was placed on his vehicle as it stood parked overnight next to his home. The device consisted of a 1.5 pound mixture of TNT and plastic explosive and a radio receiver fusing mechanism, all contained in a loaf pan, which was taped to the undercarriage of the car. The bomber's attempts to tape the pan with the bomb to the transmission area of the car proved futile because the black electrical tape he was using was not adhering to the greasy, dusty underside of the car. After numerous attempts, which all went undetected over a lengthy time period, one of the bombers was finally successful at fastening the device to the car.

The next day, as Letelier drove his vehicle to work, the bombers allegedly followed him in a second vehicle carrying the radio transmitter firing mechanism plugged into their vehicle's cigarette lighter to generate the necessary electricity to transmit the activating signal. According to testimony of the bombers' prison mate (questionable and still considered speculative), when the bombers transmitted the fire command to the radio receiver in the bomb, the explosive device failed to detonate. The bombers claimed that after a number of unsuccessful attempts to fire the device, they decided to repair the faulty wiring connections. Thus, they had to gain access to the vehicle a second time, remove the bomb, take it back to the workshop, correct the faulty wiring, and gain access to the car a third time to replace the bomb. The bombers bragged that they were able to remove, repair, and replace the bomb and finally detonate the device as Letelier drove. The explosion killed Letelier and a passenger, leaving one survivor.

Bombers recognize the problem that limited accessibility presents to their successful placement of the bomb within a vehicle. Hence, quick and easy placement is facilitated through the use of foreign military limpet mines or homemade soap dish bombs. Limpet mines and soap dish bombs are equipped with magnets or suction cups to adhere them to the gas tank or other surface. Soap dish bombs, in which approximately ¼ pound of explosive is contained in dime store soap dishes, are mass produced by some terrorist organizations.

Bombers often select the gas tank as a prime placement location because increased explosive effect can be obtained from the tank. The air-gas vapor of gasoline is highly explosive. Gas tanks that are completely filled contain little gas vapor and thus offer little explosive vapor to contribute to the force of the existing bomb. Less-than-half or quarter-full tanks supply a large quantity of air-gas vapor, which is readily consumed and adds to the explosive force of the existing bomb. In this way, a small quantity of actual explosive can yield a large blast effect.

In one incident, a small device (¼ pound explosive) placed on the gas tank of a U.S. diplomat's vehicle abroad resulted in only a negligible explosion since the gas tank had recently been filled.

Other political assassination attempts have used a bomb vehicle to house an explosive device placed along the route of the intended victim. This tactic is fairly common with terrorist groups as it is relatively safe and simple to carry out. The terrorist need only park the bomb vehicle containing the device in the vicinity of the target or along a known route and walk away. Using a remote control switch, the terrorist can observe the bomb vehicle from a safe distance and await the approach of the victim. When the victim is within range, a fire signal is transmitted to the bomb, causing it to detonate.

This tactic was used in Venezuela during the attempted assassination of President Betancourt. A 26 pound explosive device was placed on the seat of a car parked on the roadway on a known route. As Betancourt's car passed the bomb vehicle, the bomber detonated the device, spewing debris and fragmentation throughout the area. Upon investigation, remains of a black box, which proved to be a radio receiver, were recovered from the nearby underbrush.

The remotely controlled car bomb tactic is popular worldwide and frequently used in the Middle East and Northern Ireland. A remotely controlled car bomb that exploded in Hyde Park, London, in August 1982 exemplifies the effectiveness of the remote control device in creating headlines. The bomb, placed strategically on the roadway where a military parade would pass, consisted of 10 pounds of gelignite explosives and a large quantity of nails, which produced a devastating shrapnel effect. As the procession passed the bomb vehicle, the bomber waited for the opportunity that would result in the greatest number of casualties and transmitted the fire command. The explosion left four soldiers and seven horses dead and wounded thirty-two guards and civilians. A second device that exploded within two hours in a bandstand at Regents Park left two dead and twenty-eight injured. The use of two devices in conjunction to produce an even more dramatic incident is also a frequently used tactic. Perpetrated by the same bombers, the twin attacks received significant media attention, again publicizing the Irish Republican Army (IRA) cause.

Vehicles Used to Deliver Bombs

A second variation of the car bomb tactic employs the use of the vehicle to deliver and conceal the explosive device in order to gain access or improved proximity to the intended target. This method was popularized in the early 1970s by the IRA with their use of proxy car bombs and is still in use in Northern Ireland.

To penetrate security checkpoints and obtain a closer position to the targeted building, the IRA would kidnap a family member of a legitimate employee (such as a postal worker or police officer) of the intended target facility. They would then threaten harm to the hostage unless the employee delivered the bomb vehicle to his place of work or similar location. The employee had little choice but to comply, using his legitimate identity or identification pass to gain entry at check points and breach perimeter defenses. The employee acted as a proxy or representative of the bomber—hence the name *proxy car bomb*.

This tactic has been used with repeated success in the Middle East with the slight variation that the employee may or may not know that he is delivering an explosive device. In the 1983 bombing of the French embassy in Beirut, a large device was planted in the vehicle of an embassy employee. Unaware that she was delivering a bomb, the employee was recognized by the gate guard, waved through the identification checkpoint, and allowed to drive into the embassy compound, where the device detonated.

Detailed vehicle sweeps have proved successful in the discovery of explosive devices hidden in the cars of unwitting accomplices, but vehicle sweeps are time-consuming and inconvenient. In high-threat countries where car bombs are routinely employed, cars are subjected to an extensive search, or vehicle access within grounds or compound is prohibited. Employees are asked to leave their vehicles a distance from the work area outside the perimeter defenses or are encouraged to walk to work. Although somewhat inconvenient, this defense proves effective.

Another widely used tactic is to place car bombs on crowded streets, in shopping areas, or in other areas heavily trafficked by the public. Devices are timed to explode during periods when the greatest number of people are nearby, causing massive casualties to innocent bystanders and proving to be a devastating tactic of modern terrorists. The 1983 car bombing of Harrod's department store in London during the Christmas rush, killing six and injuring ninety-one, exemplifies the use of this technique.

A May 1985 bombing in a downtown section of Christian Beirut gained front-page news coverage by killing over 60 people and injuring over 200. Of the dead, 15 were children, riding in a nearby school bus. The car bomb contained an estimated 400 pounds of explosive, enough to topple building walls and set twelve surrounding cars on fire. This tactic is so prevalent in Beirut that shoppers and passersby were reportedly observed walking down the center-line of city streets in order to avoid possible car bombs parked at the curb.

Further illustrative of the prevalent use of car bombs in the Middle East was a sign observed on the Beirut corniche fronting the old U.S. embassy (site of the first large-scale embassy bombing), which was reported to have read (as translated by a native Lebanese): "Caution: All cars left unattended will be drowned." When asked to elaborate, the translator explained that all cars left unoccupied for more than 5 minutes were automatically considered suspicious and were immediately picked up by a remotely operated forklift and dumped over the seawall into the ocean.

Vehicle-Concealed Launching System

The use of a vehicle to transport and conceal a munition launching system is a third variation on the car bomb theme. This technique has been used to project rockets and mortars against buildings and their occupants.

A pickup truck that concealed a rocket launching rail was used during the attempted assassination of a U.S. ambassador in Argentina. The launch system consisted of a number of rails welded together in A-frame fashion, on which Belgian Mecar rockets were to be launched. The rockets were wired to a time-delay fusing mechanism and set to launch during the ambassador's breakfast hour. The rail frame and fusing system were placed in the payload section of the pickup, covered with a large pile of sawdust, and then parked close to the ambassador's residence, with rockets aimed at the kitchen area. The truck, though in clear view, went unnoticed until one of the rockets fired. The fact that the rocket missed and no injuries were sustained is attributed to the poor trajectory and faulty wiring of the device.

Other attacks on U.S. embassies have employed a similar method. In 1972, three U.S. military M-28 rockets were modified to fire by use of a timing mechanism, mounted within the trunk of a small sedan, aimed at the U.S. embassy in Beirut and fired after the elapsed delay. The rockets were fired from their original packaging cartons, which served as launch tubes. Launch ports were drilled in the side of the vehicle to facilitate the launch and were concealed by cardboard membranes painted to resemble autobody repairs. Two of the three rockets successfully fired. They hit the embassy structure, causing extensive damage and large penetrations; the third rocket failed to function as planned, causing no damage.

Vehicles Used to Contain Large Quantities of Explosive

In a fourth variation of the vehicle bomb tactic, massive quantities of explosive are used. Bombings have occurred where vehicles have been filled with large quantities of explosive materials in excess of 1,000 to 2,000 pounds and then parked at the target location. Trunks, door panels, station wagons, commercial truck payload areas, and vans have been filled to capacity with various types of explosive. In this application, the vehicle may serve as the container for the explosive device.

The August 24, 1970, bombing of an army research center at Sterling Hall, University of Wisconsin, used such a device. The 1,700 pound bomb was contained in a van parked on the street adjacent to the building. The explosive consisted of ammonium nitrate and fuel oil. Ammonium nitrate is the basic ingredient in commercial fertilizer and is readily available in bulk from hardware stores and garden shops. The force of the resulting explosion left an approximately 3 foot deep crater in the pavement, blew off the entire face of the building, and killed a graduate student working within the structure.

An incident involving the potential detonation of a 1,000 pound vehicle bomb occurred in Washington, D. C., during the threatened bombing of the Washington Monument in December 1982. Although no actual explosives were used, this was not determined until the conclusion of the incident. A large, white van was parked on the grounds close to the monument. The driver was a Florida antinuclear activist who threatened to blow up the monument with 1,000 pounds of TNT. All information then available to law enforcement officers indicated that the threat was in fact real. Observations and photographs of the driver showed that he carried what appeared to be a radio transmitter, similar to those used in remote-control devices to send a fire signal. The incident ended in gunfire, resulting in the death of Norman Mayer, the bomber. A search of the overturned van by trained dogs indicated that explosives were present; however, none were actually recovered. Although no live device existed, this incident illustrated the effectiveness of a bomb threat through use of a hoax device to create disruption and gain media attention. Threatened bomb attacks have proved to be just as newsworthy as actual bombings.

The suicide bomb attacks against U.S. and other targets in the Middle East illustrate another delivery method of vehicle bombs containing large quantities of explosive. These attacks have been ongoing in that region since the late 1970s and are the subject of much media coverage, which further perpetuates their use. Generally perpetrated by Iranian, Syrian, and Libyan terrorist elements, these bombings are publicly acclaimed by the Shiite Moslem group calling itself Islamic Jihad, which is generally believed to be an Iranian-controlled and-sponsored terrorist network. Although tracing those responsible for these bombings is highly complex and difficult, the cause or source of this series of suicide bombings is essentially attributed to Khomeini-inspired religious fanaticism. First employed against U.S. interests in Beirut on April 18, 1983, in the bombing of the U.S. embassy, suicide attacks were again used in three more instances against U.S. facilities where massive casualties were sustained. These attacks stunned and horrified the world because the suicide tactic was unforeseeable and incomprehensible to Western thinking.

In the first suicide bombing, a pickup truck carrying approximately 2,000 pounds of explosives crawled down the roadway toward the U.S. embassy on the Beirut waterfront. Eyewitness reports stated that the vehicle was so heavily laden that the wheels were rolling on the rims. At approximately 1:00 P.M., the truck passed through the embassy's perimeter barrier, crashed into the building, and detonated inside. The detonation caused the building to collapse, killing sixty-three, seventeen of whom were Americans, and wounding one-hundred.

The second suicide bombing took place October 23, 1983, in the bombing of the Twenty-Fourth Marine Amphibious Unit, Marine Headquarters, located at the Beirut airport. The device consisted of approximately 10,000 to 12,000 pounds (6 tons) of explosives contained in a Mercedes truck. At 6:20 A.M. the truck was driven through perimeter barriers (concertina wire, wire-mesh fence, and pipe barricades), between two sentry posts where shots were fired, and finally into the first floor of the headquarters building. The ensuing detonation was devastating, resulting in the collapse of the four-story structure and a U.S. Marine death toll of 241.

The third suicide bombing against U.S. interests occurred December 12, 1983, against the U.S. embassy in Kuwait. The 9:30 A.M. bombing resulted in six dead, seventeen wounded, and partial building collapse of the annex building. The vehicle used was a dump truck, which crashed through the gate to the embassy compound, sped toward the annex building, and exploded within the parking lot area. The explosive charge reportedly approached 4,000 pounds equivalent of TNT, of which only a quarter exploded, resulting in a partial detonation, which nonetheless achieved the terrorist goal.

The most recent suicide bombing incident against a U.S. embassy occurred at 11:45 A.M. on September 20, 1984, at the annex in Beirut. A van containing an estimated 3,000 pounds of explosive negotiated road obstacles designed to impede bomb vehicles, penetrated security checkpoints, was fired upon by security personnel, yet managed to gain close proximity to the annex structure, where it detonated. Because the explosion occurred a distance away from the building and the blast was partially deflected by a 6 foot wall, the explosion resulted in substantially less damage and loss of life than might otherwise have occurred.

Defenses against the suicide car or truck bomb are currently in the development stage. They consist primarily of physical barriers, tank-trap-type obstacles, vehicle mazes, use of increased buffer distances, and armed security guards with orders to fire on drivers of suspicious vehicles. It is not uncommon in the Middle East to see large mounds of dirt piled to block vehicle access to roads and thoroughfares. Concrete forms, spiked caltrops, tanks aimed to fire at approaching vehicles, and dump trucks filled with dirt have been employed in the Middle East to prevent vehicle bombs from penetrating into various areas. One has but only to look at government facilities in Washington, D.C., to see the impact the suicide car bomb threat has had on security in the United States.

Development of effective and practical defenses against large, moving vehicles has thus far proved difficult. Barrier walls and fences must be strong enough to withstand the impact and inertia of a crashing vehicle moving at fast speeds. The protective barrier must be placed a sufficient distance from the area being protected to provide a safety buffer; a bomb exploding at the wall must be far enough away to present minimal blast damage to the occupants of the building. Defense is thus very difficult to accomplish, since the space surrounding urban buildings is generally limited, and suitable buffer areas can be achieved only by blocking the roadways surrounding the area to be protected. The practicality of blocking off thoroughfares is questionable, yet this method has proved to be the only reliable defense against the car bomb threat.

Other security efforts to deter a suicide vehicle attack have dealt with the psychological traits of the bomber as compared to those of suicidal individuals as a whole. This has also proved a difficult task since few suicide survivors are available for study. Studies of suicide attempts have indicated that depressed individuals en route to commit suicide have failed to carry out the act when their psychological momentum is broken. Current theory suggests that suicide bombers may be subject to a similar phenomenon; perhaps the bomber's encountering of physical barriers may provide enough of a disruption of the psychological momentum to cause the bomber to abort the mission.

Use of Multiple Bombs

The fifth vehicle bomb tactic observed to date employs the use of multiple bombs aboard vehicles used for public transportation. A number of explosive devices are placed on trains or buses and timed to explode within seconds of each other for the purpose of creating mass casualties to innocent bystanders and the general public. This tactic has been used by the IRA, the PLO, and other Middle Eastern terrorist groups and more recently by the Sikhs in India. They have targeted school buses, mass transit buses, and metropolitan rail systems, all with the intent to raise public outcry and gain media coverage. The selection of public transportation vehicles as sites for terrorist bomb attacks will most likely continue because access controls have not been effectively or systematically instituted.

Booby Traps

The last variation on the vehicle bomb tactic involves the use of the vehicle to entrap bomb disposal experts and law enforcement officers with booby-trapped explosive devices. These tactics normally employ sophisticated wiring or expertly concealed devices to fool and deceive the victim. Because a relatively long time is needed to rig such a device, bombers often resort to using stolen cars, which they can hold in their possession for an indefinite period of time, enabling them to make the meticulous and time-consuming concealment preparations and wiring connections.

A 1981 incident perpetrated by the Armed Forces of Popular Resistance, a Puerto Rican group supporting the liberation of Puerto Rico, exemplifies such a device. During a convention where former Secretary of State Henry Kissinger was in attendance, police and firefighters responded to what apparently was a routine car fire located in the garage of the Contado Convention Center. After the fire was successfully put out, the car was identified as stolen and taken to the impound lot to await further disposition. A few days later, upon closer inspection, a suitcase was discovered in the trunk of the vehicle containing bomb residue (partially consumed by the fire), explosive material, fusing mechanisms, remains of pocketwatch timers, an additional clock, and a lantern battery. Also recovered was an antidisturbance switch, which could be activated by jarring the vehicle. Further examination revealed that the four doors, trunk, and hood were booby-trapped with pressure-release switches; opening the door was supposed to have detonated the device.

Because a number of high-ranking dignitaries were attending the conference and in view of the comparative complexity and sophistication of the device, many concluded that the purpose of the device was to entrap unsuspecting law enforcement officers as they performed routine area sweeps for explosive devices. Another opinion is that the multiple firing systems were designed to lure police and firefighters to the car bomb by starting a small fire with one firing system, drawing attention, and enticing subsequent opening of the vehicle, which would result in its detonation.

Other entrapment tactics have involved the repeated placement of similar bombs in vehicles. When bomb technicians responded to the bomber's alert, time after time they encountered identically constructed explosive devices. After many responses to apparently the same type of device, the technician learned to expect a particular construction and type of fusing. Once the bomber established a pattern, he or she would change the device slightly so the bomb was not as anticipated. The technician's incorrect conclusion about the construction of the device would result in an explosion. This technique is common in Northern Ireland and the Middle East.

In another recent entrapment incident, a number of firefighters were killed by an exploding van while responding to a fire alarm in Brussels, Belgium. An eyewitness to the event saw a white Toyota van pull up next to the Belgian Business Federation headquarters around midnight. Two men got out of the van, set it ablaze, and then ran from the area. Minutes later, while fire and rescue workers attempted to put out the fire, the van detonated, killing two and wounding twelve. A Brussels terrorist group, Communist Combatant Cells, claimed credit for the blast in protest of an economic summit of major industrialized nations.

The use of the vehicle bomb has been a tool of both criminals and terrorists. Criminals have used, and most likely will continue to use, car bombs as a means to carry out murders involving the usual motivations; the car will simply serve as a location to carry out traditional crimes against the occupants using one bombing technique or another.

The evolution of the vehicle bomb as a terrorist tactic has shown some definite trends, which most likely will result in its repeated and systematic application for the purpose of gaining media attention. The "bigger is better" philosophy held by many terrorist groups makes vehicle bombs the ideal tactic: the more explosives that can be detonated, the greater the casualties, which make for better headlines. Since terrorists are imitative rather than innovative and since terrorist groups closely monitor the outcomes of other groups' attacks and sometimes participate in exchange of information and technology, they have surely observed the track record of the vehicle bomb tactic. We most likely can anticipate the worldwide effects of the copy cat syndrome: the increased terrorist use of large-scale vehicle bombs on a global basis.

As the bombings continue, so do the efforts of the protectors to identify practical ways to stop the killing. To say the task is difficult is an understatement. In the case of the suicide bombing tactic, it is virtually impossible to stop penetration into an area without seriously disrupting normal daily operations. Yet law enforcement agencies, military forces, and government bureaus have continued to focus on the vehicle bomb threat with hopes of reaching a workable solution. In many respects, the responsibility to prevent or deter the bombing to the extent possible lies with the individual police officer, security guard, sentry, and bomb technician—all of whom are potentially in the position to confront the bomb on an individual basis where it is found. Whether the bomb is found on a crowded street, in a parking garage, or speeding through a gate, these people must make a split-second decision and take the correct action or perish with the device. In some instances, the explosion is inevitable.

5
Organized to Combat Terrorism

William R. Farrell

Terrorism is an affront to society and threatens the very foundations on which it rests. Often the targets of terrorist attacks are the institutions and the personages holding power within a society. The strength of a society and its government depends in part on the ability of agencies to provide for the safety and security of its people. In democratic states, there is a need for public support or, at a minimum, acceptance of the activities undertaken by a government to ensure the public welfare. The use of secret police and denial of the rights of free speech and assembly will not be tolerated, save under the most extreme circumstances.

How a democratic government responds to threats to its personnel serving overseas is also subject to domestic approval. The values that a government seeks to protect and nurture cannot be sacrificed in a response outside its borders. The legitimacy of a government may be in jeopardy if the populace sees contradictions in behavior from those staunchly advocated at home.

Responding to terrorism is difficult and complicated. The threat is usually not constant; it waxes and wanes. The characteristics of a terrorist act frequently are idiosyncratic, taking on the peculiarities of a particular group, geographic area, or manner of execution. The people of a nation deserve protection and demand it when it is found lacking. Yet an action taken by a government that is effective in countering hijacking may have no effect on reducing incidents of bombing and kidnapping. Governments have to respond to many aspects of a problem contained under the one label: terrorism. In this regard, they, through their established organizations, attempt to provide that security as required. How well and how significantly a government addresses this type of threat can be discerned through a review of official public statements, pronouncements, organizational charts, and identification of the people involved. While that may sound like a rather dry approach to an otherwise exciting subject, the results are quite enlightening.

Historical Review

The beginning of the U.S. government's response to terrorism can be traced to the massacres that occurred at Lod Airport in Tel Aviv, Israel, and the Olympic village in Munich, Germany, in 1972. The horrors of the incidents were carried into homes by television. Members of the Japanese Red Army had killed Puerto Rican pilgrims as they moved through the terminal on the way to visit holy Christian sites. The ABC television network's coverage of the Olympics ensured that the hour-by-hour trauma endured by the Israeli athletes would be seen by millions around the world. These large-scale events came on the heels of a period of years of repeated hijackings by terrorist groups.

In September 1972, President Richard Nixon sent a memorandum to the secretary of state, William Rogers, establishing the Cabinet Committee to Combat Terrorism. The committee was chaired by the secretary of state and comprised the secretary of the treasury, the secretary of defense, the attorney general, the secretary of transportation, the U.N. ambassador, the director of the Central Intelligence Agency (CIA), the assistant to the president for National Security Affairs, the director of the Federal Bureau of Investigation (FBI), and such others as the chairman might consider necessary. The cabinet committee was to be supported by a working group comprised of personally designated senior representatives.[1]

The first and only meeting of the committee was held a few days later; however, a working group was in place, centered in the Department of State, to deal with the terrorist threat. The initial chairman of the group was Armin H. Meyer. Within the department he became the special assistant to the secretary and coordinator for combating terrorism. At the time, it was the general perception that the problem of terrorism centered in the Middle East.

It is important to recognize that within State, a separate office or organization was not created at this time. Rather, it was the position of special assistant with a deputy. The actual Office for Combating Terrorism was not established until the summer of 1976. At that time the director of the office was no longer responsible to the secretary but instead came under the purview of the deputy under secretary for management.

The working group, as the sole support for the cabinet committee, was to bring "the full resources of all appropriate US agencies to bear effectively on the task of eliminating terrorism wherever it occurs." In reviewing the history of the effort by the Department of State to counter terrorism, it must be noted that the individual to chair the working group had changed seven times in as many years (1972–1978). Those who left the post either retired or were reassigned to relatively minor posts. Ambassador Anthony Quainton seemed to reverse that trend and remained in his job from July 1978 to the spring of 1982. Rober Sayer, the former ambassador to Brazil, took over the office in May 1982 and remained there until reassignment in 1984, when Robert Oakely assumed the post.

The working group during the period from 1972 to 1979 grew from the original membership of ten to thirty-one federal agencies and departments. During the administration of President Jimmy Carter, due to the inactivity of the cabinet committee, revisions in U.S. structure and policy were made. The Special Coordination Committee (SCC) of the National Security Council was to oversee efforts of the government to formulate policy to combat terrorism. In practice it was expected that the SCC would directly exercise its responsibility in the event of a major incident requiring the highest-level decisions.

In general the U.S. government's response was to be based on the lead agency concept. The State Department would have operational responsibility for international incidents, and the Department of Justice and the FBI would handle domestic incidents coming under federal jurisdiction. Aircraft hijacking was considered a special case, and Congress mandated through law that the Federal Aviation Administration (FAA) would have primary responsibility in this field. Each agency was to draw on the expertise of other agencies as required. What once were the functions of the old cabinet committee now were under the senior-level interagency Executive Committee on Terrorism (ECT), which consisted of members from the departments of State, Defense, Justice, Treasury, Transportation (FAA), and Energy, in addition to the CIA. Toward the end of the Carter administration, all the agencies that composed the working group were reorganized along functional lines (domestic, foreign, crisis, research and development, public information).

The Department of Justice oversees the FBI's and the Immigration and Naturalization Service's efforts to deal with terrorism. The FBI has been the agency that exercises principal investigative authority for criminal violations under federal law. The FBI also has jurisdiction to investigate nuclear incidents that are criminal in nature. Nuclear extortions, when there is the threatened use of a device, will be investigated as extortion and will demand close cooperation among the FBI, Department of Defense, and Department of Energy.

The CIA is a main source of intelligence on the subject of international terrorism. Little information is available in the public arena to detail the methods and sources involved in their mission. Suffice it to say that the director of central intelligence has the authority to direct the government's intelligence collection efforts.

The Department of Defense has two roles to play in countering terrorism. First, it must protect its own personnel and resources. Second, within tightly constrained legal parameters, it can render support to the efforts of other federal, state, and local agencies. There has been a long-standing tradition of not using regular military forces in any civil or criminal matter in the United States. Such involvement, even in matters of international terrorism, will be well researched and thought out prior to the employment of military units.

The primary concern of the Department of Transportation is manifest through the FAA and the need for aviation security (to include hijackings). This agency can affect the flying schedules and landing rights of both foreign and domestic lines. Should a nation fail to follow the standards of the International Civil Aviation Organization in the maintenance of proper security and protection of passengers, the secretary of transportation, with the approval of the secretary of state, can impose certain restrictions on U.S. carriers flying to that nation and that country's planes landing in the United States. Also part of the Department of Transportation is the U.S. Coast Guard. This agency works closely with the FBI and the U.S. Navy concerning threats to ports, shipping, and offshore facilities.

The Department of Treasury has a great deal of law enforcement responsibility within its authority centering around the U.S. Secret Service, Customs Service, and Bureau of Alcohol and Firearms. The Secret Service has protective responsibility for the president, vice-president, foreign heads of state when they visit, and the major presidential candidates during election periods. Additionally, the Uniform Division of the Secret Service has responsibility for protecting the White House and foreign embassies in the United States.

The U.S. Customs Service is mainly concerned with the detection of terrorists as they enter the country. The identification of the illegal exporting of firearms and munitions also falls under the purview of the Customs Service. Some of these functions are also the concern of the Bureau of Alcohol, Tobacco and Firearms. The bureau has jurisdiction over most bombings; however, when there is reason to believe that the act was carried out by a terrorist, the FBI has primary jurisdiction. The recent bombings of abortion clinics in the United States is an example of this particular jurisdictional matter. The FBI refused to characterize the incidents as being terrorist despite a good deal of public pressure to do otherwise. Alcohol, Tobacco and Firearms pursued the investigation quite successfully. If however, the Department of Justice or the president decided that the FBI should have primary jurisdiction, it could have been arranged. There is enough room in the acceptable definitions of terrorism to allow this maneuvering to take place.

The Department of Energy is involved in government nuclear materials management and security. Within the department is the Nuclear Emergency Search Team (NEST), which, with the assistance of the FBI and Defense, will provide hazard assistance in the location and neutralization of nuclear explosive devices. Also within the department is the Office of Safeguards and Security, which is responsible for the protection of special nuclear materials and nuclear facilities from theft or sabotage.

Current Structure and Policy

When one reviews the organization and policy of the U.S. government to deal with terrorism over the past decade, one is struck by the great deal of similarity. The policy on which the structure is built has remained the same.[2] The Reagan administration has continued to endorse what was stated by President Nixon in 1972: the United States will not give in to terrorist blackmail. It will not pay ransom, release prisoners or bargain for the release of hostages. Underpinning this position, is the belief that concessions to the terrorists will jeopardize the lives and freedom of additional innocent people in the future.

To carry out this policy, the government has drawn up a strategy that focuses on measures to prevent terrorist attacks (target hardening and education of personnel), measures to react to terrorist incidents (command centers, exercises, response forces), and measures to bring about international consensus against terrorism (U.N. actions, bilateral agreements).

The existing organization for antiterrorism, planning coordination, and policy formulation bears a striking resemblence to what was in place during the mid- to late 1970s. There have been some changes in terminology; for example, the senior-level executive committee is now an interdepartmental group. The office of the vice-president has been included, reflecting the crisis-response program initiated in the early years of the Reagan administration. This is the Special Situation Group, which is chaired by the vice-president and consists of the secretaries of defense and state, the director of central intelligence, chief of staff (White House), assistant to the president for national security affairs, chairman of the Joint Chiefs of Staff, and other National Security Council members as appropriate. The senior interdepartmental group would support the Special Situation Group with the necessary information concerning the incident and options available.

If one examines the U.S. effort to combat terrorism in recent years, there may be initial disappointment at the lack of spectacular responses to what were spectacular attacks. A deeper examination is more revealing and more in line with the existing structure's capability. Additionally, the comments of the secretary of state during 1984 and 1985 are indicative of potentially significant developments.

Secretary George Shultz's speeches take a giant step beyond what has been the U.S. policy to date. It is one thing to state that as a nation, the United States will not pay ransom. It is quite another to state that it must go beyond passive defense to consider the means of active preemption and retaliation. The policy of deterrence should be expanded to swift and sure measures against terrorists. Such actions should be viewed not only as a moral right but also a duty that a nation owes to its people. Shultz has correctly pointed out that the real challenges lie in those instances where international rules do not apply: terrorists striking from areas where no authority exists in a way that makes clear identification of the groups difficult at best. He is seeking to ensure that the American people appreciate before the fact that there are risks involved and some U.S. military may be lost in any response; that there are occasions when the government must act before every fact is known; that some make U.S. military and policymakers appear to be the culprits. Shultz is both educating the people and seeking popular support while sending the important signal that hard decisions such as these cannot be tied to popularity polls.[3]

On a less publicized level, interagency cooperation has led to the development of a legislative package presented by the administration to Congress to address short-falls in the counterterrorist program. Two bills deal with implementation of international conventions signed by lacking enforcement mechanisms (the Montreal Convention concerning aircraft hijacking and the U.N. Convention on hostage taking). Another authorizes the payment of rewards for information leading to the location of hostages or the resolving of terrorist incidents. These bills became legislation as Congress concluded its session in late 1984. The final bill sought to prohibit the provision of training or support by individuals and organizations (within U.S. jurisdiction) to states that practice terrorism. However, segments of the package appeared to infringe on rights protected under the Constitution and never went further than the House Foreign Affairs Committee.

Increased international cooperation has also shown itself. Both the London (1984) and the Bonn (1985) economic summits brought forth pledges of better cooperation among the United States, its European allies, Canada, and Japan to meet the threat.

The U.S. government has established the Anti-Terrorism Assistance Program to help friendly governments counter terrorism by training foreign delegations at U.S. facilities in crisis management, hostage and barricade negotiations, airport security measures, and bomb disposal methods. U.S. embassies have been subjected to hightened security plans and construction projects to protect people and facilities. Significant efforts have also been undertaken in the area of intelligence gathering and analysis.[4]

Some Reflections and Thoughts

A way to view the changes in the structure and response mechanisms that have taken place over the years could be likened to an examination of an evolutionary process. The word *evolutionary* is a deliberate choice, reflecting a time-consuming development of various forms of life that have been sustained or died off. Whether they were called working groups, executive committees, special coordinating committees, policy committees, or the current interagency groups, in fact they closely resembled what came before. Some modifications showed themselves as each sought to adapt to its environment.

The Special Security Group (SSG) and the Interdepartmental Group on Terrorism (IG/T) are sound approaches to a series of preceived needs. The elements of decision making, policy formulation, and coordination are all present, but there are some limitations. Although policymaking can involve extended periods of interagency debate, it is not a vehicle for rapid decisions. While the lead agency can implement decisions, it is not the best tool for interagency policymaking. Crisis decision makers are dependent on both policy coordination and implementation tools to be in place for them to be effective. While the IG/T is not an ad hoc structure, it is also not in continuous session. When one considers all the implications of the active responses cited by Secretary Shultz, one wonders if greater centralization may be required.

This is one of the great dilemmas within a federal bureaucracy. There exists the competing requirement of centralized coordination and decentralized execution. This is similar to the problems confronted by Alexander Hamilton and James Madison shortly after the founding of the nation: how much authority and power should be given to the executive department in order to protect the country from the dangers that threaten it. Hamilton, and many others today, would opt for greater control by the executive, for if the nation is defeated, what good are all the liberties granted to the people (especially if they hinder the formulation of effective policy for their defense)? Those who sided with Madison generally won out, and popular representation was seen as the primary objective (effective policy formulation in a strong executive). The checks, balances, and tensions that come with such a system prevail today in an open society where the media, academics, and popular opinion affect policy formulation. While we speak proudly of such a system, it can certainly be frustrating to those seeking a quick solution to a serious problem.

There have been calls in the recent past for the creation of a counterterrorism czar to meet the needs of such a complex threat. The term *czar* implies a strong element of control that in fact would not exist. As figure 5–1 shows, numerous federal agencies have statutory powers that dictate that their agency would not only be involved in the counterterrorist effort but spell out just how they will respond. Any czar would be bound by these legalized, institutionalized barriers and could only coordinate, never dictate. Change in these laws would also mean that Congress was able to view the problem as needing extensive revision of the laws they had previously established. Such unanimity may be more wishful thinking than practical reality

Another fact of life in federal bureaucracies is that the agencies charged

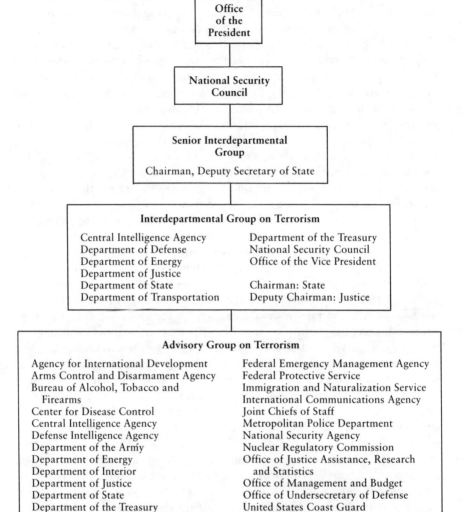

"Combatting Terrorism: American Policy and Organization," *Department of State Bulletin*, (Washington, D.C.: U.S. Department of State, August, 1982), p. 6.

Figure 5–1. U.S. Government Organization for Antiterrorism, Planning, Coordination, and Policy Formulation

with developing and executing the needed policy may not view the solution in the same way. Additionally, the issue may not be central to that particular department. For years the State Department saw terrorism as a Middle East issue and did not form the Office for Combating Terrorism until four years after the establishment of the original cabinet committee. Even then the office did not carry great weight within its parent organization, a fact not missed by those asked to coordinate with it. The Department of Transportation sees terrorism through the lens of aviation security and maritime law enforcement. For the Department of Energy, it is a matter of protection of nuclear material and facilities. The Department of Defense is not only concerned with the protection of its people and facilities but also with ensuring popular support for any undertaking on its part. In the wake of the ill-fated 1980 Iranian rescue and the bombing in Beirut, there is also a strong desire to win the next one.

Policy formulation is complicated by the fact that the threat is not constant; there are periods of drought as well as flood. The threat is also not precise (terrorism can be carried out by many types of groups, for many reasons, by many methods). Couple this with the problem being factored among so many agencies, and there is more than ample ground for reasonable people to debate constantly just what the response should be.

If a response to terrorism is to be carried out by the United States, it is more a function of policy direction from the White House than a matter of how the organizations are structured. Federal agencies have their agendas and their priorities independent of presidential direction. When cabinet officers meet, whether in the form of a lead agency or in response to the president's call, they meet as equals. They can determine if their agency will be part of a particular endeavor and to what degree. Without White House direction, their participation will be in proportion to the impact on their department.

For their part, the president and the National Security Council have dozens of items demanding their attention on a daily basis. Does the United States talk with the Soviets on arms reduction? What is to be done about the strategic defense initiative? What are the issues in Central America to be settled? What is the latest in the Middle East? What are the next steps in the battle of the budget? What will be the impact of a particular policy decision on the next election? What about the North Atlantic Treaty Organization, the Far East, Southwest Asia? The demands for attention never cease. Terrorism is one of many, but one that the media can swiftly make up front and personal.

The president has on occasion spoken out when the situation demanded. The secretary of state, an individual with the trust and confidence of the president, continues to address the issue, raising the consciousness of the American people concerning the nature and consequences of any U.S. response. Meanwhile, the agencies concerned continue to address terrorism as it affects them and their individual constituencies. In our form of government, we can expect little more. We do have the right to expect, however that those who are charged with policy development in this area will give it the attention it deserves. Failure in this regard could be costly and worthy of condemnation by the American people.

Notes

1. For a fuller review of how the U.S. government confronted the problem of terrorism from the period 1972 to 1981, see William R. Farrell, *The U.S. Government's Response to Terrorism* (Boulder, Colo.: Westview Press, 1982). Many of the points raised in the first part of this chapter are based on information taken from that book.

2. *Department of State Bulletin* (January 1982, August 1982, September 1984).

3. Ibid. (December 1984). This contains the text of one of Secretary Shultz's speeches that captures the tone on the series of talks given since the spring of that year.

4. *Gist* (September 1984). *Gist* is published by the Bureau of Public Affairs in the Department of State.

6

Target America:
The Undeclared War

James Berry Motley

> Offensive action, whatever form it takes, is the means by which the
> nation or a military force captures and holds the initiative, achieves
> results, and maintains freedom of action. . . . No matter what the
> level, strategic or tactical, the side that retains the initiative through
> offensive action forces the foe to react rather than to act.[1]

errorism is a form of unconventional warfare that the United States
has yet to come to grips with, despite the political rhetoric emitting
from Washington, D.C. From a U.S. perspective, this age-old phenomenon as a form of warfare is a relatively new concept that has received
little doctoral categorization or interpretation. More important, the resources
needed to cope with the problem are insufficient. In short, as a nation, the
United States does not understand terrorism, and as a government, it is not
prepared to deal with terrorist violence. U.S. antiterrorist policy is declaratory; its strategic thinking is reactive. Systematic state-supported international terrorism, which currently confronts the United States and which in all
likelihood will worsen, presents formidable challenges for those responsible
for U.S. national security.[2]

To accept the premise that terrorism is warfare on the cheap requires (1)
understanding the evolving historical political context within which this form
of warfare is currently being waged; (2) recognizing its purpose and by whom
it is being directed; (3) accepting the fact that in coping with terrorism, it is
highly unlikely that an American consensus will be forthcoming; and (4) acknowledging that conducting selective offensive U.S. military actions to destroy, disrupt, contain, and reduce terrorist organizations is a feasible political-military option that cannot be ignored.[3]

In the subsequent discussion, I will argue four major points. First, terrorism is a form of unconventional warfare used by the Soviet Union, its
client states, and proxies as a useful strategic and tactical weapon in the overall Marxist-Leninist world revolutionary war process. Second, state-supported international terrorism poses an increasing threat to the security and

well-being of the United States; the U.S. military has become an increasingly popular target. Third, the controversy surrounding the proposed use of U.S. military force in responding to state-supported international terrorism has not been examined in depth, given the evolving nature of the terrorist threat. Fourth, in terms of policymaking, there is a great deal of uncertainty associated with terrorist warfare. Based on current trends, however, the United States has no responsible choice other than to plan for increasing and more destructive and sophisticated terrorist acts. This planning has to be done in a pragmatic, sustained, and committed fashion, with the use of U.S. military force in the near future a distinct possibility.

Governments see in terrorism—whether they use terrorist tactics themselves, employ terrorist groups, or exploit terrorist incidents—a cheap weapon system for waging undeclared, unconventional war against the United States. I do not concur in the emerging belief held by some that the United States must fight only popular, winnable wars. When U.S. policymakers are confronted with future acts of state-supported international terrorism, they must take direct and forceful action. The decisions required may entail severe consequences, but such decisions must be made without vacillation or apology. In short, the United States, being the superpower that it is, must be prepared to retaliate against those who repeatedly employ force against U.S. interests. The United States cannot allow terrorists or those who support this form of political violence a free ride. The United States must demonstrate its resolve in defending itself without compromising its honor or ideals.

Terrorist Warfare: Old Truths–New Realities

Although an old social and political phenomenon, terrorism in recent years has received renewed attention because of the proliferation of terrorist activities. Since 1980 there has been a rise of state-supported international terrorism. More states have joined the ranks of what one U.S. senior official describes as the "League of Terror" as full-fledged sponsors and supporters of indiscriminate—and not so indiscriminate—murder.[4] Terrorists attacks supported by what Qaddafi calls the "holy alliance" of Libya, Syria, and Iran and attacks sponsored by North Korea and others have taken a heavy toll of innocent lives. Seventy or more such attacks in 1983 probably involved significant state support or participation.[5]

The involvement of Soviet and East European activities in support of international terrorism is well known, a matter I will discuss in greater detail later. At this point, it is sufficient to make three points.[6] First, the Soviet Union and its allies have provided training, arms, and other direct and indirect support to a variety of national insurgent and separatist groups. Many of these groups commit international terrorist attcks as part of their program of revolutionary violence. Moreover, some of the individuals trained and equipped by the Soviets make their way into strictly terrorist groups that have little revolutionary history or potential.

Second, Moscow continues to maintain close relations with and furnish aid to governments and organizations that directly support terrorist groups. In the Middle East, for example, the Soviets and their East European allies sell large quantities of arms to Libya and Syria and support Palestinian groups that have conducted terrorist operations. In Latin America, the Soviet Union and Cuba appear to be pursuing a long-term coordinated campaign to establish sympathetic Latin American regimes. Part of their strategy is to nurture organizations and groups that use terrorism in support of their efforts to undermine existing regimes. In other parts of the world, especially Africa, the Soviets have supported guerrilla movements and national liberation organizations that at times engage in terrorism. Finally, according to press reports, Bulgaria and other East European countries sell large amounts of Soviet-style military equipment to private arms dealers and brokers, who can resell these items. Some of this materiel is eventually acquired by groups that commit terrorist acts.

In the aftermath of the October 23, 1983, bombing of the U.S. Marine Corps battalion landing team's headquarters in Beirut, which claimed the lives of 241 U.S. servicemen, state-supported international terrorism became for a short time a major U.S. national security concern. Unfortunately—as witnessed by this incident and the subsequent September 20, 1984, suicidal terrorist car bombing of the U.S. embassy annex in Aukar, a suburb of Christian East Beirut—interest within the U.S. bureaucracy in antiterrorist and counterterrorist matters tends to rise and fall depending on the elapsed time since the most recent terrorist act.[7] (There is a critical distinction between antiterrorist and counterterrorist operations. The former denotes an offensive strategy employing a range of options to prevent terrorist acts from occurring. The latter are retaliatory measures, primarily the use of force, after the fact and thus more accurately termed a reactive strategy. Although the current U.S. program is described as antiterrorist, in reality it is counterterrorist and to date has not implemented decisive preventive-offensive action.) With the exception of a small group of professionals, the problem of coping with terrorism receives little serious study within the United States until the next major terrorist attack arouses transient interest. It is viewed by many as a low-priority national security issue, albeit an issue that competes with other programs for scarce resource allocation.

Growing state-supported international terrorism carries serious consequences for the United States. A February 1985 report by eighteen experts on terrorism concluded: "The continuing reliance by states on terrorism and other forms of subversion to accomplish political ends may lead to a diminution of international stability and unprecedented degradation of law and order throughout the world." The group further concluded that state-sponsored terrorism rivals arms control as the biggest international problem confronting the United States and that "it is imperative that the public and its governments understand the implications of this and begin to formulate the means to prevent its occurrence."[8]

One U.S. authority notes: "It [state sponsorship of terrorism] puts more resources in the hands of the terrorists: money, sophisticated munitions, intelligence, and technical expertise. It also reduces the constraints on them, permitting them to contemplate large-scale operations without worrying so much about alienating perceived constituents or provoking public backlash."[9] More specifically, the types of assistance offered terrorist groups by countries who support this form of violence include safe haven, documentation, communications, propaganda, and logistical support. In some cases, according to a U.S. official, governments have selected the target and provided operational guidance and vulnerability data on the prospective victim. Iran, Libya, Syria, and North Korea are the most blatant practitioners of this form of warfare, with the Soviet Union and Cuba taking great care to conceal their involvement with terrorists. While providing covert support to terrorist groups, these countries concurrently espouse the political rhetoric of peaceful coexistence and nonintervention, as witnessed by Soviet and Cuban activities in Central America and the Caribbean.[10]

State-supported international terrorism is warfare not readily accommodated by existing conventions and international laws. Its real targets are not American lives and property but the fundamental values of Western democracies. A successful terrorist action does not consist of killing people or destroying an installation or facility but rather achieving some larger goals. The October 1983 attack on the U.S. Marine barracks in Beirut is an excellent example of how terrorists seek to alter the political stance of an adversary. They were under no illusions regarding the U.S. ability to absorb such a military setback. Their intent, which proved successful, was to make the continued presence of U.S. forces politically unacceptable to the United States.

Notwithstanding the criticism or justification to the political aspects of the conflict in Lebanon, one thing is obvious: it introduced the United States to a form of warfare for which the nation was neither prepared nor comfortable in fighting. For the forseeable future, terrorism may well prove to be bloody and costly; there will be no easy victories. In the past, terrorism tended to be characteristic of the early stages of a conflict, but as the conflict expanded, most acts of terrorism were abandoned. Today terrorist warfare is an effective form of combat without graduating to more conventional stages. It has become the prevalent means of armed conflict confronting the United States.

States that are sponsoring terrorism are using it as another weapon of warfare to gain strategic advantage where they cannot use conventional means. It is not a coincidence that most acts of terrorism occur in areas of importance to the West. (More than 80 percent of the world's terrorist attacks in 1983 occurred in Western Europe, Latin America, and the Middle East.)[11] When Iran and its allies sent terrorists to bomb Western personnel in Beirut, they hoped to weaken the West's commitment to defending its interests in the Middle East. When North Korea sponsored the murder of South Korean government officials, it hoped to weaken the non-communist stronghold on the mainland of East Asia. The terrorists who assault Israel are also enemies of the United States. When Libya and the Palestine Liberation Organization (PLO) provide arms and training to the Communists in Central America, they are aiding Soviet efforts to undermine U.S. security in that vital region. When the Soviet Union and its clients provide financial, logistical, and training support for terrorists world-wide; when the Red Brigades in Italy and the Red Army Faction in Germany assault free countries in the name of communist ideology—they hope, as one U.S. senior official has noted, "to shake the West's self-confidence and sap its will to resist aggression and intimidation."[12]

The wave of bombings and shootings by left-wing extremists during late 1984 and early 1985 has stirred anxiety across Europe that terrorist groups are pooling skills and resources to carry out a coordinated campaign of violence against Western military and industrial targets (table 6–1). Italian Interior Minister Oscar Luigi Scalfaro believes that there may be "an organizational center" guiding "an international matrix" of terrorism. Scalfaro added, "We can be sure that there is a precise plan, a brain, a political line and that a terrorist way of waging war exists."[13]

Claude Cheysson, former French foreign minister and currently a member of the European Community's Executive Commission, draws a clear link between the terrorism in Europe and a grand strategy masterminded abroad: "Terrorism is the most efficient method of destabilizing a democracy. The encouragement of terrorism by totalitarian regimes is clear, just as the encouragement by democratic countries of human rights and freedom of expression in totalitarian regimes is clear."[14]

Terrorist Warfare: A Soviet Revolutionary War Process

Although the United States and the Soviet Union are technically at peace, Soviet-sponsored terrorism, propaganda, disinformation, subversion, espionage, and wars of national liberation continue worldwide.[15] Through its intelligence agencies, Moscow manipulates terrorism as a suitable substitute for traditional warfare. Conventional military conflict has become too expensive and is too hazardous to be waged on the battlefield except close to Soviet

Table 6–1
Terrorist Attacks in Western Europe

Date	Place	Target	Type of Action
2/29/85	Newry	Northern Ireland police station	Mortar attack
2/24/85	Paris	British department store	Bomb attack
2/22/85	Athens	Greek newspaper publisher	Slaying
2/2/85	Athens	Bar frequented by U.S. servicemen	Time bomb
2/2/85	Beja	West Germany's servicemen's cars, homes	Eight bomb blasts
2/1/85	Munich	West German industrialist	Slaying
1/28/85	Tagus River, Spain	Six-ship NATO squadron	Mortar attack
1/25/85	Paris	French Defense Ministry official	Slaying
1/20/85	Stuttgart	Computer center	Premature bomb explosion
1/15/85	Brussels	U.S. Army social center	Car bomb
1/3/85	Frankfurt	U.S. consulate	Firebomb
1/3/85	Heidelberg	U.S. Army airfield	Firebomb
1/1/85	Bonn	French diplomatic building	Bomb attack
12/31/84	Bonn	French embassy	Bomb blast
12/30/84	Düsseldorf	U.S. Army liaison office	Explosive-triggered fire
12/30/84	Mannheim	U.S. communication tower	Explosive-triggered fire
12/29/84	Wiesbaden	Lindsey Air Station (U.S.)	Home made bomb
12/27/84	Wertheim	U.S. Army chapel	Torched
12/21/84	Frankfurt	U.S. motor pool	Arson attack
12/18/84	Zaragoza	Oil pipeline linking three U.S. bases	Three bombs caused fire
12/17/84	Frankfurt	Siemens warehouse	Fire
12/11/84	Belgium	NATO fuel pipeline	Six-bomb attack
11/25/84	Lisbon	U.S. embassy	Four mortar shells

Source: Compiled by the author using assorted open source data.

borders, as in Afghanistan. By covertly sponsoring terrorist tactics, the Soviet Union is able to continue its revolutionary efforts against the United States.

The enormous power of the Soviet state is squarely behind projecting terrorist violence across national borders on a scale of intensity lower than conventional warfare. Although the nature of the war that is being waged against the United States and other non-Communist nations is not viewed as a traditional shooting war, the Soviets view this indirect strategy of state-supported international terrorism as a means of reducing U.S. influence, in addition to shifting the correlation of forces decisively in favor of the Soviet Union.[16]

The Soviet role in state-supported international terrorism should be understood without exaggeration or distortion. Since 1917, the Soviet Union has consistently, although not always successfully, attempted to change the correlation of forces through the use of the terrorist option. Inasmuch as the main struggle for power in the post–World War II era between the United States and the Soviet Union has been constrained by fear of conventional military confrontation, especially in Central Europe, and escalation to nuclear war should conflict between the superpowers occur, the role of terrorist activity has been largely ignored by Western analysts. This preoccupation has allowed the Soviet Union a great latitude in the undeclared war of state-supported international terrorism.[17]

Marx and Lenin made explicitly clear statements regarding the question of the applicability of terrorism to achieve political ends. In Marxist-Leninist ideology, terrorism is viewed as a "useful tactical weapon in the overall world revolutionary war process, to be used when deemed expedient, and as a part of the multi-faceted strategies necessary for the ultimate success of socialism." When reviewing printed material issued by the Soviet government, one cannot help but notice the constant repetition of Marxist-Leninist dogma as explanatory affirmations of party policy. In addition, Lenin remains to date the most authoritative source quoted by Soviet policymakers. Lenin espoused terrorism in the same way as he did the use of legality, diplomacy, and compromise: "as an instrument of revolution and one more weapon in the arsenal of class struggle." In this regard, terrorism is to be regarded as part of the Soviet concept of strategies of war. Lenin wrote early in 1901, "We have never rejected terror on principle, nor can we ever do so, for that is one of those military actions which can be very useful and even indispensable in certain moments of battle."[18]

The Soviet Union has found terrorist violence an excellent tactic for promoting its own political advantage. Its main objectives and modus operandi in international affairs have been well documented in Soviet doctrinal literature and political conduct for more than sixty-five years. Soviet political leaders from Lenin to Gorbachev have articulated and tried to follow coordinated, coherent, long-range plans to advance Soviet national and ideological goals and increase Soviet power in the world arena.

As sophisticated and divisive as their approach may be, Soviet sponsorship, funding, training and political indoctrination, and supply of communications and false documents facilitating acts of terror are, in part, documented.[19] But whether through ideological affinity or political naiveté, many choose to accept the assurances of noncomplicity from the Soviet Union, its client states, and proxies—despite the evidence provided by defectors, captured subversives, and Western intelligence services. Although most Americans may be outraged at terrorist acts conducted against the United States, without the smoking gun—a case in point is the attempted assassination of Pope John Paul II—there is reluctance to condemn those countries responsible for such actions.

In sum, although the Soviet Union officially denounces the use of terrorism as an instrument of state policy, there is a wide gap between its words and actions. Perhaps this point is best captured by Secretary of State George Shultz: "One does not have to believe that the Soviets are puppeteers and the terrorists marionettes; violent or fanatic individuals and groups are indigenous to every society. But in many countries, terrorism would long since have passed away had it not been for significant support from outside." He added: "The international links among terrorist groups are now clearly understood; and the Soviet link, direct or indirect, is also clearly understood. The Soviets use terrorist groups for their own purposes, and their goal is always the same—to weaken liberal democracy and undermine world stability.[20]

Facing Up to the Unfortunate Facts of Life

Although intelligence is widely recognized as the first line of defense in combating and deterring terrorism, to date, the U.S. intelligence community has been severely limited in its ability to penetrate international terrorist organizations—organizations that in recent years have had a major impact on U.S. interests worldwide, both in the number of Americans killed and injured and the millions of dollars in damage to U.S. public and private property. In 1983, for example, new records were set in total terrorist casualties (1,925) and in the number of U.S. victims (387). The high casualty levels are attributable not to an increase in the number of significant international terrorist incidents—which, in fact, have remained at about 500 in recent years—but to the deadly effectiveness of terrorists responsible for just a few major attacks. The loss of U.S. lives from terrorist violence in Lebanon (267) was greater than that by U.S. citizens throughout the world during the entire preceding fifteen years. (An additional 116 Americans were injured in 1983.)[21]

The September 20, 1984, suicidal terrorist car bombing of the U.S. embassy annex in Aukar is the most recent example (as of May 1985) of the enormous intelligence problem that the United States faces in penetrating closely knit terrorist organizations such as Islamic Jihad—the group that initially took responsibility for the bombing—in order to forestall their actions or to identify those responsible for such acts. (It was subsequently reported that U.S. intelligence agencies had evidence that a Moslem militant group known as Hesbollah, or the Party of God, was responsible for the annex bombing.)[22] Intelligence, although a vital prerequisite in the war against terrorism, will not by itself influence or determine U.S. success against state-supported international terrorism.

Although U.S. intelligence agencies have intensified their efforts at monitoring terrorist groups in the Middle East and are devoting considerable resources to improving its familiarity with terrorist groups and, where possible, to infiltrating them with agents working for the United States, progress to date appears to have been marginal. Furthermore, according to a senior White House official, attempts to improve the exchange of information about terrorism among Western intelligence services, including those of Britain, West Germany, France, and Israel, have proved inadequate.[23]

Notwithstanding declaratory statements from U.S. officials, the reality is that the United States is far from eliminating terrorism through intelligence penetration of terrorist organizations or conducting preemptive strikes or reprisal raids endorsed in principle by National Security Decision Directive 138, which President Reagan signed on April 3, 1984. In October 1983, following the bombing of U.S. Marine headquarters in Beirut, the White House announced that once the perpetrators were found, the United States would "respond to this criminal act." No U.S. action was subsequently undertaken, however. It was subsequently reported in the *Washington Post* that high-ranking members of the Reagan administration secretly debated for weeks whether to retaliate with air strikes against base camps of organizations believed to have plotted the attack. Central to the secret debate were questions of certainty and proof and of morality. Furthermore, according to the *Post*, some members of the Joint Chiefs of Staff were opposed to a retaliatory strike. Three weeks of internal debate were ended by a November 17, 1983, French air strike on a barracks reportedly used by Iranian Revolutionary Guards east of Beirut in the Bekaa Valley.[24]

The day after the Aukar bombing, U.S. government officials said that no retaliatory action was "contemplated or imminent," but possible action in the future would not be ruled out. True to its predictable behavior, no U.S. action was conducted. Subsequently, in expressing a seeming resignation over the incident, President Reagan said, "You have to live and you have to do your best to protect yourself but you have to know that these terrorist groups are threatening all over the world." Commenting on the incident, Secretary of State Shultz said the United States was taking "every measure we can to deal effectively with this problem" but acknowledged that terrorism "will be with us" for some time.[25]

As a nation that has always found it difficult to determine how to create and use military power, the United States needs to face up to two unfortunate facts of life. First, the threat confronting the United States for the remainder of this century is not the small, secret, terrorist group conducting sporadic acts against assorted targets but the organized, structured, state-supported terrorist organizations that are trained, equipped, financed, and directed by the Soviet Union, its client states, or its proxies. Second, terrorists are well aware that the United States is long on words but short on action. It talks about "swift and effective retaliation" but has yet to honor that presidential pledge. Thus, future acts of terrorism will continue to be directed against U.S. facilities and personnel. Perhaps the challenge that state-supported international terrorism poses for the United States is best captured in a 1985 Joint Chiefs of Staff report:

> The threat . . . has never been greater. . . . The lethality of terrorist violence has increased markedly, particularly during the past 5 years. . . . Future terrorism will likely be more lethal and may be more frequent. More sophisticated weapons and tactics will probably be employed by terrorists. International connections among terrorists will probably increase.[26]

The report added:

> State support for wars of national liberation and international terrorist organizations will be a special concern. Support from the Soviet Union, North Korea, Cuba and their allies and the provision of financial aid, weapons, and training from Syria, Iran, Libya, and the People's Democratic Republic of Yemen will likely continue. Terrorists may or may not be centrally controlled by their patrons. Nevertheless, the instability they create in industralized Western and Third World nations undermines the security interests of the United States and its allies.[27]

As a superpower, the United States and its status symbols inherently have high propaganda value, and U.S. military installations and personnel are some of its most visible status symbols. Data from the Rand Chronology of International Terrorism indicate that the U.S. military has become an increasingly popular target, as shown in table 6–2.[28] Between 1980 and 1983, there was a 35 percent increase in the number of incidents over the preceding five-year period, 1975–1979 (fifty-nine versus thirty-eight). This increase is particularly significant since the number of incidents in the 1975–1979 period showed no increase over the number in the 1970–1974 period (thirty-eight in each period). The largest increase between 1980 and 1983 was in the number of attacks against individuals (45 percent, from seven to thirteen); attacks on installations increased 44 percent (from sixteen to twenty-nine).

Installations are attacked more frequently because they are permanent and thus easily surveilled. Surveillance of individuals is more difficult, and they are therefore difficult to attack. (For purpose of this discussion, installations and individuals are considered sophisticated targets, and attacks against them are considered premeditated.) Premeditated attacks present greater risks for the terrorist than do random target attacks, and they require far more forethought and planning. For example, a successful assault on a

Table 6–2
Terrorist Attacks against U.S. Military Targets

		Number of Attacks		
Time Period	Installations	Individuals	Random Targets	Total
1970–1974	18	9	11	38
1975–1979	16	7	15	38
1980–1983	29	13	17	59
Total[a]	63	29	43	135

Source: Thomas C. Tompkins, *Military Countermeasures to Terrorism in the 1980s*, RAND N-2178-RC (August, 1984), p. 3.
Note: Attacks on installations and individuals are considered premeditated; random targets are targets of opportunity, and attacks against them are, by definition, not premeditated.
[a]This chronology is derived from a variety of open sources, including U.S. and foreign newspapers and magazines, as well as reports of the Foreign Broadcast Information Service. Since only open sources are used, attacks on the military that are classified are not included.

facility would require a great deal of preplanning; the firebombing of U.S. cars parked on the street would not.

An upward trend in higher-order terrorist attacks is revealed when the number of premeditated actions (installations plus individuals) is compared with the total number of attacks. Between 1975 and 1979, premeditated attacks comprised 60 percent of the total incidents (twenty-three of thirty-eight). However, in just four years, from 1980 to l983, premeditated attacks jumped to 71 percent (forty-two of fifty-nine cases) Clearly terrorists are using more sophisticated attack modes than they have in the past. The 1984 numbers support the conclusion that the U.S. military is increasingly popular as a terrorist target and that terrorists are getting better at what they do.

At the same time, random targets are becoming less prevalent. There was a 27 percent increase in random attacks between the 1970–1974 and 1975–1979 periods; there was only a 12 percent increase between 1975–1979 and 1980–1983.

These figures indicate that military installations and high-risk personnel should be the subjects of greatest concern in countermeasures planning, but education programs for less-than-high-risk targets are also advisable, if only to raise awareness levels.

The incidence of terrorist attacks, by service, is shown in table 6–3 for the period 1970–1983. The army and the air force, with a greater number of permanent installations than the navy or marines, accounted for more than two-thirds of the seventy-seven incidents (fifty-three, or 68.8 percent). The army and the air force employ about 65 percent of the personnel in the four services; thus there is a high correlation between number of people and num-

Table 6–3
Number of Terrorist Incidents in 1970–1983, by Military Service

Military Service	Number of Incidents	Percentage of Total
Army	27	35.1
Air force	26	33.8
Navy	17	22.1
Marines	7	9.0
Total	77	100.0

Source: Ibid., p. 5.
Note: Of the 135 incidents listed in table 6–2, only seventy-seven were identifiable by service.

ber of terrorist incidents. Although the navy has more personnel than the air force, it has fewer shore installations and has suffered less terrorism. The marines, being the smallest service, have had the fewest incidents, although the Beirut attack on the marine headquarters produced the largest number of casualties of any single attack.

The conclusions that one draws from the information presented in tables 6–2 and 6–3 are the following:

Terrorist attacks on U.S. military targets are increasing.

There has been significantly more antimilitary terrorism in the 1980s than at any time in the past.

Terrorist attacks requiring a higher degree of sophistication are on the rise.

Attacks on random targets are increasing more slowly than attacks on installations or individuals.

The army and the air force, having more installations and personnel, will probably continue to receive the greater share of terrorist action.

Within the U.S. government, those individuals responsible for devising policy on how to cope with state-supported international terrorism must continually step back and remind themselves that there are no magic formulas or quick fixes. The United States will be confronted by terrorist violence for a long time. Thus, the major concern for the U.S. national security community is that other nations will see terrorism as a cheap way to achieve political objectives. It worked in the Middle East in 1983, requiring a change in U.S. policy. It can work again. Thus, a key question, which to date remains unanswered, is: How will the United States cope with future acts of state-supported international terrorism? Inasmuch as the options are limited is all the reason more why U.S. military force cannot, as it has been to date, be discounted.

Responding to the Terrorist Threat: A Perspective on the Use of U.S. Military Force

In recent years, despite improved physical security around likely terrorist targets, a somewhat better understanding of the terrorists' mind-set, government policies of no concessions, and no negotiations in dealing with hostage situations, international terrorism continues to increase in number of incidents (figure 6–1) and lethality. More important, terrorists are less reluctant to inflict increasing casualties and to conduct large-scale indiscriminate attacks.

There are special problems associated with state-supported international terrorism that need to be addressed but are beyond the scope of this study. This form of political violence offers safe havens, funds, training, and logistical support to a number of terrorist organizations. Thus, how can the United States pressure members of the league of terror, and others, to cease their support? Although current experience shows that no one country can exert sufficient influence alone, whether by diplomatic measures or economic sanctions, how can the United States solve the problem?

In testifying before the Senate Foreign Relations Committee on February 6, 1985, James Schlesinger, former secretary of defense, said the United States "ought not give assurance to others that U.S. forces will never retaliate. It should not announce in advance what it will not do. That is simply unsound strategy. In the face of repeated provocations, it [the United States] must be prepared to retaliate—selectively."[29]

Since 1981 senior U.S. officials have declared that the United States will employ force to preempt or retaliate for terrorist attacks; however, the lack of action to date to back up U.S. political rhetoric has increased the perception of U.S. impotence in coping with terrorism. Although U.S. public support for some kind of action is strong in the aftermath of a major terrorist incident, it quickly evaporates in time. Many Americans, although united in their horror and frustration with acts of terrorism conducted against the United States, are uncertain if military force is the answer to coping with terrorists. There is no question that based on U.S. democratic principles, there are many unanswered questions and uncertainty as to the moral and operational aspects of this option. Certainly serious issues and questions are involved that need to be debated, understood, and agreed upon. Unfortunately, the U.S. military force option seems to have quietly dropped from public

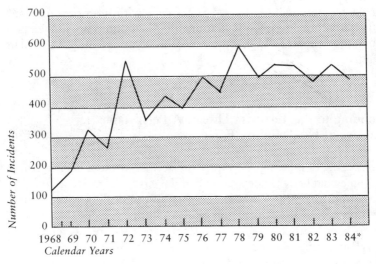

Source: Secretary of Defense, *Annual Report to the Congress*, Fiscal Year 1986, February 4, 1985, p. 23.

ᵃData through 31 August 1984

Figure 6–1. International Terrorist Incidents, 1968–1984

debate, having been overshadowed by U.S.–Soviet Union relations, the strategic defense initiative, and Central America.

From my perspective, it is highly debatable whether there is, or ever will be, a consensus in the United States in favor of a military response to terrorism. But concerned Americans should reflect upon the words of the Defense Department commission report on the Beirut bombing of October 23, 1983, which states that the suicidal terrorist attack was "an act sponsored by sovereign states or organized political entities" and that such international terrorism, while endemic to the Middle East, is "indicative of an alarming world-wide phenomenon that poses an increasing threat to U.S. personnel and facilities." (The January 1985 visit by Iranian Prime Minister Mir Hossein Mousavi to Cuba and Nicaragua may have established the groundwork within Central America for the kind of terrorist activities normally associated with the Middle East: suicidal vehicular bombings. Informed sources describe Mousavi as the "kingpin in the Iranian terrorist operation.")[30]

Terrorism is a dynamic phenomenon. By the time you figure out how to cope with today's threat, the tactics, groups, and targets may have changed, creating an entirely different set of problems. (A case in point is the replacement of embassy take-overs, which were so prominent in the late 1960s and 1970s, by assassinations and suicidal bombings in the 1980s, which have resulted in greater loss of life and more injuries.) The United States cannot live in the past. It needs to orchestrate its antiterrorist and counterterrorist policies in order to anticipate and to cope better with events far more varied and serious than it has experienced to date. Thus, the military force option needs to be assessed in far greater detail. The door should not be shut on this instrument of power as a feasible option to state-supported terrorism.

If terrorism becomes an increasingly common form of major armed conflict, the quality of its people and operations is bound to increase. Sponsoring nations may bring the full support of their established intelligence networks, their military education and training facilities, their equipment procurement and supply systems, and the other trappings of government systems to bear. If so, diplomatic channels could become more available for sensitive communications and supply (through diplomatic pouches). Clandestine support networks could be more easily tapped to acquire documents, safe houses, transportation, and other support items. In short, state-sponsored terrorists become, in essence, unconventional units. Given this situation, the Defense Department commission recommendation that active programs be implemented to combat this threat and that a broad range of U.S. military capabilities and options should be made available to meet the increasing challenge should be reassessed.

Throwing money at the problem, the common U.S. solution, will not ensure better security against dedicated terrorists. With their mobility, terrorists can strike anywhere at anytime. Thus, it is impossible to defend against terrorists statically; however, target hardening and increased security measures continue to assume a major role in the U.S. antiterrorist program. Shortly after the Aukar incident, President Reagan signed legislation providing $356 million to increase security at U.S. embassies worldwide and another $10 million to pay rewards for information about terrorist acts. Nearly half of the $366 million will be spent to relocate ten vulnerable embassies in the Middle East, Central America, and Africa. Tougher security measures, such as stronger walls, blast-resistant windows and doors, and electronic monitoring equipment will be installed. Embassies in particularly dangerous areas will be equipped with emergency satellite communications systems.[31] Although worthy and needed elements, this aspect of the U.S. program is indicative of the passive and reactive strategy that the United States has assumed in the war against terrorists. (As late as March 1985, a preliminary report of a high-level U.S. advisory panel on overseas security, headed by retired Admiral Bobby R. Inman, revealed that 139 of the State Department's overseas posts must be replaced or significantly overhauled to meet new security standards. Initial cost estimates for this undertaking are $3.3 billion.)[32]

In coping with state-supported international terrorism, the United States must accept five undisputed facts:

1. The secret nature of terrorist organizations will prevent U.S. intelligence agencies from obtaining detailed information on terrorist organizations (as recently as January 1985, President Reagan acknowledged that "one of the things that has kept us from retaliation [against terrorists] is the difficulty in getting definite information enough as to who they are and where they are.")[33]

2. Although some bilateral cooperation is underway among Western nations, limited progress can be made in the area of international cooperation. The issues of intelligence sharing, extradition, and prosecution are insurmountable.[34]

3. Diplomatic and economic pressure (even if it could be coordinated and honored) has not and will not curb states from supporting terrorist organizations.

4. U.S. self-defense target-hardening measures, as laudable as they may be, will not in themselves deter dedicated terrorists.

5. The time is fast approaching when a U.S. military response, more likely retaliatory than preemptive, against known terrorists cannot be ignored.

The use of military force as a form of deterrence and as a recommended U.S. policy against terrorists is a contentious domestic issue within the United States.[35] A major argument one hears against the use of military force to combat terrorism is that terrorism is not a military problem. It is a police problem and must be thought of in terms of law enforcement. Critics are also quick to point to the Israeli counterterrorism-retaliatory strategy, which has failed to halt terrorist attacks on its citizens at home and abroad.

Practical and policy reasons have been offered by U.S. officials why presidential authorization was not granted for a retaliatory raid against the Muslim militant group known as Hesbollah for its September 20, 1984, suicidal terrorist car bombing of the U.S. embassy annex in Beirut. A State Department official commented, "There is no sense talking about retaliation unless you know who is to be retaliated against." In cautioning against retaliatory strikes, one Middle East expert said, "If you have good intelligence there's a strong case for taking action. But if you're that good you probably knew about the plot beforehand and could have prevented it." One private authority on terrorism cautions that a bungled reprisal or preemptive strike by the United States would not only risk terrorist retaliation in the region that the United States conducted the operation but in the continental United States as well.[36]

Military and intelligence sources advised the White House that because the Hesbollah group leaders and followers do not assemble in one place, an air raid would be ineffective and would risk killing civilians. The White House was also told it would be difficult to introduce U.S. forces covertly into the Baalbek area to carry out a commando raid. Notwithstanding such concerns, Secretary of State Shultz cautioned that the United States should "expect more terrorism directed at our strategic interests around the world in the years ahead. To combat it we must be willing to use military force." He added, "Fighting terrorism will not be a clean or pleasant contest, but we have no choice but to play it."[37] Given the challenges that terrorism poses, Shultz's argument is sound. It has been reported, however, that such action has been deemed impractical, inasmuch as such strikes "would damage America's real interests" and that Shultz was "gently chided" for bringing the idea of U.S. military retaliation up.[38] Secretary of Defense Caspar Weinberger, for one, warns of the limits of military power and the need for extreme prudence in utilizing it.[39]

The military force option also entails a strong possibility that innocent bystanders will be killed, that the situation may escalate, or that the conflict will widen. Furthermore, from a U.S. perception, the use of military force for the purpose of preemption, prevention, or retaliation may be viewed as a defensive reaction.[40] Other countries may consider such actions as aggressive. If the United States remains on the defensive against terrorism, as it has to date, terrorists will continue to conduct their heinous acts unpunished. Is this what the United States wants? Or does it want the terrorists to know there is substance behind the U.S. political rhetoric expressing the willingness to use force? Perhaps selective military operations against terrorist perpetrators will reduce terrorist activities, or perhaps not. It is logical to assume that once terrorists, and those who support such forms of violence, believe that there is a credible U.S. antiterrorist military threat, they may weigh more heavily the costs and gains of their actions. Thus, maybe such violence will reverse its upward spiral.

There are more questions than answers regarding the use of military force against countries that sponsor terrorism and those that conduct the actual deed. The key question is, What is to be gained? Although there are many problems and risks associated with planning and conducting U.S. military antiterrorist operations—target acquisition, political liability, mission failure, U.S. casualties or prisoners of war, civilian casualties or property damage, reprisal raids against the United States, the likelihood that such action may have little effect on the state sponsor or perpetrator—the failure to take offensive action will only erode U.S. credibility.

It is easy to focus on the negative aspect of U.S. proactive (military force) measures against known terrorists. As with any other military operation, risks and uncertainty are factors that must be weighed by those U.S. officials entrusted to make such decisions. To commit U.S. troops to battle is not a decision to be taken lightly. The issues and decisions required will be complex and difficult. For example, in a November 28, 1984, speech, "The Uses of Military Power," Secretary of Defense Weinberger outlined a set of six tests, drawing on the lessons of Korea and Vietnam, that he said the United States would apply when deciding whether to send military forces into combat abroad.

1. Deem the act vital to U.S. interests.
2. Commit forces only as a "last resort."
3. Be prepared to fight "wholeheartedly with the clear intention of winning."
4. Have "clearly defined political and military objectives" and the means to achieve them.
5. Have "reasonable assurance" of support by Congress and the public.
6. Be ready to reassess continually and "adjust if necessary" the need to continue a military operation.[41]

Although it is difficult to argue with any of the conditions presented by Weinberger individually, collectively they make it difficult to foresee the United States initiating a preemptive, prevention, or retaliatory military counterterrorist operation. U.S. policymakers should, however, continually reassess the force option by asking what potential advantages might be gained by the United States in using military force against terrorist adversaries.

Let me offer four advantages to the military force option. First, a surgical airstrike or commando raid could reduce the terrorists or their state sponsor's capabilities to continue their terrorist campaign. Target selection is essential. Second, such action may discourage states from adopting terrorism as a form of unconventional warfare. It is well to remember the cliché, "Actions speak louder than words." Third, the military force option may persuade U.S. allies to assume a more forceful stand against terrorists. Fourth, a well-planned, successfully executed U.S. military antiterrorist or counterterrorist operation may restore the image of the U.S. military as a professional fighting force and satisfy the U.S. domestic demand for action.

In sum, the following observations can be drawn from this discussion of using U.S. military force against state-supported international terrorism:

In terms of policymaking, there is a great deal of uncertainty associated with the military force option.

Taking no action against state-supported terrorism is not without peril. If there are no costs imposed on terrorists or their sponsors, they have no incentive to cease and desist.

U.S. military antiterrorist and counterterrorist options, as limited as they may be, do not negate the need for a dedicated capability to conduct such operations.

A U.S. commitment to establishing a long-term proactive strategy, coupled with preventive intelligence, against state-supported terrorism may reduce the future vulnerability of the United States to more destructive and increasing acts of terrorism.

Conclusion

In December 1983, the *Report of the DOD Commission on the Beirut International Airport Terrorist Act,* reflecting the importance of terrorism as a strategic weapon of violence, concluded that "terrorist warfare can have significant political impact and demonstrates that the United States and specifically the Department of Defense is inadequately prepared to deal with this threat. Much needs to be done, on an urgent basis, to prepare U.S. military forces to defend against and counter terrorist warfare."[42] In effect, the commission argued that contemporary terrorism has become an important part of the spectrum of warfare that requires that the U.S. military to develop new concepts, to include identifying the enemy, determining the magnitude of the threat, measuring U.S. vulnerability to terrorist attacks, and determining how U.S. military forces might be employed to deter terrorist attackers. Events of 1984 and 1985 have validated the Defense Department commission conclusions, as well as recent concerns expressed by the Joint Chiefs.

In its military posture statement for fiscal year 1986, the Joint Chiefs of Staff states, "The use of terrorism against the United States . . . continues to pose a formidable challenge. . . . The threat from international terrorism has never been greater. . . . In addition to the renewed activity of terrorists indigenous to countries in Western Europe, the threat is growing from Muslim transnational groups which originate in the Middle East and are influenced by Iran, Libya and Syria. These groups pose a significant threat to U.S. interests both in the Middle East and in Europe."[43]

The following conclusions may be drawn from this study on state-supported international terrorism:

It is a form of unconventional warfare that entails the deliberate use of violence by some states to frighten or intimidate others in order to gain a political advantage.

It has proved to be a suitable substitute for traditional warfare. Although few terrorist organizations have met their grandiose ideology objectives, many have achieved their tactical objectives.

It is a strategy of surprise, which is at the heart of terrorist success. Terrorists' targets are symbolically related to the organization's ideological beliefs.

It is a weapon of the strong, as well as the weak, which uses both overt and covert activities. The Soviet Union views state-supported international terrorism as a means of reducing U.S. influence, in addition to shifting the correlation of forces decisively in favor of the Soviet Union.

Just as the ambiguity of traditional warfare imposes risks in the defense of U.S. interests, so does the battle against terrorism also impose risks. U.S. policymakers are elected to make decisions. To attempt to deal effectively with terrorism on the basis of a consensus, democratic principles notwithstanding, or search for perfect intelligence is a laudable but impossible and unwise path to follow. The point I intend to make is succinctly stated by a former U.S. official: "inaction in the face of terrorist assaults is a far greater risk in the long run because it convinces assorted hit men and fanatics—and the calculating governments who help them—that we are too confused or too fearful to resist. The gap between our resounding rhetoric and our demonstrated resolve may be the most dangerous imbalance of all."[44]

The use of selective military force against terrorists is not without drawbacks. Military planning may lack, and probably will lack, the detailed intelligence normally associated with military operations. Proactive U.S. military operations will require well-trained, specialized units prepared for rapid deployment and capable of carrying out tactics that emphasize precision. To maintain such a capability will require resource allocation from all uniformed services that are historically skeptical of elite units, strong leadership, joint training exercises, and the best equipment available. The performance of the U.S. military since the end of World War II has led some to question the ability of the services to defeat an enemy in the event of war, as well as the services' overall readiness. Critics of the U.S. military have claimed that the Pentagon cannot devise successful military policies; Korea, Vietnam, the aborted Iranian hostage rescue mission, and the Beirut tragedy are cited as examples of U.S. postwar military malaise. Even the recent Grenada operation has received its share of criticism.[45]

In sum, from the perspective of coping with the undeclared war of terrorism, have U.S. policymakers, both civilian and military, become so entrapped with the concern over a popular and winnable war—the no-more-Vietnam syndrome—and the possibility of a cycle of terrorist retaliation that the selective use of military force against known terrorists has become, in U.S. government jargon, a nonstarter? Has the U.S. military become a highly specialized on-the-shelf contingency response system, which plans and trains for a variety of missions only to realize that when the time comes, the U.S. bureaucracy is unwilling to make the commitment to use that capability? Or worse still, has the U.S. military leadership become reluctant warriors?

As the ultimate enforcer of U.S. interests, the senior military leadership is very much aware that in war there are no guarantees. What terrorists will do next; when, where and how they will strike is an uncertainty. But reality is that there will be new victims and new attacks, and the United States will be a major target. The question is not if the United States should use military force to combat state-supported international terrorism but when and how this instrument of policy should be used.

Notes

1. Headquarters Department of the Army, *Field Manual 100-5 Operations* (Washington, D.C., August 20, 1982), p. B-2

2. There are a wide variety of definitions that describe the phenomenon of terrorism. For the purpose of my discussion, I consider terrorism to be premeditated, politically motivated violence perpetrated against noncombatant targets by subnational groups or clandestine state agents. From a broad perspective, state-supported international terrorism—terrorism involving citizens or territory of more than one country—alludes to those countries that support international terrorist groups or engage in terrorist attacks to influence policies of other countries, to establish or strengthen regional or global influence, and, in some cases, to eliminate or terrorize dissident exiles and nationals from adversary countries. U.S. Department of State, *Patterns of Global Terrorism: 1983* (September 1983), and U.S. Department of State, *Patterns of International Terrorism: 1982* (September 1984), p. 13. A comprehensive discussion of the age-old process of terror is that by William D. Neale, "Oldest Weapon in the Arsenal: Terror," *Army* (August 1973): 11–17. Neale's basic theme is that the skills of the terrorist have been enhanced by technological advances into a major weapon in international politics, whether wielded by governments or freelance revolutionaries. He addresses terror as used by Stalin, Hitler, the Front de Liberation Nationale (FLN), and others. One of the more current scholarly books on the study of state terrorism is *The State as Terrorist*, ed. Michael Stohl and George A. Lopez (Westport, Conn.: Greenwood Press, 1984).

3. *Report of the DOD Commission on Beirut International Terrorist Act, October 23, 1983* (Washington, D.C.: Government Printing Office, December 20, 1983), p.128. This report is commonly referred to as the Long commission report. For years, a small group of experts posited that terrorism was a rapidly increasing national security threat; the United States was unprepared to counter what would eventually be the major mode of warfare of the future; however, before the Long commission report, this view was not generally accepted. See, for example, James Berry Motley, "International Terrorism: A New Mode of Warfare," *International Security Review* (Spring 1981): 93–123.

4. Address by Secretary of State George Shultz before the Jonathan Institute's second Conference on International Terrorism, Washington, D.C., June 24, 1984. U.S. Department of State, "Terrorism: The Challenge to the Democracies," *Current Policy No. 589*, p. 1.

5. Noel C. Koch, "Terrorism! The Undeclared War," *Defense 85* (March 1985): 7.

6. These three points are extracted from *Patterns of Global Terrorism*, p.18. A

more detailed examination of Soviet involvement in international terrorism is found in Roberta Goren, *The Soviet Union and Terrorism* (London: George Allen and Unwin, 1984), and Ray S. Cline and Yonah Alexander, *Terrorism: The Soviet Connection* (New York: Crane, Russak, 1984).

7. The word *bureaucracy* is used broadly here to mean any organization characterized by task specialization, explicit rules, centralized authority, and established routines—in short, any organization where each member has a task to perform, that operates by standard operating procedures, has a chain of command, and where activity follows established patterns, fits this definition. The term is not a slur. For a series of articles that provide an overview of U.S. bureaucratic behavior on defense policymaking, see John E. Endicott and Roy W. Stafford, Jr., eds., "The Theory of Bureaucratic Decisionmaking," in *American Defense Policy* (Baltimore: Johns Hopkins University Press, 1977), pp. 204–253.

8. *Washington Post*, February 15, 1985, p. A32. Members included Zbigniew Brzezinski, Robert Kupperman, Richard Helms, and Max Kampelman. The group further reported that the 1981 assassination attempt on Pope John Paul II is a classic case of state-sponsored terrorism and the Soviet KGB almost certainly was behind it.

9. Brian Michael Jenkins, "The U.S. Response to Terrorism: A Policy Dilemma," *Armed Forces Journal International* (April 1985): 41.

10. Koch, "Terrorism!" p. 9. Regarding Soviet and Cuban activities, see the Department of State and Department of Defense booklet, *The Soviet-Cuban Connection in Central America and the Caribbean* (Washington, D.C., March 1985).

11. U.S. Department of State, *Current Policy No. 589*, p. 3.

12. Ibid.

13. *Washington Post*, February 10, 1985, p. Al.

14. Ibid.

15. For a detailed treatment of how the Soviets over a long period have systematically blended overt propaganda with covert political techniques to manipulate the internal affairs of Western states and to undermine the NATO alliance, see Richard Shultz and Roy Godson, *Dezinformatsia* (McLean, Va.: Pergamon-Brassey's International Defense Publishers, 1984). Also see U.S. Department of State, "Soviet Active Measures," *Current Policy No. 595*, May 30, 1984.

16. The correlation of forces is a sweeping concept. As a practical tool for understanding international politics, however, the concept is almost worthless—at least in its present rudimentary form. The Soviets confess the near-impossibility of calculating something as elusive as "the level and nature of the political and economic development of the two social systems, the military potential of different countries, the influence on the masses of various views and ideas, the role and influence of social movements, the prestige and appeal of state policies." For an excellent discussion of this concept, see Robert Legvold, "Military Power in International Politics: Soviet Doctrine on its Centrality and Instrumentality," in *Soviet Power and Western Negotiating Policies*, ed. Uwe Nerlich (Cambridge, Mass.: Ballinger, 1983), esp. 1: 130–131, 154.

17. Goren, *Soviet Union*, pp. 196, 198, argues that for the Soviet Union to effect paramilitary power projection, it has "systematically supported terrorist groups, whether the 'right,' 'left,' or 'extreme left,' to achieve its politico-military ends," and

that several critical variables tend to reinforce the likelihood that the Soviet Union will increase its reliance on international terrorism as a major factor in Soviet power projection.

18. Ibid., pp. 27, 88.

19. For a sampling of the literature, see *Patterns of Global Terrorism: 1983,* esp. p.18; *Patterns of International Terrorism: 1982,* esp. p. 14; Goren, *Soviet Union;* Cline and Alexander, *Terrorism;* U.S. Senate, *Hearings before the Subcommittees on Security and Terrorism,* "The Role of the Soviet Union, Cuba, and East Germany in Fomenting Terrorism in Southern Africa," March 1982, vol. 1, 2; *The Grenada Papers,* ed. Paul Seabury and Walter A. McDougall (San Francisco; Institute for Contemporary Studies, 1984); Claire Sterling, *The Terror Network* (New York: Reader's Digest Press, 1981).

20. *Current Policy No. 589,* p. 3.

21. *Patterns of Global Terrorism: 1983,* pp. 1, 6.

22. U.S. officials said the Party of God, based in the Bekaa, Lebanon's eastern valley, is composed of a variety of Shiite Moslem militants linked to Iranian Revolutionary Guards who settled in Baalbek several years ago and continue to support Iran's leader, Ayatollah Khomeini. This is the same organization involved in the 1983 terrorist attacks against the U.S. embassy in Kuwait and the U.S. embassy and marine barracks in Beirut. *New York Times,* October 5, 1984, pp. Al, A7.

23. Ibid., September 21, 1984, p. A13.

24. *Washington Post,* April 6, 1984, p. A19.

25. *New York Times,* September 21, 1984, pp. A2 and A12.

26. Organization of the Joint Chiefs of Staff, *U.S. Military Posture FY 1986,* pp. 94-95.

27. Ibid., p. 95.

28. The subsequent analysis of material appearing in Tables 6–2 and 6–3 is extracted from Thomas C. Tompkins, *Military Countermeasures to Terrorism in the 1980s* RAND, N-2178-RC (August 1984), pp. 4–6.

29. *U.S. News and World Report,* February 18, 1985, P. 46. Also see *Washington Post,* February 7, 1985, p. A32.

30. For details, see *Washington Post,* January 25, 1985, p. A1.

31. In addition to these security measures, the State Department plans to buy 120 armored limousines and to ask for 307 additional marines for embassy guard duty. In Washington, the State Department intends to establish a special threat analysis working group with access to a government computer program that stores worldwide terrorism information and earmark $2.6 million to improve security at State Department headquarters. *Washington Post,* October 20, 1984, p. A14; *Newsweek,* October 15, 1984, p. 65.

32. *Washington Post,* March 2, 1985, p. A1.

33. *New York Times,* January 27, 1985, p. 12.

34. One of the more recent acts of bilateral cooperation to cope with the wave of terrorist acts occurring in Europe was the agreement between France and West Germany to create a joint antiterror working group and a special hot line to accelerate the exchange of information. For details, see *Washington Post,* February 6, 1985, p. A1.

35. The controversy sparked by Secretary Shultz's October 26, 1984, speech highlights this point vividly. Shultz argues for the importance of using armed strength as an instrument to combat global terrorism. Secretary of Defense Weinberger, however, warns of the limits of military power and the need for extreme prudence in utilizing it. For a succinct discussion of these contrasting views, see *U.S. News and World Report*, December 24, 1984, pp. 20–21. For a succinct and scholarly discussion of appropriate and effective U.S. policy responses to terrorism, see Martha Crenshaw, "Incentives for Terrorism," *Outthinking the Terrorist: An International Challenge*, Proceedings of the 10th Annual Symposium on the Role of Behavorial Science in Physical Security, Washington, D.C., April 23-24, 1985, pp. 15-24.

36. *Newsweek*, October 1, 1984, p. 20; *New York Times*, September 21, 1984, p. A12; William Quandt, Brookings Institution, *Time*, October 1, 1984, p. 37; Robert H. Kupperman, in *Washington Post*, October 16, 1984, p. A19.

37. *New York Times*, October 1984, p. A7. On the question of military force, Shultz is adamant that the public understands the risks involved. Ibid., October 26, 1984, p. A12.

38. *U.S. News and World Report*, November 26, 1984, p. 23.

39. For a discussion of the two contrasting views of Shultz and Weinberger, see Ibid., December 24, 1984, pp. 20–21. For a discussion of Weinberger's conditions of employing military force abroad, see *New York Times*, November 29, 1984, pp. A1, A4.

40. Anticipatory strategic military actions to remove an enemy's capabilities are generally categorized as preemption and prevention. The former occurs when an enemy attack is considered imminent. It aims at halting an adversary poised to strike. On the other hand, prevention is intended to incapacitate an enemy who plans a future attack but has not yet mobilized. Both preemption and prevention requires exceptional intelligence. NSDD 138, which established the foundation for an active U.S. defense against terrorism, endorses the principle of preemptive strikes, in addition to reprisal raids against terrorists abroad. Under National Security Defense Directive (NSDD) 138 guidelines, preemptive action is to be taken based on a specific planned event and only after complete information about a terrorist plan has been gathered. These guidelines require the kind of timely and detailed intelligence in which, to date, U.S. policymakers have felt less than confident. For a more detailed discussion of NSDD, based on public source material, see James B. Motley, "Terrorism," *National Defense* (January 1985): esp. 41–42.

41. *New York Times*, November 29, 1984, pp. A1, A4.

42. *Report of the DOD Commission*, Executive Summary, paragraph 1.

43. *U.S. Military Posture FY 1986*, pp. 94–95.

44. Alexander Haig, former secretary of state. Haig believes had President Reagan ordered a preemptive attack on Syrian troops in Lebanon, the 241 U.S. Marines would not have died in the October 1983 terrorist bombing in Beirut. *U.S. News and World Report*, February 18, 1985, p. 47. Also see *Washington Post*, February 8, 1985, p. A12.

45. See, for example, Edward N. Luttwak, *The Pentagon and the Art of War* (New York: Simon and Schuster, 1985); Arthur T. Hadley, "Inside America's Broken War Machine," *New Republic*, May 7, 1984; Jeffrey Record, "It's Full of Bureaucrats

Instead of Warriors," *Washington Post*, January 29, 1984; Report on Grenada to Congressional Military Reform Caucus by Bill Lind on April 5, 1984, reprinted in press release of Congressman Jim Courtier (R-N.J.). While claiming that most operations went well when U.S. forces invaded Grenada, senior military officers acknowledged that problem areas did exist, such as the lack of good maps and trouble with communication between army and marine forces on different parts of the island. According to Congressman Jim Courtier, a member of the House Armed Services Committee, "The mission was accomplished but it was a good deal less than the totally successful operation they claimed. It took some luck, an overwhelming force ratio, and we lost more equipment than we should have." *Washington Post*, January 26, 1984, p. A21. For a detailed assessment of the Grenada operation, see James Berry Motley, "Grenada: Low Intensity Conflict and the Use of U.S. Military Power," *World Affairs*, (Winter 1983–1984): 221–238.

7

The War of Words:
Can Diplomacy Be Effective?

Robert M. Sayre

International terrorism is by definition an international problem. The United States will be successful in fighting back against international terrorism only if it cooperates successfully with other nations. Effective diplomacy is the key to a strong cooperative network among nations.

Cooperation with other nations is essential because every terrorist act occurs on some nation's territory, and it is the laws of that nation that apply and the police authority in that nation that must act. The United States cannot act in other countries with its own officials when its citizens and interests are affected without the approval and active cooperation of the host government. An excellent example of strong and effective cooperation was the recovery by Italian authorities of U.S. Army General James Dozier in 1981 from Red Brigades kidnappers. In contrast, it was not possible to accept repeated suggestions that the U.S. government investigate in Italy those who might have been involved in the attempt to assassinate Pope John Paul II. No U.S. citizen was involved. The investigation was a sovereign duty of Italy, and it would have been a violation of both Italian and international law, as well as a vote of no confidence in Italy, if the United States had undertaken to interfere.

What is the international framework within which the United States must work, the tools it has to work with, the international law on the subject, and the political atmosphere? A common and understandable suggestion for better cooperation is to work through the United Nations. Since terrorism began to develop as a serious international problem, the United Nations has made limited but useful contributions, especially on aircraft hijacking (Hague Convention, 1970), aircraft sabotage (Montreal Convention, 1971), international protected persons (New York, 1973), and the taking of hostages (New York 1979).[1]

The United States cooperated fully in developing these conventions but then did not act until 1984 to implement the aircraft sabotage convention after terrorists resorted more extensively in the early 1980s to place explosives aboard aircraft to destroy them instead of hijacking. The United States also approved the hostage convention in 1984.

The basic concept of the hijacking convention is to make those who engage in skyjacking international outlaws much as pirates were considered in the nineteenth century. But the international community, primarily because of Soviet opposition, has been unable to extend this concept to other types of terrorist activity.

The United Nations has not been effective except on developing law and marshaling political pressure on those few issues on which there is an international consensus: protection of commercial aviation and diplomats. Its contribution has been limited because the difference in legal systems and political orientation results in strong disagreements over the definition of international terrorism and who is a terrorist. The nub of the problem is that the Soviet Union does not want terrorism defined except on its terms. It has insisted that those who engage in wars of national liberation regardless of the tactics used should be protected under international law. The United States regards violent clandestine acts to make political statements and directed essentially against innocent third parties as particularly repugnant and is unwilling to cloak them in the mantle of legality. On this basic legal and philosophical position, most of the world is ranged on the side of the United States. In any given case, however, the constellation of those supporting international law, those opposed, and those that would rather not commit themselves changes depending on how the case affects them. The best recent example of this ambivalence was the reaction of individual states to the shooting down by the Soviet Union of a Korean passenger airliner in September 1983. Even in this blatant case, it was not possible to marshal the votes of nation-states to condemn such illegal conduct.

The Soviet Union, joined by its satellites and a number of less developed countries depending on the issue, constitute a bloc in the United Nations sufficient to make that organization impotent in dealing with terrorist acts except those that may touch Soviet interests. The Soviet Union has also used the United Nations to promote a consensus on its thesis on wars of national liberation.

The United States came dangerously close to endorsing the Soviet views on wars of national liberation and terrorism when its delegation joined in signing the 1977 protocol to the Geneva Convention on prisoners of war (1949). This protocol (Article 1) would define wars of national liberation to be international conflicts and thus bring the participants under the protection of the Geneva Convention on Prisoners of War (1949). It would also have the effect of giving international sanction to such activity because it would no longer be a violation of the U.N. Charter provision on nonintervention for a third country to support an indigenous group's claim to the right of self-determination. This change would in effect give implicit approval to the Communist doctrine on world revolution.

In Article 44, the protocol would essentially excuse the irregular combatants from the openness requirements of the Geneva Convention to identify themselves by arms, insignia, and uniform, which are designed to distinguish between civilians and combatants and ensure humanitarian protection to civilians. The effect would be to provide legal protection to terrorists who hide in the civilian population but who show their weapons (bombs and guns) to the adversary just before they commit a violent act and disappear back among the civilians, for the only requirement in the protocol is that the irregular combatant show his or her weapon just before the attack. The worst feature of this proposed regime would be that it blurs effectively the distinction between civilians and combatants and helps destroy the humanitarian protection for civilians in the Geneva Conventions.

The sponsors of these new legal definitions would provide a legal mantle for terrorism and undercut the legal position of the Western democracies. The United States already has enough difficulty making its case even with its own citizens for support on the one hand to combatants who meet the standards of the Geneva Convention and its opposition on the other to terrorists in the Middle East, Central America, and elsewhere who do not.

Another example of the subtle use of the United Nations to achieve political objectives in support of terrorism and other clandestine political activity is the Soviet effort to liberalize the rules on the diplomatic bag, which is protected by the Vienna Convention. Through the International Law Commission, a working group chaired by a Bulgarian official has been seeking to expand the use of the diplomatic bag. The bag is already a very expandable concept and has been used to ship arms to terrorists in Western Europe, to provide cover for the shipment of truckloads of special equipment and materiel out of Central Europe to the Soviet Union, to carry unexplained cargo from the Bulgarian embassy in Rome to Sofia immediately after the attempted assassination of the pope, and even to attempt to move an ex-minister of an African government out of London in a crate. What is needed is close attention to the implementation of the existing rules and not a liberalization of the interpretation of existing law on diplomatic immunity and inviolability.

When one shifts from the global approach exemplified by the United Nations to the more specific, one looks for groups of nations that are directly afflicted by the terrorist problem and would therefore have a more immediate interest in dealing with it. The data on international terrorist incidents indicate that Western Europe, the Middle East, and Latin America are the primary victims of terrorism. Although these are the geographic areas of the highest number of incidents, the data also show that the United States is most often the target. One would expect, therefore, a strong effect on the part of these countries in cooperating with the United States and opposing terrorism. But existing multilateral levers in these areas that are available to the United States are few. (Another interesting fact about this pattern of terrorism is that it is most prevalent in the strategic areas of greatest rivalry between the United States and the Soviet Union.)

The North Atlantic Treaty Organization (NATO) appears to be the best forum for developing a policy consensus on the response to terrorism, especially because of the direct attacks by terrorists on NATO officials including Generals Alexander Haig (1979), Frederick J. Kroesen (1981), and James Dozier (1981) and recent attacks on NATO installations. For many reasons, however, the European members resisted efforts of the United States to get NATO to play that role. Their basic rationale was that such efforts would divert NATO from it primary role as a military alliance and from its primary area of responsibility in the North Atlantic area. Other NATO members are also chary of the thesis that some in the United States, including some officials, believe that the Soviet Union is responsible for all international terrorism. It is not that they do not believe that the Soviet Union and its satellites use terrorism when it serves the Soviet Union's political ends. They do. But Europeans do not believe that the available evidence supports the conclusion that a single mastermind is behind all international terrorism.

NATO members are concerned about the protection from terrorist acts of NATO installations and units, and they consider that they are dealing with those risks. But specific acts against NATO officers are considered the responsibility of the victim country (in almost all cases the United States) and the NATO country in which the incident occurs.

The rash of attacks against NATO installations over the past year and the apparent coordination of terrorist groups in France, the Federal Republic of Germany, and Belgium have caused NATO to review its position and to consider at the political level a unified response.

There is justification for the basic NATO rationale because defense against terrorism is essentially a police matter for ministers of interior and national police authorities. NATO should not become involved in any operational response except at NATO installations. But when one goes to the police level, there is a problem of interface of national police between the United States and the Western European countries because the United States does not have a national police authority as do all of the Europeans. There are other constraints also, such as wide differences in laws, and it is not easy to develop an effective working relationship to do the daily job of countering the terrorist threat. The United States has a national investigative organization, the Federal Bureau of Investigation (FBI), but that is not the same. It also has good working relations on intelligence matters but not at the police level on the types of intelligence used for law enforcement.

A major concern of the Europeans is national sovereignty. The exercise of police authority and the execution of national laws touches too closely the issue of national sovereignty, and they prefer that the United States, as well as their European neighbors, stay at arms length on such sensitive matters. One need only consider the extreme sensitivity in the United States between police jurisdictions at both the state and federal levels to appreciate the views of other sovereign nations. Terrorists understand this and take advantage of it. Ways must be found to bridge more effectively these organizational and jurisdictional issues in dealing with international terrorism.

Another factor that inhibits multilateral effort even among close allies is the sharing of intelligence. Intelligence services guard their information jealously (even in the United States) and must be careful about making information available to third parties. They will invariably insist that the third party go to the source. An intelligence briefing at a multilateral meeting usually proves to be so general that it tells the other participants nothing that they do not already know.

The most effective multilateral vehicle for developing an international political consensus and action on terrorism has been, interestingly, the annual economic summit meetings with allies. It has long been known that the political system is the vehicle through which economic decisions are made, but with respect to terrorism, there has been somewhat of a reverse twist. The economists who prepare these meetings are not comfortable with political issues, especially political violence.

Terrorism was first addressed at an economic summit in Bonn in 1978 because international terrorism had become a serious threat to an economic interest: commercial aviation. The participants agreed that they should seek to deny the benefits of commercial aviation in their countries to other countries that did not deal with the terrorist threat to aviation. But the summit leaders—the United States no less than the Europeans—have been reluctant to address in these economic meetings the threat posed by terrorism when it is an essentially political matter. They did find a basis for urging cooperation on the protection of diplomats at their meeting in Venice in 1980, and this has promoted extensive cooperation among allies at diplomatic posts around the world. The terrorism issue was not addressed in final statements and communiqués at the summit meetings in 1982, 1983, and 1985, although the terrorist problem continued to grow more serious. So in the last four summit meetings, terrorism has been on the agenda only once, in 1984.

Because of the coincidence of places and events—Libya's abuse of its diplomatic premises in London in April 1984 and the London summit meeting in June—the summit leaders addressed in strong language in the London Declaration the issue of state-supported terrorism. International terrorism became a subject of intense discussion with U.S. allies after the bombing in Lebanon of the marine barracks in October 1983, and with the added incentive of Libyan misconduct, the London summit provided a convenient time and place for the allies to express their solidarity and support.

Experts of the Summit Seven countries meet periodically to discuss implementation of the Bonn Declaration and other statements of the summit leaders on terrorism. The chairperson is the expert representative from the country acting that year as host for the meeting. But there is no secretariat, and the Europeans especially have resisted the formation of another international organization to deal exclusively with terrorism.

The Europeans themselves have a number of organizational arrangements in which to address the terrorism issue, at both a political and a police level. The Council of Europe has helped to develop a political consensus among the Europeans, and there is a European *Convention on the Supression of Terrorism* (1977). But key countries such as France have not ratified this convention. The ministers of interior of the European Economic Community meet regularly and have improved substantially their cooperation at the operational level. These efforts are to be applauded, but the fact remains that the United States is on the outside of these European multilateral groupings and is likely to remain so.

In the Middle East, there is no multilateral grouping in which the United States plays a role or can address the issue of terrorism. In the Western Hemisphere, there is the Organization of American States (OAS). The approach there has been to develop a legal framework as in the United Nations, and the inter-American Convention on Terrorism is much the same as the U.N. Convention on protected persons. (The full title is *Convention to Prevent and Punish the Acts of Terrorism Taking the Form of Crimes against Persons and Related Extortion That Are of International Significance.*) Seven countries, including the United States, have ratified this convention. The OAS has no operational arrangement to coordinate efforts against terrorism.

In the multilateral context, then, there are only a few cases when the allies have taken strong action. Constant vigilance is required to keep the issue in front of the world community. Also necessary is watching Soviet efforts to support terrorist activities such as trying to broaden the use of the diplomatic pouch under the Vienna Convention and to bring terrorists within the definition of combatants under the Geneva Convention.

Most of the diplomatic work to combat terrorism takes place daily in a bilateral context, working on a one-to-one basis with friends and allies and sometimes opponents. Within the framework of U.S. policy, international law, and the policy consensus the United States has been able to develop with its friends and allies on such issues as aircraft hijacking, the Department of State and U.S. diplomatic missions around the world must carry on a persistent effort to enlist the cooperation of other governments in fighting back.

The United States has some 140 embassies in 153 countries. But that does not begin to describe the complexity of the matter because it must deal through foreign ministries, which for the most part lack an operational interest on international terrorism. Even among European countries where diplomats have been the targets, the usual interlocuters tend to be ministries of interior. Thus, the United States deals with a broad range of ministeries and agencies in other governments with responsibility for law enforcement, border controls, aviation, intelligence, and all other aspects of the terrorist problem. When one considers that the federal policy group on terrorism includes ten major departments and agencies in addition to the Office of the Vice-President and the National Security Council staff and that the advisory group includes another two dozen agencies, one can readily appreciate the intensive effort that must be undertaken to achieve policy agreement and carry out actions.

What actions can be taken? Can preemptive action be taken? Are political and economic sanctions useful and effective? Fundamental to effective action against international terrorism is good intelligence. Unless the United States and its friends are prepared to expend the time, effort, and resources to identify terrorist groups, their participants, their modes of operation, and their supporters, no effort will be successful. This is exceedingly hard when dealing with modern techniques that produce fraudulent passports and other documentation, remote detonating devices, fast trips by commercial air and closely knit family groups. Strategic intelligence is useful, but tactical intelligence is essential if the police are to act.

What is needed next is well-trained police who know how to use the intelligence provided. The FBI has an outstanding record in the preemption of terrorist activity. The number of terrorist acts in the United States dropped from over fifty in 1981 to a handful in 1984. When the Italian police decided to find and release General Dozier unharmed in 1981, they mounted, with the active cooperation of the United States, a major effort and were successful not only in their immediate goal but in dealing a crippling blow to the Red Brigades. The Federal Republic of Germany and the United Kingdom also have impressive records. Working in such diverse places as Honduras, Costa Rica, the Sudan, the Middle East, and other places , there have been successes. Most of the successes outside the United States have been in the resolution of cases without concessions, but the Europeans are having more and more success at preempting terrorism.

The success of the FBI teaches that preemption is a viable option if nations are ready to devote the resources necessary to upgrade the police intelligence effort and to train foreign police to deal with terrorism. President Reagan asked early in 1982 for a program to train in the United States law enforcement officers of other countries on combating terrorism. The Congress acted in late 1983. Currently twenty foreign countries are participating in this program administered by the Department of State. By the end of 1985 there should be some thirty. Actual training is provided by federal and state law enforcement training centers. The closest U.S. allies have similar but smaller programs, and all of these efforts are closely coordinated. Strengthening this program and expanding it to all of the most threatened countries should be the highest priority in fighting back. Terrorists, whether acting for states or national groups, have to be stopped by national police forces.

Other major advantages of training foreign law enforcement officers on dealing with terrorism include better protection for Americans in foreign countries, a better working relationship with the countries that participate not only on terrorism but other law enforcement problems, and a growing network of law enforcement officials around the world who know each other and have a common doctrine for dealing with a threatening common problem.

Another high-priority matter is the attention governments give to the problem and their attitude toward it. The United States has not had a high level of terrorism within its own territory, and the effective efforts of the FBI have reduced even that. The problem for the United States is overseas. It has been slow to recognize that other governments must deal with the terrorist problems and to cooperate with them in training their police and in other ways. Some governments, even in Western Europe, which has been plagued with terrorism, have taken a permissive attitude in dealing with terrorists and have permitted them to live and operate in their countries so long as they do not bother nationals of the country. Still others give sanctuary to terrorists. The international community has some distance to go in recognizing that terrorism, like drugs, cannot be tolerated because in the end it undermines the social and moral fabric of the country.

None of the actions discussed here deal directly with states that sponsor terrorism. The main actors have been Libya, Syria, South Yemen, Iran, Cuba, and North Korea. The Soviet Union and its Eastern European satellites are active suppliers of logistical support and training under the guise of supporting movements of national liberation.

The most effective and consistent action that has been taken against states engaging in terrorism is to expose that activity to public view. States do not like to get caught with their hand in the cookie jar and held up to worldwide condemnation and ridicule. They like to consider themselves respected members of the international community. That is not to say that they will stop engaging in such criminal activity, only that they will be constrained and worry about what others may do or say and how these reactions may adversely affect their interests.

U.S. friends and allies are generally willing to cooperate in denying states that engage in terrorism the specific means to do so. Some have been willing to go even further and deny military equipment and training in general. This does not mean that states engaging in terrorism cannot get sophisticated timing devices, new types of explosives, weapons, and other materials. In the end, they will be able to get what they need and someone to carry out the act if the price is right. But sanctions on supplies and equipment do exact a price and make terrorist acts more difficult. And the terrorist state's efforts to overcome the difficulties may provide intelligence on what it is planning.

Economic sanctions are a different problem. The prevailing view is against sanctions, even in the United States, because they disrupt trade. Strong evidence supports the view that economic sanctions do not really work; they may in fact cost the state applying the sanctions more than the one against which the sanctions are directed. States are willing to consider economic sanctions only after the greatest provocation. The United States, for example, applied sanctions against Libya because of its consistent support of international terrorist activities. The number of Americans working there dropped but has since risen. European countries that have Libya as an important trading partner have not been willing to act, except the United Kingdom, which was the target in April 1984 of severe Libyan provocation. Even in that case, the action was termination of diplomatic relations. Despite the Bonn Declaration against aircraft hijacking in 1978 by the Summit Seven, only Afghanistan has been subjected to the termination of commercial air service for harboring terrorists.

Termination of diplomatic relations is often thought of as a sanction. Governments are reluctant to take such action because diplomatic posts are important for a whole host of reasons. One need only look at the list of countries on the U.S. terrorist list to note that the United States does not terminate diplomatic relations for terrorism reasons alone.

Finally, the diplomat has a real challenge when terrorism occurs in a country where there is no government. That was the problem in Iran at the beginning of the hostage crisis. As a practical matter, the government with which the United States had to deal for much of the time on this crisis was the mob that held the hostages. The other example is Lebanon, where the United States sent marines to participate with other military peacekeeping forces in trying to create a peaceful atmosphere in which a government could be created and function. Even now, the writ of the Lebanese government hardly runs beyond parts of Beirut—certainly not throughout Lebanon. The lesson in these cases is that if the United States proposes to enter an area where there is no government, it must be prepared to enforce international law for the time that it is present or take effective action with allies to ensure that a national government is established that will be responsible for enforcing national and international law.

The diplomat is crucial in combating terrorism. The tasks of the diplomat are to open the door and to sustain the tedious, painstaking, and long-term effort to deal with terrorism for what it is: a criminal activity carried out to achieve the political objectives of changing governmental policy and even changing governments. The tools available to the diplomat are few; the efforts require ingenuity, creativity, and persistence for success. But if the total effect is successful, democracy and diplomacy benefit, for the principal targets of the terrorists are the democratic nations and the diplomats who serve them.

Note

1. *Convention for the Suppression of Unlawful Seizure of Aircraft* (Hague Convention), 22 UST 1641, U.S. PL 93-366, 88 Stat. 413; *Convention for the Suppression of Unlawful Acts against the Safety of Civil Aviation* (Montreal Convention), 24 UST 564, U.S. PL 98-473, 98 Stat. 2187; *Convention on the Prevention and Punishment of Crimes Against Internationaly Protected Persons*, 28 UST 1975, U.S. PL 94-467, 90 Stat. 1997; *Convention against the Taking of Hostages*, vol. XVIII, International Legal Materials, No. 6 (1979) 1457, U.S. PL 94-873, 98 Stat. 2186.

8

Executive Protection: Living Long in a Dangerous World

Harvey J. McGeorge II
Charles F. Vance

Terrorism is moving inexorably westward. The opportunities for media gratification, expropriation of capitalist wealth, and disruption of the politicoeconomic status quo are too tempting to be passed up indefinitely. In the 1960s and early 1970s, the flame of domestic terrorism lit briefly, flickered, and dimmed to an ember. This ember of domestic strife is once again igniting and asserting its influence. The string of organized bombings directed at major defense contractors in the United States and at military bases abroad is proof enough.

As the body count from this current round of terrorism begins to mount, the affected populace will develop a series of concerns. Why is this happening here and now? What is the government prepared to do? What can a potential target do to protect himself or herself? This last question of self-protection is our subject here.

Self-protection is a two-part question comprised of the intertwined necessity to protect specific people (ourselves and our loved ones) and specific property (that which we own and cannot readily replace). These two concerns are intertwined because although the adversary's target may be either people or property, the two are rarely separated. To protect either, we must in fact protect both.

The first step in determining a procedure for securing the safety of people or property is to evaluate and define the threat. The threats being considered here include assassins, terrorists, and kidnappers. Although other types of threat certainly exist, these are the classic ones and are sufficiently broad to encompass the predominant incidents of violence.

How does the adversary pick a target? Six factors must be evaluated. Not every terrorist group considers all six factors, but at least several are generally taken into account.

1. Criticality: How critical is the individual or place to the continued functioning of the organization to which he, she, or it belongs?

2. Accessibility: Can the terrorist gain access to this critical individual or place?

3. Recuperability: How quickly can the organization recover from the loss?

4. Vulnerability: How vulnerable is the individual or facility to the destructive assets that the adversaries can bring to bear against them?

5. Effect: Will a kidnapping or assassination invoke such a level of retribution on the terrorists that they are unable to function in the future?

6. Risk: Will the adversaries survive? Few terrorists wish to become martyrs; they want to live to keep their cause alive.

One school of thought on how to protect someone or something from these adversaries suggests surrounding the threatened individuals or facility with wide concrete walls, high barbed-wire fences, attack dogs, and a moat full of man-eating fish. Such barriers are, in the case of individuals, hardly realistic. People must have relative freedom to continue to lead their lives. How can a balance be achieved between the safety of restrictive barriers and the danger of free motion? A four-step protective process, known as hardening the target, is used. The four steps are initial assessment, protective detail, technical security, and intelligence.

Initial Assessment

The initial assessment, sometimes called a target study, consists of five steps: threat modeling, data collection, formulation of scenarios, vulnerability assessment, and the identification and implementation of countermeasures.

Threat Modeling

The threat model phase requires defining the adversaries' assets. How many people are likely to mount an attack? What are their methods of operation? This information is just as, if not more, important as knowing their numbers. How do they achieve their goals? By kidnappings? Do they dress as police officers? Their methods of operation must be clearly described.

Next, consider the equipment available to them. Do they have rockets? Do they shoot submachine guns? Do they use silencers? These terrorist weapons would complicate the protective strategy.

What is their level of skill? Are they experienced, accomplished professionals, or are they likely to make errors? How dedicated are they? Will they continue to press home the attack in the face of opposition? Relatively few groups will. Some do, however, and the level of dedication has become an important consideration.

Data Collection

In the data collection phase of an initial assessment, data should be collected about the target from the point of view of *the adversary*. What we think about ourselves or what we think our weaknesses are is not very important. How our adversary views the target is what matters, because the adversary will be doing the attacking. What sort of information will this person or group collect?

A description of daily activities comes first. Are certain trips made at the same time every day? Are the same roads taken to predictable locations? Is there any visible security? The adversaries will almost invariably do such things as take photographs, make sketches, and draw maps, to show the habits or characteristics of the target.

The goal of data collection is to define where the victim is likely to be at any given time and by what route he or she will arrive at that location. If the adversary can predict with some certainty where the victim will be, when he or she will be there, and how he or she will get there, then the success of the operation is virtually assured.

In facilities protection, the data collection goal focuses on access to the facility, particularly at night. Does the lighting permit an adversary to approach under cover of darkness? How easily can an unauthorized person gain entry at any time?

Formulation of Scenarios

The next step in initial assessment is the creation of a series of scenarios. The threat model and the collected data are combined to devise a series of attacks. Once the attack scenarios have been formulated, the existing defenses must be assessed to determine whether they are sufficient to stop the anticipated adversary. If so, then no further evaluation is required to harden the target. If not, which is more often the case, the next step is undertaken.

Vulnerability Study

What is the vulnerability? That is, what terrorist threat poses the greatest hazard? Is life endangered or just property? What countermeasures can be put in place to minimize this vulnerability?

Implementation of Countermeasures

Countermeasures include technical security devices such as intrusion detection systems, lights, locks, barriers, safe rooms, bullet-resistant materials, and perhaps protective details for particular individuals.

Protective Detail

A protective detail can be viewed as a three-phase operation made up of the working shift, the command post, and the advance team.

Working Shift

The protective detail's working shift consists of the agents who are visible: the people carrying guns, wearing sunglasses, and occasionally trotting along beside the protected person. There may be quite a few of them, as in the case of the president of the United States; however, a typical corporate-level detail has one protective agent for each protected person.

The stereotypical agent or bodyguard is often viewed as a combination of or variation on three themes: gunslinging mercenary, karate killer (ready to judo chop his way through gun-toting adversaries), and muscle-bound knuckle dragger. None of these three types of people will have any significant impact on the outcome of an armed attack. In virtually every instance when a protected individual was attacked, the bodyguards or protective agents were killed. The primary emphasis must be on preventing the attack from taking place while continuing preparations to react in the event of an attack. This proactive strategy separates the true professional security agent from the classic or stereotyped large-bodied bodyguard.

Intelligence and mature judgement are required of a good protective agent. Every day a protective agent is put in the position of making judgmental decisions as to whether an apparently hazardous or dangerous situation is a coincidence or an ambush. The car backing suddenly across the street and the strange car parked on the street two days in a row near the victim's driveway are examples of the need for quick, mature judgment.

The agent must have a high degree of initiative. The successful protective agent has to be a take-charge person. There is a considerable amount to do and usually very little time in which to get it all done.

The agent has to be in good physical condition. Often the protective agent is the first person the protected person will see in the morning and the last person he or she sees at night. Long hours are routine, and good physical health is required. Thus an agent should be generally fit and possess stamina.

An agent is most successful when his or her appearance or demeanor blend with that of the person being protected. Whether the protected person normally wears sports shirts or business suits, the agent should conform to this attire. The agent's demeanor will have a lot to do with success on the job; he or she must fit in with the protected person's work and social environments. This places an unusual demand on the agent, who may not have the sort of background that allows natural adaptation to a wide variety of roles.

Appropriate background experience for a protective agent rarely includes prior service in the marine corps, special forces, or other throat-cutting organization. The best combination of experience probably includes one tour in the military to teach discipline and self-reliance and time spent in federal law enforcement in one of the major agencies to acquaint the individual with law enforcement procedures and to establish some of the contacts that he or she will need as sources of information and assistance.

Command Post

The protective detail's command post is the hub of information. The command post keeps track of the location of the protected person and the protective detail and coordinates fulfilling any needs for supporting services. Command posts need not be elaborate; an existing guard shack is often quite adequate. Hotel rooms are commonly adapted for use as a command post. A command post should have, at a minimum, a radio or some form of communication with the protected person, a telephone to communicate with police and other supporting agencies, a copy of the protected person's itinerary to show where he or she is supposed to be and when, and the routes that will be taken, and a log book.

The normal operation of a command post includes noting when the protected person leaves and keeping track of when the detail should be calling in to advise of their arrival at the destination. If the command post has not received that call, they initiate an inquiry on the status of the protected person. If they do not get a satisfactory answer, they immediately summon assistance.

Advance Team

The third element of protective detail is the advance team or advance person, possibly the most important element of a protective detail's operation because this person or group of people keeps the protected person out of trouble. The advance team's job is to go ahead and survey any areas to be visited prior to the protected person's arrival. Advance work is the primary proactive step in executive protection.

During a typical survey, the following steps are taken. First, there is a series of predeparture preparations. These include acquiring copies of the anticipated itinerary: destination, time at destination, what the protected person will do while there, and how he or she will get to the next location. Second, liaisons are established. They might include meeting with the local law enforcement authorities or with an airport manager and contacting the local hospital or deciding which to use in case of an emergency. Then a series of site surveys is performed. These are the actual visits that the advance person makes to the site that the protected person will be visiting, such as a restaurant, another individual's home, or a banquet hall. The purpose of the survey is to identify what will be done, and where, once the person reaches this location. Where will the car be parked? Where are the emergency exits? Where will the protected person and agent(s) sit? Where are the telephones? Attention to these details ensures a pleasant, efficient, and secure trip. The advance work should be done whether the protected person is going to an office, a social gathering, or on vacation.

Other advance team responsibilities include the coordination of ground transportation, establishment of procedures to be followed in the event of medical emergency, and the significant responsibility of handling technical support requirements.

Technical Security

Technical security measures are equally important to the protection of people or places. The most educated protective detail can neither sniff out an explosive device nor adequately ward off a hail of machine-gun fire. Conversely, excessive reliance on technical solutions always results in procedures that are cumbersome, arbitrary, and soon bypassed.

Each set of circumstances has its unique technical security requirements, generally involving a combination of communications, physical security, surveillance countermeasures, explosives and munitions protection, finally bullet-resistant materials.

Communication

Communication among all parties in any security plan is vital. Without clear communication, confusion and error or perhaps tragic consequences will almost always inevitably result. What level of communication is required? Between a protected person and the agent, there should be some form of communication in addition to verbal. The person can carry a panic switch in a pocket or leave it alongside the bed at night. The switch is readily available in the event of anything that requires an agent or other help immediately. Communication between the protective agent and the command post is usually accomplished by a radio. Small portable radios, usually multiple channeled, are the instrument of choice for this purpose. There must be provision for communication between the command post and the response force—fire, police, ambulance, or proprietary guard force, for example—in the event of a problem. This assistance is normally summoned by telephone.

Communications requirements for facilities protection differs only in scale. Security guards need immediate contact with the guard shack, which must be able to summon the appropriate response force.

Physical Security

Physical security typically includes barriers, intrusion detection devices, panic alarms, and fire detection and associated reporting means. Good physical security is based on the simple philosophy of detect, communicate, delay, and respond. Intrusion detection systems note the presence or encroachment of an adversary and communicate this information to a response force. The adversary's movement toward the intended target is then delayed through a series of barriers, enabling the response force to arrive in time to interdict the intruder before he or she can reach the objective.

An intrusion detection system is a combination of some form of sensor that detects motion, heat, or sound and a device to relay this information to someone who can establish the validity of the alarm and summon a response force. This goal can be achieved with a proprietary system where plant guards themselves monitor the system, a contract system with a commercial firm monitoring the status of alarms in the building, or a local alarm with just a siren on the outside of the building, which relies on happenstance for someone to recognize that an alarm is going off and that help needs to be summoned. Except for banks, rarely are alarms connected directly to police departments today.

Intrusion sensors can be classified in two principal ways: active and passive. Active systems use light beams or radio frequency energy in the form of sonic, ultrasonic, and microwave motion detectors. Light beams, normally infrared, depend on the anticipated movement of an intruder through some choke point, such as a hallway, for their effectiveness. When the light beam is blocked by the intruder's body, the sensor triggers an alarm.

Radio frequency or volumetric systems emit radio frequency energy at a specific frequency. The configuration and contents of the room modulate this energy and reflect it back to the sensor. When an intruder moves through this radiated energy, the reflected pattern undergoes a significant and rapid change, a Doppler shift, which triggers the alarm.

Passive systems can be mechanical in action, using trip wires, lead tape, or microswitches that depend on being pulled, broken, or moved, or they can be heat sensors that look for a specific pattern of radiated heat from the area being monitored. A third type of passive sensor is the acoustic sensor, which picks up noises made by the intruder. These are amplified, and when they exceed the normal threshold, they signal an alarm. This sort of system is quite popular in schools where the public announcement systems that are usually located throughout the school are turned into a monitoring system at night.

If the sounds detected exceed the normal squeaks and groans emitted by the building, an alarm is triggered. These systems are cost-effective and reliable.

Panic alarms are related to intrusion detection systems. Panic alarms can be used by a protective detail, with the protected person using a pocket-sized transmitter to summon the security agent. Besides protective detail use, panic alarms are frequently used in the home or business in conjunction with an intrusion detection system. Pushing the panic button signals the monitoring service that there is an emergency.

Barriers can take many forms. The typical perimeter barrier is the chain link fence, though it is not an effective barrier unless it is quite high. A standard 8 foot chain link fence can be scaled in about 4 to 5 seconds. If the fence is 12 feet high, almost 30 seconds are needed to scale it. A chain link fence stretched around a sizable piece of property can cost hundreds of thousands of dollars to install, yet it delays an intruder only for seconds. Other common barriers include barbed wire attached to the top of a chain link fence at an angle, which adds little to the deterrent value of the fence. Similarly, the concertina-like rolls of barbed tape, which look fierce, are simple to penetrate. A simple means by which determined adversaries penetrate these razor wire rolls is through the use of a strip of carpet, which they lay on top of the concertina to provide a safe walkway. Another technique is to use four-by-eight sheets of thin paneling material, which the adversary throws on top of the razor wire and walks across.

Other barriers include bars on exterior windows, reinforced exterior doors and door frames, and multiple locked interior doors within the house or office building. Finally, a safe haven somewhere in the building, typically off the office or the bedroom, should be established as a place where those who are being pursued can retreat to await rescue.

Audio Surveillance Countermeasures

Gathering information about the target is a vital step in the planning phase of a terrorist action. If kidnapping or assassination is intended, foreknowledge of the target's immediate itinerary is particularly useful. Conversely, if economic terrorism is the goal, sensitive financial information, often much more difficult to acquire, is desired. One route to achieve either of these potential goals is to monitor the conversations of the targeted individual or group through mechanical or electronic bugging. The procedures used to prevent or minimize this vulnerability are known collectively as technical or audio surveillance countermeasures.

Audio countermeasures is a three-phase program, based on the prevention, detection, and nullification of surveillance devices. Prevention involves two primary steps: initial assessment and physical security. The initial assessment should determine the likelihood of an audio surveillance attack. What information should be gathered by an audio survillance? What is the value of this information, both today and tomorrow? Time is needed, sometimes days for recorded information to get into the hands of those who can exploit the information. Who are the adversaries who might profit from this information? What are their resources to mount such an audio surveillance attack? Because audio surveillance can be expensive, the cost to acquire the information, coupled with the time delay involved in exploiting it, often far outweighs the value of the information.

The physical security step of the prevention phase focuses on preventing the surveillance device (microphone, transmitter, modified telephone) from entering the targeted area. If the device cannot be emplaced, no surveillance will occur.

The detection phase consists of physical searches and electronic inspection. The physical search requires a detailed inspection of everything in and around, underneath and above, and alongside the area likely to be targeted. Everything that can conceal a surveillance device or that could be used to facilitate the survillance has to be identified and carefully inspected. Frequently this includes the removal of all baseboards in the room, the dismantling of all electrical appliances to look for carrier current devices, the inspection of the interior of all air ducts, the X-raying of all desk ornaments and other knickknacks, and an incredibly detailed look at everything that exists in the executive's environment.

The electronic inspection uses expensive, specialized equipment to perform a number of electronic checks. These include a broadcast spectrum analysis done with a special radio receiver or a spectrum analyzer, which can cost up to $35,000 to $40,000 each. This equipment looks for operating radio transmitters. A telephone analyzer is used to examine the telephone instrument itself, searching for modifications that allow it to act as a microphone when it is in the on-hook position. Every component in the telephone is carefully inspected, and each wire is compared against all other wires under a number of different conditions in an attempt to detect improper passage of voice communication.

The telephone line itself can be inspected in a number of ways. Time domain reflectometers are used to detect anomalies such as series or parallel taps on the pair of wires that connect the home or office with the telephone company's central station.

Electrical power lines in the building can be inspected with carrier current detectors. A carrier current device, actually a form of radio transmitter, is typically secreted in an electrical appliance such as a lamp. The device will operate continuously as long as the lamp remains plugged into a wall socket. The device's microphone picks up room sounds, which are then altered in frequency and superimposed on the building's electrical power circuits. A nearby conversation is thereby transmitted throughout the building and out the main power line until it reaches the first transformer. The conversation can be monitored at any point with a suitable narrow band FM receiver. Radio Shack's wireless FM intercom system, which retails for less than $40, is an example of the commercial application of this principle.

Fixtures and furniture in the room can conceal drop transmitters and should be inspected with portable fluoroscopic equipment like a small X-ray machine or with a nonlinear junction detector, which can cost up to $20,000.

The nullification phase of audio countermeasures presupposes that operating surveillance devices are present but were not found. The goal is then to nullify their effectiveness. Several techniques are available to interfere with surveillance devices. Because air carries conversation, successful surveillance does not require putting a microphone in the room; bringing the air from the room to a microphone will suffice. Acoustic barriers can be created by identifying and blocking off air passages with something as simple as duct tape. Audio masking is another technique. A noise generator is used to saturate an area with obscuring noise, which makes obtaining a distinct recording difficult. Blinds and draperies drawn across windows will significantly, if not totally, eliminate the potential for eavesdropping by means of laser devices. Minimizing the wiring in a room, around the room, through the walls and the ceiling, to that which is required makes the installation of wired microphones difficult. Another common technique is installing telephone disconnects, usually in combination with a nonresonant ringer. When the telephone is not connected to the wiring, it cannot be utilized as a surveillance device. Scramblers and encryption devices are used in conjunction with a telephone when sensitive discussions are necessary. Both scrambler and encryption devices, though they work differently, can be effective, as well as expensive, typically costing up to about $10,000 each. The telephone instruments at either end of the conversation require an identical scrambler or encryption device.

Explosives and Munitions Protection

Although small arms, particularly small automatic weapons, have traditionally been the principal weapon of the terrorist, the tide is turning in favor of bombs and other explosive devices. The Department of State recently predicted that all major incidents of terrorism in the coming year will involve the use of explosives. Any security plan therefore must contain a strategy for dealing with explosive devices, which can range from a few ounces in an envelope delivered by mail to a thousand pounds or more concealed in a car or truck.

Protection from explosive devices requires coordinating threat response, searches, and the handling of suspect items. Threat response requires deciding whether to take a communicated threat seriously. Although the majority of attackers with serious lethal intent—suicidal drivers of car bombs—do not provide warning, a sufficient percentage of threats are real. Thus, threats cannot be ignored. Since there is no clear, accurate means of assessing whether the threat is real, the determination of its validity becomes a matter of subjective judgment. If the threat is to be treated as valid, then a decision is required: evacuate or search? Evacuation is rarely a good policy because the vast majority of threats are hoaxes. When it becomes known that the intended victim will evacuate when a bomb threat is received, then the number of these bomb threats will dramatically increase, particularly on sunny days.

Preferably searches should be conducted by the occupants of the area to be searched, and bomb teams are usually reticent to perform a search anyway. Only the occupants of the area know what items do not belong there. For example, they know that the briefcase left by the salesman yesterday has nothing in it because they saw it opened. A bomb team conducting the search would not know this. If a suspect item that cannot be identified is found, the bomb team should be called.

Bullet-Resistant Materials

Until terrorists abandon the use of firearms, there will be a continuing need for bullet-resistant materials or armor. The available types of bullet-resistant materials are as varied as their many uses.

Armor can be transparent or opaque. It can be rigid, like steel or glass, or flexible, like the Kevlar fabric used to manufacture the majority of bullet-resistant vests used by law enforcement and threatened individuals worldwide.

Transparent armor comes in three principal varieties: glass, acrylics, and polycarbonates. The bullet-resistant glass in use today is usually constructed of multiple layers of soda lime float glass laminated together with a bonding agent and backed with a layer of acrylic or polycarbonate material. The number of laminations of glass is determined by the level of threat to be defended against. Small caliber handguns can be stopped with a single ⅜ inch layer of glass, whereas protection from twelve-gauge shotguns and large caliber handguns may require two laminations of glass. Protection from high-powered hunting or military rifles may require three or four laminations of glass, in addition to the polycarbonate backing material, making a total composite of 2½ to 3 inches thick. This becomes a massive piece of glass, very heavy, and particularly expensive to produce with an acceptable level of visual clarity.

Acrylics are considerably stronger than glass from the standpoint of resistance to shattering. They are also lighter and much easier to work with than glass. Their major drawback is susceptibility to scratching and flammability. They are normally formed as a homogeneous one-layer type material, up to several inches thick.

Polycarbonates, while considerably stronger than acrylics and approximately 300 times more resistant to breakage than glass, are restricted to thinner laminated sheets. The polycarbonates are also flammable and prone to scratching but represent the state of the art in transparent bullet protection.

Opaque bullet-resistant materials include metals, ceramics, glass-reinforced plastics, and fabrics. The two metals most commonly used in armor applications are steel and aluminum. Steel armor, usually in the form of high-hard or dual-hard sheets, is used where maximum protection is required from high-powered rifles and machine guns. The hardness of the steel causes the projectile to shatter before it can penetrate the armor material. The doors, roof, and other opaque areas of armored cars are the most common applications of steel armor. The other metal commonly used for bullet protection is aluminum. Aluminum armor is appropriate for those applications where only handgun or submachine gun level protection is required; 2024-T3 is by far the most common aluminum used. A quarter-inch of this material, which can be cut with a band saw and drilled with a normal quarter-inch home workshop drill, will stop most 9 mm submachine gun ammunition. There are probably more armor vehicles fabricated with aluminum than any other material.

Ceramics like aluminum oxide and boron carbide are occasionally used as bullet-resistant material. Aluminum oxide is the cheaper of the two and the more common. Ceramics are fabricated in a number of different ways but typically as small hexagonal tiles bonded to another material. The ceramic's extremely high hardness is used to shatter the incoming projectile while the material that the ceramic is bonded to absorbs the impact and dissipates its energy. Ceramics are most commonly found in helicopter seats and other aircraft armoring applications because of their light weight and excellent ballistic properties. They are, however, extremely expensive and used only where light weight is the dominant criteria.

Glass reinforced plastics (GRP) are usually a high-pressure lamination of fiberglass cloth and epoxy resins that produce a rigid material with excellent ballistic properties. GRP can be used alone to stop handgun ammunition or used in combination with ceramics, as a lightweight composite system, to defeat more severe threats.

Kevlar, the fabric woven from the aramid fiber, has made possible an entire industry devoted to the production of bullet-resistant garments. The level of protection afforded by a garment is directly proportional to the number of layers of Kevlar used in its construction. Approximately seven layers are required to protect against low-powered handguns, eighteen to twenty-three layers for protection against medium-power weapons such as a 9 mm submachine gun, and thirty-five or more layers for protection from the .44 magnum cartridge. Kevlar by itself is not practical for protection against rifle fire.

Intelligence

Since it is always easier to avoid or defeat an anticipated attack, intelligence is a necessary integral part of the overall security plan. Two questions dominate any discussion of intelligence: What should be collected, and where does this information come from?

Collection efforts should focus on the methods of operation employed by potential adversaries. Earlier in this chapter we reviewed the construction of a threat model. Intelligence collection should be directed toward creating or refining the threat model. It should avoid the common pitfall of devoting excessive time to researching and cross-indexing the names of adversary groups or particular individuals, information that rarely proves useful.

Intelligence is derived from three primary information sources: police, commercial sources, and print media. Law enforcement personnel usually have the best understanding of their jurisdiction, and they have a vested interest in preventing terrorist incidents. In some cases, however, they are reluctant to confide in civilians, regardless of an apparent need to know.

Numerous private firms collect information and offer it for purchase in the form of broad-scope newsletters or more narrowly focused special reports. These firms typically charge up to several thousand dollars a year for their services and may offer only a small quantity of information actually relevant to any particular security program.

The in-house media analysis effort or clipping file remains one of the most cost-effective ways to collect and organize relevant information. For maximum effectiveness, a variety of publications should be used. *Time* magazine, the *Washington Post* and the *Christian Science Monitor* are good examples.

Summary

The protection of people and places is slowly evolving from an antiquated reliance on masses of underpaid and poorly trained guards to a scientific discipline steeped in state-of-the-art technology. This evolution is slowed by an almost universal reluctance to spend more than a pittance on protection in the absence of a manifested threat. The fallacy is clear: to wait until the bombs begin to explode and then depend on luck to see you through as you gather your defenses is foolish. Luck smiles on those who are prepared.

9

Proactive Responses to Terrorism: Reprisals, Preemption, and Retribution

Neil C. Livingstone

> Our goal is to deter aggressors from taking terrorist actions against us. We should work to make terrorist acts so counterproductive and costly, or seem so costly, that potential perpetrators will think twice before carrying out, or threatening to carry out, terrorist acts. In that context, even preemptive and retaliatory acts carried out for their deterrent effect may, under carefully controlled circumstances, be moral.
>
> —Admiral James D. Watkins*

The Reagan administration came to office in 1981, on the heels of the Iranian hostage crisis, with tough new rhetoric concerning terrorism. The president promised "swift and effective retribution" against terrorists, and Secretary of State Alexander Haig said that efforts to suppress and control terrorism would receive the same emphasis as human rights did under Jimmy Carter's presidency. Despite such pledges, however, the Reagan administration's actions were little match for its words. During the first two-and-a-half years of the administration's tenure, few substantive initiatives, either legislative or administrative, addressing the subject of terrorism were undertaken. Then, beginning in April 1983, came a rapid and unprecedented succession of attacks on U.S. diplomatic facilities and military installations in the Middle East.

Iranian-backed Shiite terrorists bombed the U.S. embassy in Beirut in April, the headquarters of the U.S. Marine peacekeeping force in Beirut in October, the U.S. embassy in Kuwait in December, and the U.S. embassy annex in Beirut in September, 1984. Although all four attacks horrified the nation and produced calls from those in Congress and the media for action, it was the suicide bombing of the marine headquarters building at the Beirut airport with the loss of 241 lives that truly represented a watershed in the thinking of many in the administration with respect to terrorism. No longer

---

*Admiral James D. Watkins, "Countering Terrorism: A New Challenge to our National Conscience," *Sea Power*, (November, 1984), p. 37.

simply a nuisance or "cost of doing business in the world," as one government official put it, terrorism had finally become an issue on the front burner of public policy concerns, capable of undermining the U.S. presence in the Middle East and challenging the basic assumptions of U.S. foreign policy. The Reagan administration, despite its hard-line rhetoric to the contrary, seemed as incapable of dealing with the problem as had Carter four years earlier during the Iranian hostage crisis.

Part of the problem stemmed from the nature of the new enemy, the Shiite Moslem fanatics and followers of Iran's Ayatollah Khomeini. They were unlike any terrorists the United States had encountered before, except on an individual and then only sporadic basis. For the members of the so-called Islamic Jihad and its constituent group, Hesbollah, life is viewed as a series of punishments and rewards, with the ultimate punishment—death—being the ultimate reward. The United States found itself confronting "mad dog" terrorists indoctrinated in the view that the United States was the "great Satan" and bent on eliminating all Western influences from the region, including the eradication of the state of Israel.

Security at the four sites that had been targeted had been inadequate at best and incompetent at worst, in part a function of a poorly defined mission (the U.S. Marine Headquarters) and too little understanding of the threat environment (the US. embassy in Beirut). But it was clear to most thoughtful observers, both inside and out of government, that physical security alone was not enough to thwart committed state-sponsored terrorists. Something more was needed. One way was for the United States to adopt a lower profile in the region and to pull its forces out of Lebanon, which it did shortly after the October attack. But many found this an altogether unsatisfactory response. As a great power with global interests, the United States could not afford to pull up stakes and withdraw in the face of every terrorist challenge. Indeed, there were even those who had opposed the introduction of U.S. Marines into Lebanon as part of the multinational peacekeeping force but who now felt—in the wake of the attack on the marine headquarters—that the marines should stay indefinitely, whatever the cost, since it would be disastrous to be perceived as having been forced to withdraw.

At the same time, others, like Secretary of State George Shultz, began looking for more effective answers to the problem. Shultz, in particular, had been profoundly affected by the bombing of the marine headquarters since he had been very much a part of the decision to introduce the marines in the first place. A former marine himself, Shultz believed that the bombing had occurred on his watch and that he bore a strong responsibility to see that the murder of so many young Americans did not go unpunished. Those who knew Shultz best say that they had fully expected him to leave the Reagan cabinet at the end of the first term, so discouraged was he over the frustrations of the office and the inability to get things done, but that the bombing lit a fire inside of him and gave him the impetus to redouble his efforts.

The trouble was that very few practical options were available to policymakers for dealing with terrorism. U.S. intelligence, which provides the first line of defense to terrorism, was still suffering from the damage done to it during the 1970s, when an overzealous Congress and two administrations turned needed efforts at reform into mindless persecution. Particularly hard hit was humint (human intelligence) collection, especially important with respect to identifying terrorists and tracking their movements and activities. Not only were many of the top officials in the intelligence community during this period chiefly advocates of electronic collection methods, but they tended to fear humint collectors as the kind of people who were hard to keep in check and occasionally bolted the reservation and thus were at the root of many of the public's negative perceptions of the agency and the intelligence community in general.

Under CIA director William Casey, important steps were being undertaken to redress the overwhelming technological bias characterizing intelligence collection methods, to improve analysis of data that was collected, and to restore the agency's paramilitary capability. But the work of developing new assets abroad, especially in the troubled Middle East, could not be accomplished in the space of a few years; rather it would take at least a generation. Thus, the United States was, in effect, flying blind in many parts of the world with respect to hard intelligence about terrorist operations and activities, and this insufficiency of accurate and timely intelligence would play a crucial role in creating the U.S. vulnerabilities perceived by Islamic terrorists in Lebanon and Kuwait. Moreover, it reduced the ability of the United States to respond meaningfully in the aftermath of the terrorist attacks that occurred in 1983 and 1984. Although certain allied intelligence services cooperated with the United States to relieve this intelligence deficiency, their assistance, welcome though it was, was no substitute for a formidable U.S. capability.

In the wake of the attacks on U.S. embassies and military installations, a crash program to upgrade embassy security and tighten base security was initiated around the world. Following threats of suicide bombers in Washington, D.C., barriers were even erected outside the White House, the U.S. Capitol and other government buildings to prevent Kamikaze-style vehicle attacks. So acute was the threat deemed to be that sand-filled dump trucks were positioned in front of the White House gates and at the six entrances to the Capitol building until more permanent barriers could be put in place. Pop-up antitank barriers and metal barricades were also installed at the Department of State. Metal detectors and X-ray scanners screened visitors to the Capitol building and the various Senate and House office buildings, at the Defense Department, and other locations, and new identification badges were issued to congressional staffers. Washington rapidly came to resemble a beseiged city, or as *U.S. News and World Report* observed, "a fortress."[1]

Congress appropriated $50 million to the Defense Department to assist in the security of the Los Angeles Summer Olympics, and the effort took on a new urgency after the rash of bombings abroad. As a part of its Olympic preparations, the Federal Bureau of Investigation (FBI) conducted a public demonstration for the press and invited dignitaries of its fifty-man antiterrorist SWAT team. The unit, though primarily skilled in hostage-rescue operations, would be deployed at major national events, according to FBI director William Webster, and on call in the event of a major terrorist crisis in the United States.

Federal authorities adopted new plans to provide more coordinated responses to terrorist attacks at home and abroad, though knowledgeable critics still characterized the planning activities as inadequate. At the Pentagon, a special task force was created to develop new strategies and technologies for combating terrorism, and new priority reportedly was given to counterterrorist activities at the Central Intelligence Agency (CIA) and National Security Agency (NSA). New efforts to coordinate intelligence collection and sharing by Western governments were set up, and the CIA's directorate of operations was expanded in an effort to beef up U.S. covert and clandestine antiterrorist capabilities, which had been cut back under the Carter administration.

Growing Discord within the Administration

Despite the frenzy of activity and plethora of pronouncements by the administration following the terrorist attacks in the Middle East, the administration's posture with respect to terrorism was still primarily defensive and designed not so much to engage and defeat terrorism but to avoid better their attacks and in the event of an attack to provide more rapid and effective assistance to those stricken.

On April 3, 1984, President Reagan signed National Security Decision Directive 138 (NSDD 138), which, in the words of Defense Department official Noel Koch, "represents a quantum leap in countering terrorism, from the reactive mode to recognition that pro-active steps are needed."[2] Although the main elements of NSDD 138 are still classified, the chief themes underlying the policy directive are these:

No nation can condone terrorism.

Every country has the right to defend itself.

Terrorism is a problem for all nations.

The United States will work with other governments to deal with terrorism.

U.S. policy aims to deal with all forms of terrorism but regards state terrorism as a special problem.

States that use or support terrorism cannot be allowed to do so without consequences.

The United States will use all available channels to dissuade states from supporting terrorism.

The United States will heighten its efforts to prevent attacks and to warn and protect its citizens and allies.

The United States will seek to hold acts of state terrorism up to the strongest public condemnation.

When these efforts fail, the United States has a right to defend itself.

The final element of the new decision directive is a clear reference to article 51 of the U.N. Charter, whereby states reserve the inherent right of self-defense, barring other remedies. The new decision directive, however, did not spell out how far the concept of self-defense might extend, though some, like Noel Koch, wanted it to sanction both preemptive raids and reprisal attacks against terrorists abroad. Nevertheless, it was clear that events had compelled the administration to cross the threshold into territory that during the 1970s would have been considered unthinkable. The United States was, furthermore, serving notice that it would no longer submit to terrorist outrages without reserving the right to respond in kind, and whereas in the past it was generally accepted that the United States would develop the capability to intervene in hostage crises and other ongoing terrorist incidents to bring about their successful resolution, Washington was now taking the posture that it would consider military action in advance of actual incidents to prevent them from occurring or to punish terrorists in the aftermath of an attack. Such a proactive policy, however, raises a plethora of political, moral, legal, and practical questions, which have produced one of the most vituperous and hotly contested behind-the-scenes debates in recent Washington memory, pitting not only liberal opponents against the Reagan administration but creating a firestorm of conflicting views within the administration itself. In the months that followed, senior administration officials nearly came to blows over how the new policy would be implemented and who would implement it. Late-night telephone calls laced with profanity and accusations were exchanged by key administration figures; some engaged in turf battles; and others were fearful of the consequences of an all-out war against terrorists. Some senior CIA officials accused proponents of the new policy of wanting to transport the agency back to "the bad old days" when it was vilified by the Congress and in the media because it was felt that the implementation of proactive policies would be too high risk and not fully understood or supported by the public. It was all right for some agency or government entity to pursue such tactics, they argued; just leave the CIA out of it.

Many in the Pentagon also had serious reservations about putting the prestige and power of the U.S. armed forces on the line in combating terrorism. Fighting terrorism was viewed as a sordid kind of warfare that would inevitably tarnish military reputations and destroy careers. Secretary of Defense Caspar Weinberger picked up this theme, maintaining that combat forces should be used extremely cautiously and then only with "clearly defined political and military objectives."[3] Weinberger went on to cite six tests that should be met before any decision to employ military force abroad is taken, which are a clear legacy of the military's Vietnam experience and reflect the Pentagon's unease over engaging in low-intensity forms of conflict. Weinberger even suggested that there might be a role for the United Nations in combating global terrorism, despite the international organization's shameful effort to address the subject during the early 1970s when, after two years of debate, it gave up after failing to arrive at a common definition of terrorism. This is not to suggest that Weinberger's views reflect a total consensus within the Pentagon, for a number of senior Defense Department officials, including Noel Koch and Chief of Naval Operations James D. Watkins, continued to press internally for tough policies to meet the terrorist challenge.

The Defense Department position was in sharp counterpoint to the bellicose rhetoric of Secretary of State Shultz on the subject of terrorism. In a speech to the Trilateral Commission on the day President Reagan signed NSDD 138, Shultz called for a bold new policy to combat terrorism, including retaliatory and preemptive actions. He described terrorism as a form of warfare and said, "It is increasingly doubtful that a purely passive strategy can even begin to cope with the problem."[4] He also chided the nay-sayers and faint of heart at the Pentagon who constantly raised the ghost of Vietnam as justifiction for adhering to a no-risk, high-threshold policy with respect to projecting force into the Third World or aggressively combating terrorism. "The need to avoid no-win situations cannot mean that we turn automatically away from hard-to-win situations that call for prudent involvement. These will always involve risks: we will not always have the luxury of being able to choose the most advantageous circumstances. And our adversaries can be expected to play rough."[5] Less than three months later, he told a conference on terrorism sponsored by the Israeli-based Jonathon Institute, "Experience has taught us over the years that one of the best deterrents to terrorism is the certainty that swift and sure measures will be taken against those who engage in it."[6] He called on the United States to give far more consideration to active means of defense, again raising the possibility of preemptive action.

In a speech on October 25, 1984, at the Park Avenue Synagogue in New York City, Shultz's frustrations over U.S. inaction in the face of the mounting terrorist challenge boiled over. In the strongest speech on the subject yet delivered by a senior U.S. policymaker, Shultz declared that the United States must be ready to use military force to fight international terrorism and perhaps even retaliate before all of the facts about a specific terrorist attack are known, noting that "we may never have the kind of evidence that can stand up in an American court of law."[7] He said the United States should also be prepared to accept the loss of some innocent lives as a collateral result of its retaliation. "We cannot allow ourselves to become the Hamlet of nations," he concluded, "worrying endlessly over whether and how to respond. A great nation with global responsibilities cannot afford to be hamstrung by confusion and indecisiveness. Fighting terrorism will not be a clean or pleasant contest, but we have no choice but to play it."[8]

Shultz's remark set off a heated controversy. Even Vice-President George Bush took exception to some of the secretary of state's strident statements. The *Baltimore Sun* declared "Shultz Off Course," and the *Philadelphia Inquirer* labeled his speech "How Not to Fight Terror," as other newspapers across the country lashed out at his tough rhetoric. Shultz, however, refused to back off his attack or to be intimidated by Congress and the media. He added fuel to the debate in December when, on a flight to a three-day meeting of NATO ministers, he reasserted to accompanying reporters the need for preemption and other retaliatory actions against terrorism.

Although no consensus emerged from the debate that raged in the wake of Shultz's pronouncements, most of the issues had at last been laid on the table. Was the United States, after years of tough talk but little action, finally ready to strike back militarily at international terrorists? Shultz seemed to be laying the groundwork and preparing the public for the employment of force against U.S. terrorist tormentors, and he was clearly sending a message to terrorists and their patrons in the hope that it would have a deterrent effect on them. He was, moreover, venting his own anger and frustration and attempting to move the administration in the direction of a firm and resolute response to what, after October 1983, Shultz saw as a growing threat not only to U.S. foreign policy but to what noted British historian and civil servant Harold Nicholson referred to as the "diplomatic method," that set of practices and procedures that had evolved over the centuries governing the relations among nations.

Nicholson believed that modern diplomacy owed a great debt to the ancient Greeks, who were the first to discover that an orderly international system must be governed by certain universally established and recognized principles, the most important being the principle of diplomatic immunity. In earlier times, diplomatic envoys were often held hostage to guarantee their nation's adherence to a treaty or arbitrarily put to death by sovereigns displeased with their messages. Once diplomats were accorded the status of protected persons, they finally became free from intimidation and threats against their personal safety. This, in turn, brought the world closer by ensuring improved channels of communication, information, and understanding.

The inviolability of diplomatic persons is recognized in most quarters as necessary to the conduct of diplomacy. Yet by 1984, attacks on diplomats and diplomatic facilities had reached epidemic proportions. This could be attributed in large measure to the fact that diplomats and foreign embassies are often the most visible and accessible symbols of their governments abroad; hence they make inviting targets. And as one terrorism expert noted in explaining why terrorists strike at U.S. embassies rather than at targets in the continental United States itself, "It is easier to walk across the street to carry out an attack than to cross a border or an ocean."[9]

During the past fifteen years, diplomats from 113 countries have been targets of acts of terrorism occurring in 128 different nations. In some instances, the host nation itself collaborated with the terrorists, as in the case of the seizure of the U.S. embassy in Tehran in 1979. In other cases, as in Lebanon, the host government was too weak and disorganized to provide adequate protection to foreign legations or to curb terrorist gangs operating within its borders.

Add to this situation further abuses of the diplomatic method such as the smuggling of arms and explosives across national frontiers by nations like Libya for the use of terrorist organizations, or the murder of a police officer and the wounding of anti-Qaddafi protestors by a gunman firing from within the Libyan "embassy" in London. In June 1984, Italian prosecutors strongly suggested that one of the Bulgarian officials implicated in the assassination attempt on the pope in St. Peter's Square was smuggled out of Italy in a sealed truck in a consignment of diplomatic bags and crates.

It was clear that modern diplomacy was under assault as never before by international terrorists, and Shultz and many others at the Department of State worried that unless steps were taken to remedy the situation at once, diplomacy as we know it will become a thing of the past. Some have suggested that traditional diplomacy is already dead, having been rendered superfluous with the advent of modern office machines, instantaneous communications, television, and jet travel. Critics contend that diplomats are no longer the principal source of information about foreign governments and are necessary only to perform consular functions, such as granting visas. The traditional function of diplomacy, they maintain, can better be performed by high-level shuttle diplomacy or even through teleconferencing. Maintenance of large foreign legations, especially in troubled parts of the world, such critics contend, is an invitation to terrorists and may actually foster conflict—as in Iran—rather than serve as a means of lessening confict.

By contrast to such views, however, the weight of informed opinion still sees virtue in the traditional diplomatic method. Despite television and the communications revolution, embassies are still vital listening posts to ascertain the mood and temper of the host country. This is especially true of smaller, more remote countries without major media centers and closed societies where alternative sources of information are unavailable. A majority of the personnel, moreover, at most U.S. embassies are engaged in tasks far afield from those associated with traditional diplomacy, such as promoting trade and cultural exchanges and administering foreign assistance and agricultural programs. Although the modern ambassador is increasingly becoming a manager of programs and resources rather than a front-line policymaker, this in no way diminishes the practical value of the functions he or she performs. In view of increased global interdependence, the role of the modern embassy may in fact be more important today than ever before.

Shultz and his advisers knew that nothing less than the future of modern diplomacy was at stake. Unless something was done to lessen the threat from international terrorism, they believed, not only would U.S. foreign policy be undermined but pressure would build to redefine substantially the role of the foreign service and the U.S. diplomatic presence abroad.

Yet despite the serious terrorist threat to U.S. diplomats and embassies, David Stockman, director of the Office of Management and the Budget, demonstrating a removal from reality and disregard of the potential implications of his actions, tried to cut monies for the security improvement of U.S. embassies in the fiscal year 1985 budget. Only the direct intervention of a furious George Shultz saved the funds from being axed.

By the beginning of 1985, Shultz's views, although not yet implemented in any meaningful sense, were gaining increased momentum in the administration policy debate and picking up influential allies. While attacks by Shiite extremists had tapered off, new threats had emerged, especially what appeared to be a concerted effort of leftist terrorist groups to strike at U.S. and NATO (North Atlantic Treaty Organization) military-related targets in Europe. On March 25, 1985, national security adviser Robert C. McFarlane downplayed the debate over military responses to terrorism embodied in the divergent views of the secretary of state and the secretary of defense:

> Secretary Shultz has stressed the need to consider the use of force as a realistically available option for certain terrorist acts. He has carefully pointed

out the risks and problems we must consider before deciding upon the use of force including the problems of securing the support and cooperation of other governments. Secretary Weinberger has underscored the very real, practical difficulties that exist for the military planner in attempting to apply small amounts of force, especially over great distances. He has accurately noted, I think, the difficulty of assuring success, and has echoed the need for public support for any sustained resort to force by the United States in defending us against terrorist attack.[10]

McFarlane, however, went on to make it clear that his own views were very much in concert with those articulated by the secretary of state. "We must be free," asserted McFarlane, "to consider an armed strike against terrorists and those who support them where elimination or moderation of the threat does not appear to be feasible by any other means."[11] He described how terrorists "have been skillful in forcing or sometimes persuading innocent bystanders to shield them from reprisal," and embraced Shultz's contention that such considerations cannot be allowed to freeze us into paralysis."[12] Reaffirming that the United States would not bargain with terrorists, McFarlane then pledged, "We cannot and will not abstain from forcible action to prevent, preempt, and respond to terrorist acts where conditions merit the use of force."[13] To renounce force as an option in countering terrorism, he concluded, is to invite more, not less, terrorist brutality. President Reagan, he said, fully supported such a proactive stance, believing as he did that "international terrorism is the ultimate abuse of human rights."[14]

The reference to human rights was timely and important since one of the great fallacies perpetrated during the Carter years was that an aggressive counterterrorism policy was inimical or contradictory to effective advancement of human rights around the world. Proponents of this view noted that many U.S. allies were wholesale violators of human rights and that U.S. efforts to assist them in dealing with outbreaks of terrorism and insurgency only contributed to a perpetuation of injustice and oppression and therefore prolonged the human rights abuses of such governments.

There is little question but that advancement of human rights should be the soul of U.S. foreign policy. It is one of the chief moral weapons of the West in its ideological struggle with the Soviet Union, and if U.S. foreign policy is deprived of this content, it runs the risk of being perceived as a policy of expediency and the United States solely as a land of merchants and capitalists. Nevertheless, as the national security adviser noted in restating the president's position, freedom from arbitrary death and maiming at the hands of international terrorists must constitute the most fundamental human right, and those who resort to violence against innocent people as a means of advancing their political agendas and philosophies deserve universal condemnation.

A week later, Reagan made his voice heard directly on the matter of state-sponsored terrorism. He told reporters that the United States should go to the source when other governments are found to be supporting terrorists, instead of tracking down terrorists individually, but he provided no specifics as to what such action would entail.[15] The following day, however, the United States reportedly sent a strong message to Iran warning that government of serious consequences flowing from any attempt by pro-Iranian terrorists in Lebanon to create a new hostage crisis by kidnapping U.S. citizens. A similar warning had been transmitted to Libya the previous day threatening that country's mercurial strongman, Muammar Qaddafi, that he would be held accountable for any new Libyan-backed attacks against U.S. interests and citizens. On April 17, 1985, CIA director William Casey told a Cambridge audience that terrorist "attacks have not passed without significant response," although, like the president, he did not shed any light as to the nature of the responses employed.[16]

"High officials from the President on down have regularly excoriated terrorism, terrorists and the people who support them," observes Hugh Tovar. "Yet, to date, in the face of this rhetoric, force has never been used to redress the situation."[17] Nevertheless, after more than four years of wrestling inconclusively with the problem of international terrorism, the Reagan administration finally seemed poised to use force to protect the United States and its citizens from terrorists and their state patrons. Many questions, however, remained unanswered. What kind of force would be employed and against whom? Who would carry out the new policy of counterattack, and what instrumentalities would be required? During previous months, various force options had been referred to, but little thought had been given to the specific elements of each. What were the advantages and disadvantages of the force options that had been discussed, and in what circumstances would each be employed?

Proactive Responses

The options for combating and suppressing terrorism can be visualized as a continuum of response moving from stoicism, static defensive measures, and diplomatic initiatives at one pole to the force options at the opposite end of the spectrum. In this connection, proactive responses to terrorism can be separated into three categories: reprisals, preemption, and retribution. All can be viewed as coercive measures short of war, although each is also applicable in the context of general warfare. All three proactive forms of response have a legal justification under Article 51 of the U.N. Charter, which reserves to nations the inherent right of self-defense. If we accept the fact that terrorism, especially that sponsored and supported by foreign governments, is a form of aggression, then the United States may adopt and employ proactive measures as a traditional form of self-help while still attempting to find peaceful long-term solutions to the problem.

Tovar has argued that force should be used "whenever we judge that it is justified and feasible" and not simply as a last resort, maintaining that to regard it as a final option would, in effect, mean that it would never be employed.[18] Although the United States should be free to consider armed strikes against terrorists at any time, nevertheless every feasible and effective option short of force should be explored before crossing the force threshold. The operative term here is *effective*. If the only effective response is force, then the liberal democracies of the West should not shrink from using force to protect their interests, citizens, and property. Force, moreover, may be used in some cases even more effectively in combination with other forms of retorsion and coercion short of hostilities designed to isolate, weaken, and punish sponsoring states. For example, commercial restrictions on states that sponsor terrorism may in fact have a greater restraining impact on them in some cases than the application of limited amounts of force. "Inasmuch as neither Qaddafi or Khomeini has any apparent hesitation at paying a human price to advance their political goals," writes Tovar, "the question is whether they would balk at paying a material price if it were sufficiently high. If the economic viability of their fragile regimes is at stake, they may have to balk."[19]

Force is a deterrent to terrorism. Nevertheless, the resort to force by a democratic society is always a difficult and usually reluctantly reached decision. Because democratic societies are founded on the rule of law, there is a natural tendency to want to solve international problems by diplomacy and recourse to other legal devices rather than by force. However, the threat posed by international terrorism and its patrons is so serious that there is a need by the liberal democracies of the West to protect their moral order and values with the judicious use of force.

Reprisals

Reprisals, defined as coercive measures directed by a state against another state in response to (or 'in retaliation for') illegal acts of the latter for the purpose of obtaining, either directly or indirectly, reparation or satisfaction of the illegal act," are as old as history itself and recognized under international law.[20] Reprisals involve the exaction of punishment on those who have committed an illegal act for which there is no other form of peaceful redress. For them to be legal and recognized under international law, reprisals cannot be capricious and open-ended and must conform to certain carefully defined conditions and limitations. An obscure military incident in Portuguese Angola during World War I resulted in an arbitration award in 1928 that set forth some of the major limitations on reprisals. But for the legal issues raised by the incident, the skirmish at Naulilaa would have been long forgotten.

In October 1914, a small party of Germans approached the Portuguese border post of Naulilaa. Portugal at that time was neutral and had not become a belligerent in the war. Owing to their inability to communicate in a common tongue, the commander of the Portuguese garrison believed that his post was being attacked and ordered his men to fire. In actuality the Germans had come to discuss the importation of food supplies from Angola into German Southwest Africa. In the ensuing hostilities three Germans—two military officers and one official—were killed, and the remaining two members of the party were interned. The Germans, in response, carried out various reprisals against the Portuguese colony, including attacks that destroyed the Portuguese fort at Cuangar and four border posts and forced the evacuation of the garrison at Naulilaa. This, in turn, apparently triggered a native uprising in the Portuguese colony, resulting in extensive looting and losses to the Portuguese.

Submitted to arbitration after the war, the three-man tribunal found that Germany had been guilty of using excessive force, not to mention other deficiencies, in mounting its reprisals and therefore was liable for compensating Portugal for damages that it had suffered. The panel found, that to be legitimate, reprisals must be precipitated by a prior illegal act, preceded by an unsatisfied demand for peaceful redress of the injury, and in proportion to the initial action.

Other limitations governing reprisals including prohibitions against injuring innocent third parties, continuing reprisals after reparations have been made by the guilty state, engaging in reprisals against reprisals, and resorting to reprisals before all peaceful means to obtain redress have been exhausted. To be legal, reprisals must also be carried out by states. Until the 1856 Treaty of Paris, private citizens who had suffered injury or loss at the hands of a national from another country could receive authorization from their own government to carry out reprisals—usually the seizure of property—against fellow citizens of the national who was responsible for the original offense. Even the U.S. Constitution provides for the granting of letters of marque and reprisal by the Congress, a privilege specifically denied to the states.

One of the problems with the traditional legal limitations on reprisals is the insistence that all peaceful remedies be exhausted before carrying out any form of retaliation. As the Israelis have maintained in disregarding efforts at peaceful redress before undertaking military reprisals in southern Lebanon, such efforts would be a waste of time and unlikely to produce tangible results. Furthermore, many observers hold that only a very short window exists wherein reprisals against terrorists are relevant and can be effectively linked to a precipitating terrorist incident. Under normal circumstances, such a window for military action is probably no more than seventy-two hours. After that, the horror of the original terrorist incident generally recedes, and both the public and world opinion begin to have difficulty in connecting the original action to the response. To be most effective, recent military experience suggests, reprisals should be swift and discriminating, or in other words whenever possible directed at those specifically responsible for the actual terrorist incident.

Public attitudes in the West reject notions of collective responsibility where members of a whole group or nationality are held responsible for the actions of a minority—which in most cases they are powerless to influence—and punished accordingly. During the 1984 hijacking of a Kuwaiti jetliner to Tehran by Shiite terrorists, two Americans were brutally murdered and others abused and tortured simply because they were Americans. The American public was outraged at the thought that nationality alone was justification enough for murder. Such attitudes are a throwback to the French anarchist Emily Henry, who tossed a bomb into the crowded Café Terminus and maintained at his trial that he felt no remorse inasmuch as there are "no innocent bourgeois" since it was society itself that permitted children to starve to death in French slums. To adopt a policy of indiscriminate reprisals against whole populations for the terrorist crimes of a few is to accept the distorted value system of the terrorists and become like them.

Criticism of reprisals also comes from those who believe that they are a cruel and ineffective strategy for dealing with terrorism. In this connection, the Israelis have carried out reprisals in southern Lebanon for more than a decade following terrorist attacks in Israel or against Israeli citizens on the theory that such attacks will drive a wedge between the host population, which fears further air raids and ground attacks, and the terrorist "fish" that swim submerged within their number. The Israelis also customarily raze the homes of Arabs on the occupied West Bank whose relatives have been implicated in terrorist attacks or identified as supporters of outlawed organizations like the Palestine Liberation Organization (PLO), in the hope that such retaliation will serve as a check on terrorist activities.

Critics of such Israeli policies contend that reprisals of this kind simply feed the cycle of violence in that tortured part of the world without materially affecting the terrorists and guerrillas who are the real source of the problem. Similarly, the 1983 shelling of the Chouf Mountains in Lebanon by the U.S. battleship *New Jersey* following attacks on U.S. Marines could not reasonably have been expected to punish those specifically responsible for the incidents. Although enemy command and forward observation positions were hit, reportedly killing high-ranking Syrian military personnel, the naval bombardment also inflicted casualties on the civilian population of the region without having a real impact on those who actually carried out the attacks on the marines. Using the *New Jersey* to fight terrorists is rather like employing a sledge hammer to kill a bothersome flea.

When considering military reprisals against terrorists, a number of suggestions relating to practical, legal, moral, and public relations issues must be given careful weight. Reprisals should be carried out as soon after the terrorist attack as possible so as not to permit the public to lose sight of the original incident which provoked the retaliation. And whenever possible, there should be a direct, provable link between the target of the reprisal and the terrorist incident. Striking at a terrorist training camp, for example, where members of a particular group that carried out the terrorist attack were trained, or at a facility where a particular bomb was assembled would generally be good targets that the public would understand.

The law of proportionality should always be borne in mind. Public opinion in the United States will never accept massive retaliation for a minor offense; it will be regarded as mean-spirited and beneath the dignity of a great power.

According to Michael Walzer, although a terrorist attack may be aimed at innocent civilians, "the reprisal must not be so aimed. Moreover, the 'reprisers' must take care that civilians are not incidental victims of their attack."[21] Thus, whenever possible, civilian targets should be avoided, although as Secretary of State Shultz has contended, some civilian casualties may be an inevitable product of reprisal scenarios. Terrorists have a propensity for locating their installations near hospitals and in heavily populated civilian districts precisely because to do so affords them protection and raises the stakes to any nation eager to carry out reprisals. Nevertheless, to punish large numbers of innocent civilian noncombatants as a side product of military strikes against terrorists is generally a poor policy and one likely to bring censure on the country initiating the reprisals. Such behavior runs the risk of making the states in opposition seem little different from the terrorists and augurs for smaller, more surgical operations designed to minimize casualties to innocent parties.

Reprisals against states that sponsor terrorists and use terrorism to achieve their national purposes always run the risk of precipitating either a general state of war or additional terrorist attacks. Shortly after Iran's role in the bombing of the U.S. embassy in Beirut was established, targets in Iran were selected by the Pentagon for possible retaliation. However, such plans were abandoned because policymakers did not feel that the United States was ready to deal with the possible secondary and tertiary consequences that might flow from such reprisals, especially the prospect of suicide bombings in the continental U.S. or an Iranian attack on Kuwait or Saudi Arabia.

Reprisals should be overt, rather than covert, if they are to have a cathartic effect on the victimized nation or serve as a deterrent to future attacks. While deniable missions and other black work can disrupt terrorist operations and punish terrorists for past transgressions, reprisals must be publicly acknowledged to have maximum impact.

Finally, the choice of the appropriate instrument with which to carry out a reprisal is all important. Without a full range of options in this regard, a nation can find itself employing the wrong instrument to achieve the right effect, a sure formula for eventual disaster. A measured response to intimidation and violence is required, ranging from low-signature, highly surgical operations to air strikes and full-scale military operations.

By contrast to Napoleon, who viewed reprisals as "a sorry recourse," reprisals have utility in combating terrorism. Nevertheless, they must be employed with restraint and then only when other alternatives do not exist. There is moral and legal justification for states carrying out reprisals against terrorists and their supporters, but reprisals remain an imprecise method of dealing with the problem. To be successful, reprisals generally require a rational adversary who can be intimidated into showing restraint rather than suffering the consequences that might flow from a particular reprisal. Moreover, if reprisals are to serve as a real deterrent, the state that threatens retaliation in the event that it suffers some injury at the hands of terrorists must be prepared to carry out its reprisals expeditiously and without hesitation or vacillation if an attack occurs. Otherwise threats of retaliation will have little credibility, and the victimized nation will suffer the second indignity of being seen as a paper tiger.

Preemption

Preemption can be defined as striking in advance of hostile action to prevent its occurrence and to avoid suffering injury. Preemption involves many more difficult questions than reprisals since it takes place before an actual terrorist attack or injury is suffered and therefore amounts to a response without a prior illegal action. Preemption is not designed to punish or deter, as are reprisals, but rather to protect; in other words, it is designed to prevent a terrorist attack from being carried out and thus to avoid the related deaths, injuries, and destruction.

Preemptive responses run the risk of relinquishing the moral high ground that derives from being the victim of an attack and therefore entitled to some form of redress, including the possibility of reprisals. In fact, a nation carrying out a preemptive attack may appear to the rest of the world as an aggressor rather than a potential victim, and in order to win acceptance of its action, the nation engaged in the preemptive attack will have to make a strong and persuasive public case to justify its action. This, however, can be exceedingly difficult and in some instances impossible. Few potential terrorist attacks can be verified in advance. Intelligence collection and analysis is an imprecise science, and policymakers often are required to make decisions based on imperfect intelligence where conclusions represent only probabilities, not hard facts. As a result, intelligence officials may only be able to advise policymakers that there is a 70 or 80 percent probability of a particular attack occurring, and they will be forced to decide whether that level of certainty is enough to act upon. The lower the level of certainty, the greater the incumbent risks in taking preemptive action. One can anticipate the problems arising from an incident where the United States acts preemptively to thwart a potential terrorist attack only to find that its information was incorrect. The media, the Congress, and U.S. critics abroad would likely have a field day with such a situation, although the preemptive strike was launched acting on what was considered to be accurate intelligence and with the best possible motivation: that of saving lives.

In other cases, it may be impossible for the United States to reveal fully to the public the reasons that compelled its actions since to do so would compromise intelligence sources and methods deemed critical to continued national security. Thus, preemptive strikes against terrorists raise serious practical and public relations issues, which will tend to discourage policymakers from such a course of action in all but the most high-consequence and solidly documentable circumstances.

"When you see a rattlesnake poised to strike," President Franklin Delano Roosevelt once observed, "you do not wait until he has struck before you crush him."[2] Nowhere is it written that the United States must absorb terrorist onslaughts before striking back. From the standpoint of self-defense, offensive action may well be justified; hesitation by policymakers to strike first in the face of a bona-fide threat from terrorists will be roundly condemned by their own citizens, especially if their restraint permits a terrorist outrage to occur that results in extensive destruction and loss of life.

The problem of preemption is brought into sharp focus by the prospect of terrorists armed with weapons of mass destruction or conspiring to strike at a critically sensitive or high-consequence target. The outcome of such an attack would likely be too terrible for a president to accept, and therefore he would have to make every effort to prevent the attack from occurring.

In this connection, preemption need not automatically entail air strikes or the insertion of commando teams to attack a specific facility or group of people. The United States has, for example, been engaged, along with other Western nations, in a quiet struggle to disrupt terrorist operations and communications through a process of disinformation, dirty tricks, and so-called black work. For example, Western intelligence operatives posing as illicit arms merchants, have sold terrorists defective weapons and equipment. In one case ultrasensitive detonators were given to a group of terrorist bomb builders who lost their lives when the bomb they were loading into a vehicle went off prematurely.

The following guidelines are proposed to govern acts of preemption. Just as conspiracy to commit a crime is illegal from the standpoint of domestic law, so too should conspiracies by foreign terrorists to harm the interests, citizens, and property of the United States be deemed illegal in advance of the actual attack and as appropriate justification for preemptive action. In this regard, the United States should invoke the right of self-defense and mount an effective campaign to explain the underlying reasons motivating its action.

Preemptive action should represent a last resort when no other remedy exists to prevent a terrorist attack from occurring. When advance information is obtained describing a forthcoming terrorist attack, publicly or privately threatening a patron state or the country where the attack will occur with certain reprisals if it permits the attack to be carried out may be a more effective strategy than preemption. Because preemptive strikes necessarily involve violations of another nation's sovereignty and thus could be considered a form of aggression, every effort should be made to get the nation where the terrorists are located to deal with the problem utilizing its own methods and legal procedures. If, however, a nation repeatedly demonstrates an inability (Lebanon) or an unwillingness (Libya) to take appropriate action, then it should not be necessary for a potential victim nation to waste time once more and leave itself vulnerable to attack before striking to eliminate the threat.

The amount of force used should be adequate to remove the threat and no more. Any disproportional use of force runs the risk of undermining the position of the threatened state and ultimately is itself a threat to the peace (with the preemptive strike viewed simply as a pretext for aggression). Moreover, any preemptive action should be highly discriminate and clearly defined so as to prevent the needless loss of life.

If the United States desires to prevent injury from occurring to its national interests, citizens, and property, it must be prepared—as a last resort—to preempt terrorist attacks. Anything less is a policy without teeth.

Retribution

In response to the bloody massacre of Israeli athletes at Munich in 1972 and a wave of attacks on Israeli diplomats, aircraft, supporters abroad, and other targets, the government of Prime Minister Golda Meir concluded that "current methods of dealing with terrorists had become obsolete overnight" and that a "new approach to the terrorist threat had to be devised."[23] The enemy in this case was the shadowy Palestinian group known as Black September, which had been established by Yasir Arafat and the high command of the PLO as a deniable unit without offices and formal infrastructure that could carry on the terrorist struggle while the PLO itself moved toward public respectability.

The Israeli answer to the challenge was to create a new organization committed to fight fire with fire. Known as the Mivtzan Elohim ("Wrath of God") its members were drawn from the Israeli defense and intelligence establishment. In the months that followed, the Israelis relentlessly struck back at the Black September terrorists, conducting daring raids into Beirut to kill the top leadership of the organization, tracking down Palestinian operatives in Europe and other locations and assassinating them, and broadcasting a message to terrorists everywhere that Israeli lives could not be taken with impunity.

In July 1973, a Wrath of God operation in Norway went sour, and a young Moroccan waiter was mistakenly killed in the belief that he was Black September's operations chief, Ali Hassan Salameh. Apparently the waiter, who bore a striking resemblance to Salameh, had been set up by Black September agents who knew that the death of an innocent man would bring public censure down on the Wrath of God. Although the Wrath of God purportedly was disbanded after the Norwegian incident, its work continued under the direct auspices of the Mossad, and it was not until 1979 that Salameh was actually killed. By late 1973, however, Black September had ceased to exist, its remaining members demoralized and fearful of being assassinated. The activities of the Israeli counterterrorist operation had not ended Palestinian terrorism but had certainly disrupted its operations and undermined its capability to carry out sophisticated attacks. Experienced operatives like Mohammed Boudia, Wadal Abdel Zwaiter, and Hassan Ali Salameh could not easily be replaced; effective planners and logisticians are rare in comparison to the large number of men and women willing to carry out an operation or even to the small number willing to drive a truck loaded with explosives into a building.

Today the United States should give serious consideration to restructuring its antiterrorist force to approximate the unit created by the Israelis. This new unit should be given the responsibility of taking the offensive against international terrorism, and should be trained to deal with this challenge equally well on paramilitary, intelligence, and investigative levels. This force would carry the war to the terrorists, turning the hunters into the hunted by disrupting their lines of communications and supply, gathering intelligence, infiltrating their organizations, sabotaging their weapons and plans, exposing their operations to friendly governments, and buttressing normal police investigative and assault tactics. The United States should work closely with and support any friendly government and its police and security apparatus to track down terrorists and ensure that they are punished for their crimes, no matter how long the hunt may take or how far afield it may range.

Today terrorists are still one of the least likely categories of international criminal to be caught and punished, and this has a corrosive impact on the international order because it serves to embolden terrorists who otherwise would have to be fearful for their own lives. The only durable way to remedy this situation is to turn up the heat and by so doing make it clear to terrorists that they will be pursued until they are caught and punished. This determination will communicate to state sponsors of terrorism that a cost will be attached to their support and they themselves are not immune from the retribution exacted by victimized Western governments.

"Keep running after a dog," goes the old saying, "and he will never bite you." By taking the war to the terrorists, it will be possible to keep them off balance, sow suspicion within their ranks, undermine their sources of support, and erode their confidence. They will be forced to stay constantly on the run and to expend scarce resources for their own security that might otherwise have gone to buying arms and underwriting new operations.

A policy designed to target the actual terrorists responsible for specific crimes is infinitely more humane than blasting heavily populated villages in reprisal air raids or shelling them with 16 inch guns from a battleship. By targeting clearly identified terrorists and relentlessly pursuing them, it will be possible to ensure that the guilty are punished and the innocent spared. Although the United States has not decided to train and employ its military and paramilitary forces in this fashion, it is time that serious consideration be given to such a policy. The essential elements of that policy, if adopted, might be as follows.

A new elite, civilian-run paramilitary unit that draws heavily on the CIA and Department of Defense should be created for the purpose of carrying out special operations against terrorists. Its charter would be tightly drafted and high restrictive. Members of the unit could only be given their orders and deployed by the president of the United States, the unit could never be deployed on U.S. territory, and its members would hold special military commissions and be subject to rigorous discipline. Both official and unofficial cover would be used to mask the activities of the unit and its members. Members of the unit would be drawn from a broad age spectrum, be highly compensated (with a great premium placed on retention of personnel), and manifest a wide range of life-styles and experience. A mechanism for prudent congressional consultation would be created to ensure proper oversight of the unit. Finally, the unit might consider the recruitment of a limited number of foreign nationals, along the lines of the French Foreign Legion. Such individuals would be drawn from various cultures and linguistic groups so as to improve the unit's ability to operate successfully in all environments and against all types of terrorist challenges.

Conclusion

The United States may yet perish as a nation of the delusion that it is necessary to be more moral than anyone else. There exists today a void in the international milieu composed of countries that do not subscribe to the laws and civilized norms that are the bedrock of the international system—nations like Libya and Iran, which observe traditionally accepted rules of behavior only when it serves their purposes. Similarly, transnational terrorists and third-force groups have added a new dimension of instability and peril to the international scene, sometimes at the behest of patron states and at other times to achieve their own agendas. To maintain a posture of national innocence and inaction in the face of such threats is to run the risk of catastrophe. When living in the jungle, it is best to observe the law of the jungle.

All three force responses discussed represent a significant departure from past U.S. efforts to address the threat of international terrorism, and each involves considerable risk and controversy. In some respects, all three options fly in the face of traditional U.S. self-perceptions, which hold that the United States does not need to resort to so-called dirty forms of warfare, even in self-defense, because to do so would compromise its own values and standing in the world community. The United States perceives of itself as a good and benign nation, slow to anger but righteous in its wrath, the kind of power reminiscent of old Hollywood adventure films where the hero throws away his sword after knocking the villian's weapon from his hand and then disposing of the fellow with his fists.

This does not mean that moral and legal considerations should be disregarded; quite the contrary. It is merely to suggest that we do not cease to be moral beings simply because we engage in nasty, low-intensity forms of conflict. The various proactive strategies for dealing with terrorism must be judged in the context of the circumstances in which they are employed, the limitations placed on the use of force in any of its manifestations, and the ends that each response is designed to achieve. In the words of Admiral James D. Watkins, "No response to terrorism ever will be absolutely clean or pure in its morality to all people. We do not live in a world of perfect absolutes, so we must do the best we can with the information available to us."[24] Those who allege that the Western democracies run the risk of becoming like the terrorists they oppose by adopting proactive options to suppress and defeat them are engaging in a cruel form of deception and falsehood, which only encourages and emboldens terrorists who want the United States to be paralyzed with indecision and moral vacillation. It is a sad commentary on the times that it is necessary to reassert our obvious superiority, by any conceivable yardstick, to the terrorists and their sponsors whose only politics are those of fear and murder and whose only law flows out of the barrel of a gun. It is time to stop apologizing for taking appropriate measures to protect societies from enemies bent on destruction.[25]

The demand for probative, or court-sustainable, evidence of a particular foreign terrorist group's culpability or affirming the complicity of a specific sponsoring state is an impractical standard and has contributed to the impression on the part of terrorists that the United States is inhibited from responding meaningfully to their outrages. The amount and quality of intelligence available will always fall something short of optimal, and as Tovar has stated,

"There is a very real danger that the pursuit of more and better intelligence may become an excuse for non-action, which in itself might do more harm than action based on plausible though incomplete intelligence."[26] Thus the United States should not insist on absolute evidence before employing force against terrorists; a functional standard of guilt appropriate to the threat will suffice.

Neither should there be an absolute requirement to obtain public endorsement and support of every contemplated action against international terrorism. This, too, would have a chilling effect on the ability of the United States to wage war against terrorists. The president and other elected officials should do what is required to protect the nation regardless of considerations relative to the support any action enjoys in the polls. Force, in the abstract and irrespective of an actual terrorist incident, will never garner a great deal of public support. Public officials therefore must be prepared to lead public opinion rather than simply follow it.

In conclusion, Oliver Wendell Holmes Jr., once observed, "Between two groups that want to make inconsistent kinds of worlds, I see no remedy except force."[27] The obvious superiority of the Western liberal democracies over the forces challenging them gives moral authority and license to their actions. Terrorists and their sponsors operate on the assumption that the United States will never use force. It is time to prove them wrong.

Notes

1. "Washington Turns into a Fortesss," *U.S. News and World Report*, February 6, 1984.

2. "Preemptive Anti-Terrorist Raids Allowed." *Washington Post*, April 16, 1984, p. 19.

3. "U.S. Will Not Drift into Combat Role, Weinberger Says," *New York Times*, November 29, 1984. See also Philip Taubman, *New York Times Magazine*, "The Shultz-Weinberger Feud," April 14, 1985.

4. "Shultz Defends U.S. Use of Force, Suggests Need for Anti-Terrorist Action," *Washington Post*, April 4, 1984.

5. Secretary of State George Shultz (speech to the Washington Plenary Meeting of the Trilateral Commission, April 3, 1984.)

6. "Shultz Urges 'Active' Drive on Terrorism," *Washington Post*, June 25, 1984.

7. Secretary of State George Shultz, "Terrorism and the Modern World" (speech to Park Avenue Synagogue, New York, October 25, 1984), p. 23.

8. Ibid.

9. Yonah Alexander, statement to author, 1984.

10. Robert C. McFarlane; "Terrorism and the Future of Free Society" (speech before the National Strategy Information Center, Defense Strategy Forum, Washington, D.C., March 25, 1985), p. 19.

11. Ibid.

12. Ibid.

13. Ibid.

14. Ibid.

15. "A Reagan Interview," *Washington Post,* April 2, 1985, p. A12.

16. William Casey (speech to the Fletcher School of Law and Diplomacy, Fourteenth Annual International Security Studies Conference, in Cambridge, Massachusetts, April 17, 1985).

17. Hugh Tover, "Low-Intensity Conflict: Active Responses in an Open Society" (paper prepared for the Conference on Terrorism and Other "Low Intensity" Operations: International Linkages, Fletcher School of Law and Diplomacy, Medford, Mass., April 1985), p. 14.

18. Ibid., p. 17.

19. Ibid., p. 25.

20. Wolfgang Friedmann, Oliver J. Lissitzyn, and Richard C. Pugh, *International Law* (St. Paul, Minn.: West Publishing Co., 1969), p. 880.

21. Michael Walzer, *Just and Unjust Wars* (New York: Basic Books, 1977), p. 217.

22. Franklin Delano Roosevelt, "Fireside Chat," September 11, 1941.

23. Michael Bar-Zohar and Eitan Haber, *The Quest for the Red Prince* (New York: William Morrow and Co., 1983), p. 135.

24. Admiral James D. Watkins, "Countering Terrorism: A New Challenge to Our National Conscience," *Sea Power* (November 1984): 37.

25. See Sam C. Sarkesian, "The Open Society: Defensive Measures" (paper prepared for the Conference on Terrorism and Other "Low Intensity" Operations, International Linkages, Fletcher School of Law and Diplomacy, Medford, Mass., April 1985).

26. Ibid., p. 24.

27. Oliver Wendell Holmes Jr., letter to Sir Frederick Pollock.

10
Covert Responses:
The Moral Dilemma

Guy B. Roberts

The Dilemma

Terrorism is not a new weapon; however, the threat it poses to security and society is growing. From 1973 to 1984, there were over 5,000 terrorist incidents recorded worldwide that took over 4,000 lives and wounded twice that many. In 1983, 40 percent of the attacks were directed at U.S. interests. In that year, more Americans were killed or injured by international terrorists than in any other year. Today more than 50 percent of terrorist attacks involve human targets. In December 1984 alone, there were over a dozen terrorist incidents, including one well-publicized airline hijacking in which two Americans died.

One need only think of the recent destruction of the U.S. embassy annex and the 1983 tragedy at the marine barracks in Beirut; about the bombing of the U.S. embassy annex in Kuwait; the bombing at Harrods in London and the recent attack on Prime Minister Margaret Thatcher; the murder of four members of South Korea's Cabinet in Rangoon; and the recent Belgium bombing by the so-called Free Communist Cell to get a perspective of the challenge.

Today several unscrupulous sovereign nations are sponsoring terrorist training camps on their soil, and thousands of trained assassins are being tutored at these universities of murder, mayhem, and destruction. This league of terror includes Libya, Syria, Iran, North Korea, and Bulgaria in its membership, and Soviet support for these terrorists and their activities is widely known. A recent issue of *Humint* magazine described "the hidden KGB hand behind terrorism, like that of the Islamic Jihad" in Lebanon and the Middle East.

Paper presented at the Joint Services Committee on Professional Ethics Conference on Terrorism, National War College, Ft. McNair, Washington, D.C. January 10-11, 1985. The views expressed in this chapter are those of the author only and do not necessarily represent the views of the U.S. Marine Corps, the Department of the Navy, or the U.S. government.

In response to the challenge of state-sponsored and other acts of terrorism, the United States has developed a national strategy based on four broad areas of response:

1. Prevention: Initiatives to discourage support of terrorism. This initially is an education and informational effort.
2. Deterrence: Described as protection and security efforts or measures to discourage the terrorist. This involves primarily internal security efforts.
3. Prediction: The intelligence and counterintelligence effort and support of the other three components.
4. Reaction: Action or operations in response to specific acts or incidents of terrorism.

My purpose here is to discuss one aspect of the prediction strategy to counter terrorism and terrorist acts: the legal and ethical issues associated with using government employees, military and civilian, to gather intelligence information to combat terrorism.

Counterterrorism depends entirely on intelligence. As secretary George Shultz has remarked, the first line of defense against terrorism is intelligence capability:

> Determination and capacity to act are of little value unless we can come close to answering the questions: Who? Where? And when? We have to do a better job of finding out who the terrorists are, where they are, and the nature, composition, and patterns of behavior of terrorist organizations. Our intelligence services are organizing themselves to do the job, and they must be given the mandate and the flexibility to develop techniques of detection and contribute to deterrence and response.

Although I am personally not aware of any covert intelligence-gathering project or operation, nevertheless if such projects are undertaken, the question is to what extent the United States should be willing to condone the commission of violent or illegal acts by its own agents in order to provide the intelligence information necessary to allow for a viable, acceptable reaction to counter or eliminate the terrorist threat. To set the stage, I will briefly outline the legal parameters that affect covert intelligence-gathering operations.

Legal Parameters

I define covert operations as government personnel engaged in a relationship with a target of a foreign counterintelligence or an international terrorism investigation where the contact is expected to continue over a period of time and where U.S. government employment is concealed.

Second, for want of a better definition and recognizing that there are several definitions or interpretations of terrorism, I will use the definition of international terrorism contained in the Foreign Intelligence Surveillance Act [50 U.S.C. § 1801]. That act defines international terrorism as activity that

1. Involve[s] violent acts or acts dangerous to human life that are a violation of the criminal laws of the United States [or of any state, or that would be a criminal violation if committed within the jurisdiction of the United States or any states];
2. Appear[s] to be intended
   A. To intimidate or coerce a civilian population;
   B. To influence the policy of the government by intimidation or coercion; or
   C. To effect the conduct of a government by assassination or kidnapping; *and*
3. Occur[s] totally outside the United States or transcend[s] national boundaries in terms of the means by which they are accomplished, the person they appear intended to coerce or intimidate, or the locale in which their perpetrators operate or seek asylum.

The Department of Defense is given authority to conduct intelligence-gathering activities in accordance with executive order 12333, which directs the secretary of defense to "conduct counterintelligence activities in support of Department of Defense components outside the United States in coordination with the CIA, and within the United States in coordination with the FBI pursuant to procedures agreed upon by the secretary of defense and the attorney general." The order also gives the various service components the authority and responsibility of conducting counterintelligence activities outside the United States in coordination with the Central Intelligence Agency (CIA). It has been implemented within the Department of Defense (DOD), by DOD Regulation 5240.1.

Several statutes restrict the activities of individuals who would be assigned to covert operations. Briefly, these prohibit the following:

1. Any acts of violence including, but not limited to, murder or manslaughter of foreign officials, official guests, or internationally protected persons. An internationally protected person is defined as "A chief of state or a political equivalent, head of government, or foreign minister, whenever such person is in a country other than his own and any member of his family accompanying him; or any other representative, official, or agent of the United States government, a foreign government or inter-

national organization who at the time and place concerned is entitled pursuant to international law to special protection against attack upon his person, freedom, or dignity, and any member of his family then forming part of his household." Title 18 of the U.S. Code (18 U.S.C. § 1116) provides jurisdiction by the United States over the offense committed as described no matter where the offense occurred if the alleged offender is present within the United States.

2. Title 18 (18 U.S.C. § 877) also provides for extra territorial jurisdiction in any case of mailing threatening communications from any foreign post office to any person. Special penalties (18 U.S.C. § 878) are provided in cases of a willful threat to kill, kidnap, or assault foreign official guests or internationally protected persons.

In addition to domestic legislation providing for extraterritorial jurisdiction, the United States is party to several international treaties or agreements that proscribe terrorist acts. These include the following four broad categories:

1. Aircraft hijacking: The Tokyo (1963), Hague (1970) and Montreal (1973) conventions, codified in Title 49 (49 U.S.C. § 1301 *et seq.*), confer extraterritorial jurisdiction to try alleged offenders and provide for the death penalty when the death of another person results from the commission or the attempted commission of the offense.

2. Crimes against internationally protected persons: Any act, wherever located, against any internationally protected person is included in this protection by statute.

3. Crimes committed during armed conflict: Common Article 3 of the Geneva Convention related to the protection of civilian persons in time of war also provides that the commission of any violence to life and person, including murder, mutilation, cruel treatment, and torture; taking of hostages; outrages upon personal dignity, in particular humiliating and degrading treatment, is considered a grave breach of the laws of war and subject to criminal sanction in any country in which the alleged offender is found. This applies to all armed conflicts between states even if a state of war is not officially recognized by either party.

4. Use of mails for terrorist acts: The United States is a party to universal postal conventions. Under domestic legislation, crimes commited in violation of those conventions are subject to extraterritorial jurisdiction.

Several of the conventions, particularly the conventions on aircraft hijacking, also include provisions by which the contracting states have an obligation either to extradite the alleged offender found in their territory or to submit his or her case, without exception, to its competent authorities for the purpose of prosecution.

Finally, in addition to the statutes and international agreements, the president has issued executive order 12333, which contains a prohibition on assassination: "No person employed by or acting on behalf of the United States government shall engage in or conspire to engage in, assasination." Two points should be made regarding that prohibition. First, an executive order does not have the force of law, and an act in contravention of that order is not prosecutable. Second, no attempt was made within the executive order to define assassination. *Webster's Dictionary* defines *assassinate* as "to murder a usually prominent person violently or to injure, wound, or destroy unexpectedly and treacherously." Could a military operation designed to eliminate a terrorist threat conceivably involve assassination?

Prosecution, Enforcement, and Oversight

Any violation of these laws is investigated and prosecuted, in accordance with Title 28 (28 U.S.C. § 535), by the attorney general and the Federal Bureau of Investigation (FBI). The head of any government department or agency receiving any information regarding federal criminal violations involving government officials and employees is required to report the same to the attorney general unless the investigative responsibility is otherwise assigned. Exceptions include offenses by military personnel and postal offenses. The Department of Defense and, more specifically, the service concerned retain cognizance over offenses committed by military personnel wherever they may occur. Military personnel are always subject to prosecution under the Uniform Code of Military Justice; however, civilian personnel of the Department of Defense are subject to investigation and prosecution by the attorney general.

In addition, to oversee intelligence operations in general, executive order 12334 established the president's Intelligence Oversight Board. That board is responsible for informing the president of any intelligence activities that any member of the board believes violates a law, executive order, or presidential directive. It reports these activities to the attorney general, it is responsible for reviewing the practices and procedures of the various agencies involved in intelligence activities to discern whether any illegal activity is being conducted, and it is authorized to conduct any investigation necessary to carry out its function as an intelligence oversight board. Within the Department of Defense, an independent oversight of all intelligence activities was established by DOD directive 5148.11, which requires an assistant secretary of defense to make a quarterly report to the Intelligence Oversight Board on all significant oversight activities and any activities of questionable legality.

A Hypothetical with a Twist

Human intelligence is the most productive intelligence discipline in combating terrorism. Usually the terrorist has neither elaborate communication systems, which can be exploited by signals intelligence, nor can the terrorist's intentions and preparations be determined through imagery. Terrorist groups are usually very small groups of five or so members. It is very difficult for anyone to work his or her way into the group, especially when the members are fanatical, deeply religious or ideologically motivated, and dedicated. Suborning a member of these groups has proved, in most cases, impossible. It is not an easy task to go out and, say, recruit a hundred Lebanese and tell them to join the so-called Islamic Jihad to gather information.

So when you talk about preventing a terrorist attack on a specific target, how do you find these terrorists? The people who actually would execute the operation usually number no more than two or three. Additionally, there is nothing unusual about the means in which they employ their weapons of destruction—specifically, a nondescript vehicle containing several hundred pounds of explosives. Consequently, identifying terrorists and their targets is like finding a needle in a haystack.

Historically, an inside man, whether a U.S. agent or informant, has proved to be the most valuable in obtaining information on these characteristically small terrorist groups. Assume for the moment that a U.S. citizen, a DOD civilian or service member, is ordered to seek out and join a specific terrorist group. Also assume that he or she is successful in that effort. Most terrorist gangs are known to some extent, and they all are characterized by their proclivity to do violent acts. Another obvious characteristic is the intensity and fanaticism of the individuals involved. If this is the case, how does a U.S. agent or informer manage to become a member so that he or she can provide the necessary information needed to stop and eventually eliminate this threat? The obvious answer is that the informant will have to join and participate in some of the group's activities.

To the extent the informant actively participates in the group's activities three problems need to be addressed.

First, assuming that the information the undercover agent has been directed to retrieve is vitally essential to the national interest of the United States, what should be his or her brief regarding the parameters of participation in that group? Should the informant be allowed to participate in the targeting of foreign nationals (statesmen, diplomats, or citizens, for example) of allied nations? Of hostile nations? If not participate, should he be allowed to help plan or support? If the individual has prior knowledge of the pending attack, what is his or her responsibility regarding that information?

This question has serious foreign policy, as well as moral, implications. If a U.S. agent participates in criminal acts in a foreign state, he or she has committed a crime in that country subject to its jurisdiction. If it is an allied country and the U.S. agent is caught, there obviously will be some hard feelings regarding the lack of cooperation, assuming there was none. If it involves a hostile nation, the policy implications can be even greater, leading possibly to reprisals and retaliation.

Second, what is the legal, social, and moral responsibility of the supervisor(s) in charge of these operations? Often there will be a conflict between the legal restraints placed on the ability to conduct such operations and the clear, practical situations faced by the field agent. What guidance should the supervisor provide when placing an agent in a position that the supervisor knows or reasonably should know may require the agent to commit or participate in illegal acts (for example, distinguishing between committing an illegal act and compromising his or her cover or, worse, losing his or her life)? Must certain information be obtained at all costs? If not, what should be the guidelines to the supervisor to give to the field agent regarding the political, social and moral implications of assigned endeavors?

Third, what of the moral dilemma and consequences we place on the individual involved in such situations? What criteria and training do we give him or her to make the necessary choices? What guidelines do we give or should give to draw the line between the objective to be achieved and the cost in terms of lives, property, or foreign relations? Or should we give them any guidelines? Should we hold only the agency (or the government) responsible and not the individual for the acts he or she committed or participated in? Are we to congratulate an agent for a successful intelligence-gathering operation and then prosecute the person for the illegal acts he or she committed in obtaining that information? By statute, government agencies are required to report any criminal act. They are also required to investigate and, when appropriate, prosecute for the commission of illegal acts in which the United States has extraterritorial jurisdiction. Additionally the United States has an international obligation to investigate and prosecute for those acts committed in violation of our treaty obligations.

The Rowe Case

The following actual example points to the kind of dilemmas that the United States will face in this area. From 1960 to 1965, the FBI paid Gary Thomas Rowe, Jr., to inform on the Ku Klux Klan as part of their domestic counter-intelligence program. This was a time when all of the South, as well as the rest of the United States, was in the throes of a violent civil rights struggle. The FBI believed that hard-core Klansmen in the Alabama Ku Klux Klan were responsible for much of the violence. Rowe was recruited to infiltrate their ranks. He did and rose rapidly within the ranks of the Klan, soon becoming a confidant of several Klan leaders. He gave the FBI more and better information than any other Klan informant in Alabama.

Following FBI policy, Rowe's handling agents first instructed him to get close to the Klansmen to find out what they were doing but to stay away from violence. Both Rowe and his supervisors soon recognized, however, that he would never penetrate the inner circle responsible for the violence without taking part, at least to some extent, in its planning and execution. Nonetheless, Rowe was warned that if he did participate in violence, the FBI would disown him and treat him like a criminal. As events were to prove, this was an empty threat.

Rowe faithfully reported his participation in Klan-provoked beatings, harassment of local black leaders, firebombings, and other illegal acts. These acts were never reported by his supervisors to local authorities nor was he terminated as an informant. He was considered too valuable an informant to abandon.

By late 1963, Rowe was doing so well in the Klan that he had become the leader of one of the Klan's most violent action squads. (This points out another problem in intelligence-gathering operations. Agents are usually so well trained and so good at what they do that they often rise to positions of responsibility within the infiltrated organization. If they refuse to assume these additional responsibilities, they may be suspected of either not being faithful to the cause or being an informant.) On March 25, 1965, a civil rights worker from Detroit, Viola Liuzzo, was shot and killed while driving her car following the Selma-to-Montgomery freedom march. After the shooting, Rowe immediately reported to the FBI that he was in the car from which the fatal shots were fired. The FBI, after investigation, arrested the car's three other occupants. Rowe was given immunity and was the government's star witness in two state murder trials and one federal civil rights trial. The other three men were convicted for violating Liuzzo's civil rights and sentenced to serve a ten-year prison term.

Rowe was not charged in connection with the Liuzzo killing until 1978, when he was indicted for murder by an Alabama grand jury after two other members of the gang in the car accused Rowe of murdering her. Certainly, if Rowe did not actually shoot Liuzzo, he did fire shots at the vehicle and was involved in the initial planning of the act. At the very least, a strong case could be made that he was an accessory. FBI evidence established that the murder weapon did not belong to Rowe but belonged to the man who was driving the car; however, no one claimed that the driver fired it because be was driving at an excessive rate of speed, which made it virtually impossible for him to have used his weapon. Indeed, two of the occupants in the car testified that Rowe had borrowed that weapon, fired it at Liuzzo's car, and later had given the weapon back to the owner. Rowe was never convicted of any criminal act relative to this incident. He was given $10,000 as severance pay and provided with a job and new life in California.

Although the task force investigating this case could find no document that definitively set forth whether there was a permissible level of violence by informants such as Rowe, it was clear that the handling agents allowed (either explicitly or implicitly) Rowe to participate in illegal acts, and he was led to believe that he would be immune from being called to account for those acts.

As a consequence of this case and others, in 1976 attorney general Edward H. Levi promulgated guidelines designed to govern the FBI's use of informants in domestic security criminal cases. The guidelines, known as the Levi guidelines, now require agents to instruct their informants that in carrying out their assignments they should not:

1. Participate in acts of violence.
2. Use unlawful techniques to obtain information for the FBI.
3. Initiate a plan to commit criminal acts.
4. Participate in criminal activities with persons under investigation, except insofar as the FBI determines that such participation is necessary to obtain information for purposes of federal prosecution.

Thus, on a domestic level, as a matter of policy, there are social, political, and moral bounds beyond which the United States has determined its agents will not go in gathering intelligence information to combat criminal activities. How workable are these guidelines on a day-to-day basis? Further, how workable are they or have they been in combating domestic terrorist groups such as the radical FALN (the Puerto Rican terrorist group) or the new phenomenon of drug traffickers engaged in terrorists acts? As the Rowe investigation established, the FBI was unable to get reliable information about one of the oldest terrorist groups, the Ku Klux Klan, without having an agent on the inside. And that agent could not get there unless he was able to prove his propensity and willingness to be an active member of the group.

In many ways the Rowe case is a good example of the moral issues involved in the use of U.S. agents in covert operations. It may be necessary to come up with guidelines that prohibit or proscribe certain activities of undercover agents. But in the fight against terrorism, if we realistically want a viable intelligence capability, the harsh truth is that the U.S. public must understand that fighting terrorists will not be a clean or pleasant contest in which everyone agrees to play by the rules.

One Possible Approach

The Rowe case and its aftermath portrays an actual example that poses the dilemmas facing those engaged in the war against terrorism. These dilemmas must be resolved by the implementation of a national policy that takes into account the values of U.S. society. If one concludes that to combat terrorism, good intelligence and, in many cases, an informant or inside agent is necessary, then the questions I have posed will always be with us. With that in mind, let me suggest an approach.

First, the agencies involved should review at the outset all possible implications of using an undercover agent, whether a U. S. citizen or otherwise. The various responsible intelligence-gathering agencies should establish a review procedure of covert operations with specific guidelines establishing the parameters of possible actions and consequences. This should take into account national policy, foreign policy considerations, societal values and morality, and the law.

Second, if it is reasonably contemplated that criminal acts may have to be committed in order to gain the information necessary, the appropriate agencies, and in most cases this would include the Department of Justice, should be consulted. Agreement must be reached beforehand that would in effect act as a waiver of prosecution for acts committed that may be classified as crimes. All of this should be done on a classified basis.

Third, these actions, if undertaken, should be subject to an independent review by an independent agency, such as the present Intelligence Oversight Board, to ensure that the actions contemplated by a particular agency or agencies comply with national policy and are, in view of the results to be achieved, an acceptable temporary sacrifice of society's values, if that has occurred, for the greater cause of eliminating the immediate terrorist threat.

I do not mean to suggest that the United States should abandon its basic values. On the contrary, if Americans truly believe in these values, they have a duty to defend them. As Secretary of State George Shultz stated, "[When] we fight this battle against terrorism, we must always keep in mind the values and way of life we are trying to protect. Clearly, we will not allow ourselves to descend to the level of barbarism that terrorism represents. We will not abandon our democratic traditions, our respect for individual rights and freedom, for these are precisely what we are struggling to preserve and promote. Our values and our principles will give us the strength and the confidence to meet the great challenge posed by terrorism."[2]

The Challenge

The intelligence services have come a long way in organizing themselves to do the job of combating terrorism—that is, to discover who the terrorists are, where they are, and their patterns of behavior. Covert intelligence operations are necessary for identifying and targeting terrorist bases and training camps and providing an effective warning of potential terrorist attacks. Secretary Shultz said, "If terrorism is truly a threat to Western moral values, our morality must not paralyze us."

I do not believe his comments were meant to suggest that neither morality nor law should restrain American behavior. Neither am I compelled to conclude by examining this issue that the United States must adopt an end justifies the means mentality and sanction any and all aspects of covert operations. But on the other hand, it should not draw any absolute lines over which it is prohibited under any circumstances to cross. Americans should make no mistake that they are in a war in which their fundamental values are at stake. In such a war, the traditional theory of just war applies. It applies because the cause is just. The United States is defending itself against an unjust aggressor and protecting legitimate state interests. Providing such protection is both a lawful and moral obligation of nations, and as the chief of naval operations, Admiral Watkins, has stated, "For those serving in the armed forces it is also the foundation of our oath of duty and call to service."[3]

No response to terrorism ever will be absolutely clean or pure in its morality to all people. We do not live in a world of perfect absolutes, so we must do the best we can with the information available. But decisions must be made, and it is clear that moral decisions can be made.

As the Gary Rowe case has shown, we cannot bury our heads in the sand over the complexities that covert intelligence-gathering operations present. It is not enough to establish strict do's and don'ts in such situations because often the requirements of obtaining the necessary information to counter and eventually destroy a terrorist group do not lend themselves easily to strict prohibition of certain actions. If an agent is faced with a choice of violating the law or dying as a result of the position the government has placed or him or her in, it would be indeed a rare individual who would choose to die rather than break the law. It would serve the opposite interests of the government who put the agent in that situation in the first place. If the United States needs people to infiltrate terrorist organizations, it has to accept that they may be called upon to commit illegal acts, and those acts may have serious moral, legal, and political consequences.

Ultimately, the real question is how the U.S. public, aroused by the growing, pervasive threat of terrorism, will respond when it is asked to understand the need for such actions. Public consciousness raising is occurring every day with continued revelations of terrorist attacks.

Recently, international terrorism showed a new face when Colombian drug traffickers detonated a car bomb outside the U.S. embassy in Bogotá, Colombia. They threatened to kill five Americans for every narcotics suspect extradited. The State Department has released evidence showing that Colombian insurgents and drug traffickers have combined forces, and both have been given access to Cuba for training, supplies, and protection. This is a new challenge that must be met with renewed determination. Awareness of the growing global menace will demand action to prevent chaos.

The first duty of any government is to preserve order and defend its own existence. Chaos and constant terror cannot be permitted in a civilized world. Therefore, it is the duty of any government to use such measures as are necessary to maintain order. The challenge is to ensure that such use of the state's police power is not excessive and does not degenerate into the abuse of power; if it does, the terrorists have won. Nevertheless, one of the responsibilities of government is to protect its people from violence and itself from the injustice of terrorism and to strike first if that responsibility so requires. Cicero, in his treatise "Of Duties" said it clearly: There are two sorts of injustice; the first is caused by those who commit an injury and the second by those who do not ward off an injury to another if they have the power to do so.

Above all, a society should be given ample opportunity to foresee the problem of terrorism and to discuss in dispassionate terms the options for dealing with it. Public understanding and acceptance of the necessary tools to combat terrorism is a reflection of the resolve needed to continue to stand firmly for the set of values Americans believe in. The United States should not and will not abandon those values in the face of the threat. If Americans understand the threat and the requirements necessary to check and eliminate that threat, there will be no moral dilemma, and the U.S. tradition of democracy will continue to be nurtured and developed.

Notes

1. George P. Shultz, The Scherr Lecture, Park Avenue Synagogue, New York, Oct. 25, 1984.

2. *Ibid.*

3. Admiral James D. Watkins, "Countering Terrorism: A New Challenge to Our National Conscience," *Sea Power*, (November, 1984), p. 36.

BELOW: Fighting Back: May 5, 1980 — Members of Britain's elite Special Air Service storm the Iranian embassy in London, England to end a six-day seige. Nineteen hostages were rescued and three gunmen killed.

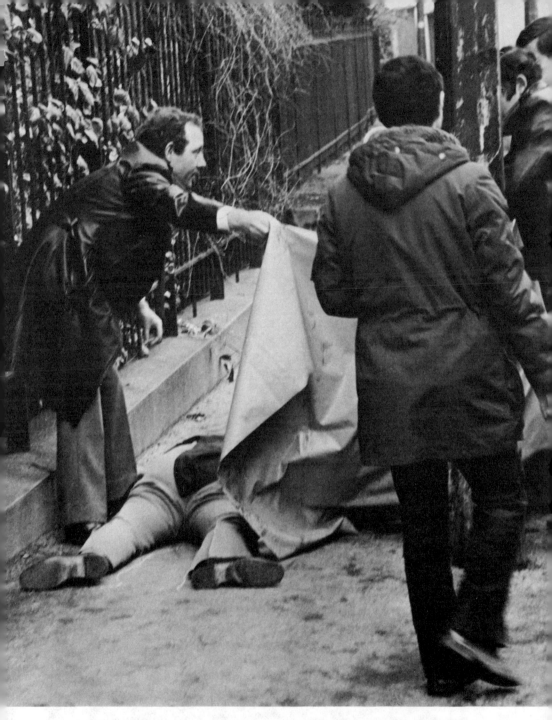

Dodge City on the Seine: A police inspector puts a blanket over the body of U.S. assistant military attache Lieutenant Colonel Charles Robert Ray minutes after he was shot dead outside his Paris apartment on the morning of January 18, 1982. Ray was murdered with one shot in the head. The killer escaped on foot from the scene.

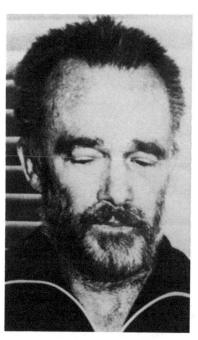

ABOVE: Americans are terrorist target #1 in the world: At left, Brigadier General James L. Dozier in a 1981 photo. At right, Dozier on January 28, 1982 following his rescue by Italian police commandos. Dozier had been held captive for 42 days by Red Brigade terrorists. BELOW: New anti-NATO terrorist offensive in Europe: Debris is scattered on the ground after a bomb exploded on June 1, 1982 at the headquarters of the U.S. Army 5th Corps in Frankfurt. An Army spokesman said other explosions occurred at U.S. Army officers' clubs in Bamberg, Gelnhausen and Hanau. A leftist terrorist group claimed the bombings were a "prelude" to President Reagan's visit.

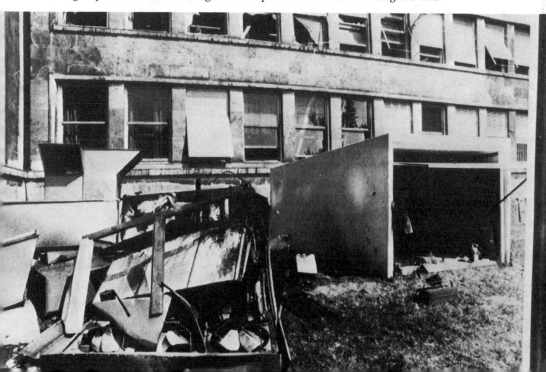

ABOVE: Diplomacy under attack: Bodies of Americans killed in the U.S. embassy bomb blast on April 18, 1983 in Beirut are honored in a quiet 35-minute ceremony before being flown to Washington. BELOW: Looking like a fugitive from the "Rocky Horror Show", Libyan leader Muammar Qaddafi, second from right, is escorted by armed female bodyguards as he walks with Tunisian Prime Minister Mohammed Mzali.

ABOVE: Diplomatic immunity has been used to cloak terrorist activities. **BELOW:** Reports link Qaddafi to Reagan assassination plot.

Television terrorism: The masked leader of a group of hijackers who took over an Air France flight talks to newsmen on August 31, 1985 at Tehran's Mehrabad airport. The group of four gunmen surrendered after Iranian officials agreed to allow them to talk to newsmen, illustrating the symbiosis between terrorism and the media.

ABOVE: The United States at War: A U.S. Marine guard watches as rescue workers search through the rubble of the Marine battalion headquarters in Beirut which was destroyed in a car bomb blast on October 23, 1983. 241 Americans were killed in the blast. BELOW: Death on wheels: Rescue and police teams search through the rubble at the U.S. embassy in Kuwait in the wake of a car explosion on December 12, 1983.

Training for the inevitable: Members of the FBI's hostage rescue team rush a mockup of a building to rescue a hostage held by terrorists in a training exercise at the FBI Academy in Quantico, Virginia.

ABOVE: Explosive end to a hijacking: Hijackers blow up a Royal Jordanian ALIA Boeing 727 at Beirut Airport on June 12, 1985. The hijackers released passengers and crew members but eight Jordanian sky marshals were still aboard the plane when the hijackers sprayed it with bullets and set off three explosive devices. BELOW: A moment of terror: An armed terrorist holds a gun on TWA pilot John Testrake during an interview on June 19, 1985 from the hijacked plane, Flight 847, in Beirut.

11
The Legal Case for Using Force

Victoria Toensing

> Men are not hanged for stealing horses, but that horses may not be stolen.
> —George Savile, marquess of Halifax, 1633–1695[1]

One by one they were captured from the public street of Beirut: two journalists, a U.S. diplomat, two clerics, two educators, and one administrator from American University Beirut.[2] And in the winter and spring of 1985, the United States sat silently by as its own citizens were held hostage and threatened by the Islamic Jihad, an avowed terrorist group demanding release of convicted terrorists jailed in Kuwait in return for the lives of the Americans. Not until TWA flight 847 was hijacked by Shiite terrorists on June 14, 1985, did U.S. outrage become public and loud. Its frustration quickly grew commensurate with its anger.

In November 1979, when the U.S. embassy was captured in Tehran, America's outrage was also loud, enduring throughout the 444 days of the embassy personnel's captivity. By October 1983, when U.S. Marines were killed and maimed by a truck bomber in Beirut, incensed Americans turned not to outcry but to internal investigations by congressional committees and the executive branch's Long commission. The result of these studies was a collective mea culpa for insufficient or underanalyzed intelligence and for lack of a strategy to respond to the attack. In 1983 there was no plan for dealing with a terrorist attack. Although two years later some headway had been made for the government to respond to terrorism, still no blueprint included a vital tool for this response: striking back with force.

It is time to discuss whether the United States can accept a domestic or international system that is either structured or construed to provide freedom from accountability to nations or groups who attack others. There are many forms of response to terrorism; chief among them is peaceful diplomacy. A comprehensive plan, however, must include an option to use force—either preemptorily or reactively—to prevent future attacks.

Lack of Remedies

Ambassador Robert B. Oakley, director of the U.S. State Department's counterterrorism and emergency planning office, told a congressional panel in March 1985, "If the need for a preemptive or retaliatory strike should occur, it would take us a year to come up with a plan and then we would be spitting into the wind."[3] Any such plan, Ambassador Oakley informed Congress, would require consultation with the White House, National Security Agency, Central Intelligence Agency (CIA) Department of Defense, and other State Department offices. And, he should have added, any attempt to formulate a plan to redress terrorism by any display of force would be countered by political, procedural, and legal obstacles built over a decade of reaction to the U.S. failure in Vietnam.

"Antiterrorist Plan Rescinded after Unauthorized Bombing" blared the May 12, 1985, headline of the *Washington Post*. The story claimed President Reagan had approved CIA covert training and support for counterterrorists to strike terrorists before they again attacked U.S. facilities in the Middle East. Some members of the group had gone astray by hiring others to detonate a car bomb outside the Beirut residence of Mohammed Hussein Fadlallah, a militant Shiite leader believed to have been behind the terrorist attacks on U.S. installations, including the U.S. embassy and marine barracks. Over eighty persons were killed, and two hundred were wounded; the Shiite target escaped injury.[4]

Robert C. McFarlane, presidential national security affairs adviser, and CIA director William J. Casey had used almost identical words in separate speeches within weeks after that bombing but prior to the *Post* allegations:

> We cannot and will not abstain from forcible action to prevent, preempt or respond to terrorist acts where conditions merit the use of force. Many countries, including the United States, have the specific forces and capabilities we need to carry out operations against terrorist groups.[5]

McFarlane's speech also outlined what he thought should be the "principles of employment": force proportionate to the threat, targeted as precisely as possible, judicious selection of where, when, and what kind of case, and the fullest possible cooperation of Congress and other governments. Above all, McFarlane said, "We want to succeed."[6]

The runaway bombing did not succeed, and the political reaction was prompt. Sunday talk shows featured senators and congressmen debating whether all members of Congress who should have been informed had been properly so and whether the plan for preemption, not the actual disclaimed attacked, was in violation of the executive order ban on U.S. personnel direct or indirect involvement in any assassination plan or operation. One administration source responded by comparing killing terrorists to "preemptive self-defense," noting, "Knocking off a guy who is about to kill you is no more assassination than a policeman getting off the first shot at a man pointing a gun at him." However, with the plan having gone awry and with the congressional furor, sources stated that covert training had been quashed. Only the hijacking of flight 847 exhumed the issue, but then the nation was in the midst of a crisis.

International redress fares no better. Current international law has gaps on paper and in practice that grant immunity to terrorists. "Law is not a law without coercion behind it," observed President James Garfield.[8] International law is unenforceable as Americans understand enforcement by a legal system that backs its laws with courts, juries, judges, and police. It is for the most part played in the courtroom of world opinion. With such murky underpinnings, there are great gaps when a response to terrorist violence is needed.

The U.N. Charter outlaws force or the threat of it:

> All members shall refrain in their international relations from the threat or use of force against the territorial integrity or political independence of any state, or in any other manner inconsistent with the Purposes of the United Nations. Art. 2(4).

The exception to this prohibition is Article 51:

> Nothing in the present Charter shall impair the inherent right of individual or collective self-defence if an armed attack occurs against a Member of the United Nations, until the Security Council has taken measures necessary to maintain international peace and security.

This exception has been interpreted by the current international legal community to permit self-defense only when an armed attack "occurs." This interpretation is based not only on Articles 51 and 2(4) but also on Article 2(3), which states: "All Members shall settle their international disputes by peaceful means in such a manner that international peace and security, and justice, are not endangered."

It is argued that one border crossing or even "isolated or sporadic" crossings do not reach the threshold of an "armed attack."[9] It is also argued that because the definition of *armed attack* is narrower than *aggression*, then "certainly self-defense against armed bands would not seem to be included within the permitted area."[10]

Such restrictive definitions of self-defense reward those who strike quickly with few cohorts and retreat—the very modus operandi of terrorists. These renditions are also contrary to the traditional self-defense doctrine, which permitted defensive action based on "instant and overwhelming necessity," thus permitting action prior to an attack's occurring.[11]

In practice, this limited right or, if not a right, this exemption from renunciation by the international community has even further restrictions. The politics of the United Nations permits self-defense for addressing grievances only for certain countries.

From 1968 to 1978, eleven Security Council resolutions discussed Israeli counter-*fedayeen* activities directed at Lebanon. All eleven "condemn Israel for violating the territorial integrity of Lebanon or for engaging in forbidden military reprisals"; none "condemn Lebanon, the PLO, or the *fedayeen*; nor on their face do they suggest that any violence on the part of the *fedayeen* preceded the condemned Israeli attacks."[12]

International law imposes on a state a duty to control activities of persons within its jurisdiction or its territory that harm citizens within a foreign state.[13] U.S. law has long recognized this duty: "The law of nations requires every national government to use 'due diligence' to prevent a wrong being done within its own dominion to another nation with which it is at peace, or to the people thereof."[14] This duty has been interpreted to mean that the host state shall not only prevent injurious acts to other states but also that it should punish persons engaging in such activities.[15]

The U.N. General Assembly has adopted declarations forbidding a state to permit its own borders to be used as a base for those who would plan violence for another state.[16] However, the technical escape clause to these declarations is that if the host state cannot control the aggressors, that state is then excused.[17] The result, therefore, is that a state can be subject to raids and kidnappings from terrorist groups and be left remediless because the host state is in disarray.

The example of Israel and Lebanon leaps out at the international observer, but it takes little imagination to envision a future scenario where Mexico and U.S. southern states could repeat their nineteenth- and twentieth-century history of border raids where innocent U.S. citizens were killed. Clearly the kidnapping and hijacking of Americans in Lebanon place the problem in the present tense. The question remains: Why isn't the tool of striking back by force in the U.S. or international arsenal for dealing with terrorist attacks?

Domestically, there is a public admission of no plan considering the use of force. Ambassador Oakley and/or the State Department are hardly to blame. The present layer of domestic legal requirements and political considerations, plus bureaucratic notice requirements, inhibit such a plan.

Internationally there are attempts to cope with terrorism, but they are limited to specific subjects, like the Montreal Convention outlawing aircraft sabotage, and they work to apprehend the perpetrators only when the states are cooperative. There is, however, no international enforcement when states cannot or will not comply. But before one denounces the United Nations for its inability to address terrorism, one might consider self-denunciation for possessing expectations too great for that body. The United Nations was and is designed to stop war as the world knew war in the 1940s. When a major international crises occurs, such as the Suez Canal nationalization in 1956, the debating process can calm the belligerent parties. The United Nations cannot enforce peace; it can only lessen hostilities. It possesses no mechanism for controlling terrorism.

In a seven-day period in June 1985 when the U.S. hostages kidnapped from Beirut streets plus forty male passengers and crew from TWA flight 847 were held somewhere in the Middle East (June 14), when a bomb had exploded at Frankfurt airport killing two young children and an adult (June 19), when twelve persons, including four off-duty U.S. Marine embassy guards, had been shot dead in cold blood in a San Salvador street café (June 20), no one sought help from the United Nations. Instead, Americans, Germans, and Salvadorans could only express frustration about not knowing how to react to the tragedies.

No international body deals effectively or comprehensively with terrorism. As soon as we accept that proposition, we can consider forming another type of alliance where states opposing terrorist violence can reach agreements on how to react when an incident occurs.

All means must be taken to resolve every episode as peaceably as possible through diplomatic channels and international tribunals. But when faced with the threat of kidnapped U.S. citizens being murdered one by one or with incursions into U.S. territory (whether continental United States or its embassies abroad), and given the United Nations's minimal ability to respond, it is imperative that the United States have plans for striking back. Both legal and moral arguments support such an option.

Legal Arguments

The U.N. Charter is interpreted much more restrictively than historical international law regarding the use of force. A system of rules that prohibits a certain act but does not have the means to enforce that prohibition becomes a farce. The present interpretation of the U.N. Charter, which precludes limited force in response to attacks and does not even permit self-defense when "acts of aggression" do not reach the threshold of "an attack," coupled with the United Nations's rarely taking up the enforcement itself, has left a void that will continue to proliferate in unchecked terrorism. Why not? What does the speedy terrorist have to lose? A surreptitious planter of a time bomb taking refuge in a weak or cooperating state is immune from punishment. Hostage takers can slip into the streets of a state in chaos and will never be hunted. Even if found, the perpetrators would not be punished or extradited by a state in upheaval like Lebanon.

The rationale supporting the U.N. position that there should be no re-action by force to force is that it would perpetuate violence. Is it not just as logical to suppose that if those who practice terrorism are unchecked, violence will also continue but the perpetrator will always be the terrorist, the victim always the innocent?

The politics and purpose of the United Nations preclude an interpretation permitting "self-defense" to be construed to include the historical notions of that term. Other international and domestic legal precedents do not preclude striking back by force. Even the plain words of Article 51 do not invite a restrictive interpretation. Indeed, the words indicate otherwise by referring to the right of self-defense as inherent.[18]

The principal case in the United States involving self-defense was one where force was used against it. The *Caroline* incident occurred in 1837 during the Canadian insurrection. Along the Canadian border, the U.S. government found it impossible to control the insurgents who sought refuge on the U.S. side where they planned and recruited for raids back into Canada. The insurgents used a small steamer, the *Caroline*, to communicate with and carry supplies to the Canadian mainland. On December 29, the *Caroline* had made several trips between the United States and Canada and finally docked on the U.S. side. There about twenty-three U.S. citizens asked to remain on ship overnight. At midnight, seventy or eighty armed men attacked with "muskets, swords, and cutlasses."[19] The *Caroline* was set adrift and ultimately plunged over Niagara Falls. The passengers and crew attempted to escape, but in the aftermath one was found dead, several wounded, and twelve missing. After the *Caroline* was set adrift, cheering was heard on the Canadian side. Investigation pointed decidedly to the Canadians as the perpetrators.

In response to the U.S. protest, the Canadians declared that the "piratical character of the Caroline seemed to be fully established; that the ordinary laws of the U.S. [were] not [being] enforced [at the border]; and that the destruction of the Caroline was an act of necessary self defense."[20] After five years of discussion and negotiation, the United States through its secretary of state, Daniel Webster, admitted "that the employment of force might have been justified by the necessity of self defense" but denied the existence of the necessity in the affair, saying that self-defense should be confined to cases where the necessity is "instant, overwhelming, and leaving no choice of means and no moment for deliberation."[21] The British apologized; the matter was laid to rest.

Even before its admission in *Caroline*, the United States established the right to invade the territory of another state to control insurgents. General Andrew Jackson wrote to Secretary of War John Calhoun in 1818 that the Seminole Indians in Florida had demanded "arms, ammunition, and provisions or the possession of the garrison of Fort Marks." General Jackson pointed out that the Spanish government was bound by treaty "to keep her Indians at peace" but had "acknowledged their incompetency" to do so.[22] The general proceeded against the Indians and afterward claimed that if the Spanish authorities had not instigated the war, they surely had provided the Indians "the means of carrying [it] on." Jackson took the fortress on May 25 and returned it to Spain three months later.[23]

President James Monroe stated later that in authorizing the attack, "care was taken not to encroach on the rights of Spain." He explained, however, there was evidence that the Spanish officers in authority had furnished munitions and other supplies of war, contrary to a 1795 treaty whereby Spain had agreed to restrain the Indians from hostile acts.[24]

Although closely related, a different rationale for pursuing those who have attacked inside U.S. territory rests in the theory of hot pursuit. In 1911, the United States had border problems caused by Mexican troops and insurgents. At various times during these clashes, shots were fired that found their way from Mexico into U.S. territory, wounding or killing innocent citizens. For several years shootings and even incursions occurred despite protests from the United States.[25]

Finally on March 9, 1916, Columbus, New Mexico, was attacked by Francisco Villa and his troops. Several U.S. soldiers and civilians were killed. President Woodrow Wilson sent an armed force into Mexico with the sole object of capturing Villa so that future raids would be thwarted.[26]

The minister of foreign affairs of the de facto Mexican government requested the same arrangement for his own pursuit of Villa. He based the request on a prior U.S.-Mexico agreement that each country could cross into the other's territory to chase marauding Indians. The secretary of state immediately agreed to the reciprocity. The U.S. Senate adopted an agreement of approval for the U.S. armed forces to apprehend and punish Villa, with the restriction that such a military expedition should not be permitted to encroach on Mexican sovereignty.[27]

A dispute arose between the de facto Mexican government and the United States regarding rules for the reciprocal incursions. In May, while both sides were trying to settle this dispute, Mexican bandits raided a Texas town, killing three soldiers and a nine-year-old boy. U.S. troops immediately pursued across the Mexican border.

The secretary of state wrote the Mexican minister of foreign affairs that the United States had "no recourse other than to employ force" against the bandits since Mexico was not preventing their attacks:

> The U.S. Government cannot and will not allow bands of lawless men to establish themselves upon its borders with liberty to invade and plunder American territory with impunity and, when pursued, to seek safety across

the Rio Grande, relying upon the plea of their Government that the integrity of the soil of the Mexican Republic must not be violated.[28]

The U.S. legal system does not impose the tight restrictions that the U.N. Charter does on the use of force. The rationale supporting the use of force under U.S. domestic law is to control the situation, not, as in war, to prove superiority over another. Notwithstanding the different rationale, the use of force by a police officer is accepted even when he or she is not under attack. In *Tennessee* v. *Garner,* the Supreme Court considered whether the Fourth Amendment prohibited a state law from permitting a police officer to use "all necessary means" to arrest a criminal suspect if the officer has given notice of an intent to arrest and the suspect flees or forcibly resists.[29]

The Court upheld the constitutionality of the statute but found it unconstitutional as applied because the fleeing burglar was an unarmed, one hundred pound, fifteen year old. However, the Court explained:

> Where the officer has probable cause to believe that the *suspect poses a threat of serious physical harm, either to the officer or to others, it is not constitutionally unreasonable to prevent escape by using deadly force.* Thus, if the suspect threatens the officer with a weapon or there is probable cause to believe that he has committed a crime involving the infliction or threatened infliction of serious physical harm, deadly force may be used if necessary to prevent escape, and if, where feasible, some warning has been given. [emphasis added][30]

Thus, under the U.S. domestic legal system, where an enforcement mechanism exists, force is permitted to capture one who is fleeing and dangerous. By contrast, present interpretation of the U.N. Charter, where there is no effective enforcement, does not permit force against terrorists fleeing across the border into another state.

Because the United Nations and its charter do not and cannot cope with present-day terrorism, it is time to look outside that body to the historical legal interpretations for reacting to violence: force can be used when there are agreed-on rules for doing so.

Moral Arguments

Cicero wrote, "*Salus populi suprema lex esto*" ("the safety of the people shall be the highest law").[31] For centuries, religions and philosophers have reasoned that violence does not require one to turn the other cheek. Indeed, there has been a recognized right to protect oneself from another's violence, even if innocent parties are harmed, even if the potential perpetrator has not yet acted. Like the legal precedents, the moral principles require a set of rules.

"If one comes to kill you make haste and kill him first," teaches the Talmud. Hugo Grotius, a seventeenth-century lawyer, humanist, and politician who had said Richelieu hated him "for the sole reason I love peace," wrote of the rules of war and peace.[32] He discussed general rules permissible in war:

> We are understood to have a right to those things which are necessary for . . . securing a right, when the necessity is understood not in terms of physical exactitude but in a moral sense. . . .
>
> Hence if otherwise I cannot save my life, I may use any degree of violence to ward off him who assails it, even if he should happen to be free from wrong. . . . The reason is that this right does not properly arise from another's wrong, but from the right which nature grants me on my behalf.
>
> Furthermore, I can also take possession of another's property from which an imminent danger threatens me, without taking account of the other's guilt; yet not in such a way as to become its owner . . . but in order to guard it until adequate security has been given for my safety.[33]

On retaliation, Grotius submits it is lawful if inflicted on those who have done the wrong. He delineates the bases for declaring war: it should have the support of the sovereign, be publicly declared, and have as its purpose the recovery of property or to repel enemies.[34]

Another seventeenth-century philosopher and political writer on the state of war, John Locke, expounded that one should have the right to destroy whoever threatens him or her with destruction,

> for by the fundamental law of Nature, man being to be preserved as much as possible when all cannot be preserved, the safety of the innocent is to be preferred, and one may destroy a man who makes war upon him, or has discovered an enmity to his being, for the same reason he may kill a wolf or a lion, because they are not under the ties of the common law of reason, have no other rule but that of force and violence, and so may be treated as a beast of prey. . . .[35]

Locke continues that it is lawful for a person to kill a thief who has not in the least hurt him or threatened to do so, for there is "no reason to suppose that he would take away my liberty would not, when he had me in his power, take away everything else."[36]

Montesquieu, writing in the eighteenth century, recognized that the right of natural defense for the individual does not imply a necessity of attacking because there are tribunals for recourse. But nations are a different matter. With "states, the right of natural defense carries along with it sometimes the necessity of attacking as for instance when one nation sees that a continuance of peace will enable another to destroy her and [attacking] instantly is the only way to prevent her own destruction."[37]

There are commentators who discuss the morality of war in a vacuum: killing of innocents is wrong; therefore we must never kill even in war because an innocent might be killed. Philosopher George Hegel responded in the early nineteenth Century with the obvious: "The welfare of a state has claims to recognition totally different from those of the welfare of the individual." The ethical substance, the state, has its right in its existence and must be guided in its conduct by that and not by "universal thoughts supposed to be moral commands. When politics is alleged to clash with morals and so to be always wrong, the doctrine propounded rests on superficial ideas about morality, the nature of the state, and the state's relation to the moral point of view."[38]

When there were no rules for war, philosophers and moralists carved out rules for using force. When Grotius or Locke or Hegel spoke of war, their reference was in a time when war had not been outlawed by a post–World War II United Nations. They never looked at force as immoral per se but only considered that its use must conform to certain rules. The historical rules for war are every bit as applicable to today's acts of violence, which are less than war: terrorism.

The United Nations bans war; thus, no state wants to declare war. But it should not follow that there is a hesitancy to apply these traditional rules for force to acts of aggression or terrorism. There is no logic to such reticence. A country that must cope with an armed attack, a hostage taking, or a bombing of a facility within its territory has as much need to know the applicable rules as those who over the centuries suffered the same violence under a formal declaration of war.

The legal and moral precedents establish that using force in times of undeclared war to respond to terrorism is acceptable. This acceptance relies on force being used in restrictive situations and with carefully defined rules. These rules of engagement are considered in depth in chapter 13. However, a review of the precedents necessitates that they include the following:

Reasonable exhaustion of other peaceful avenues for stopping the conflict.

A response proportional to the force inflicted.

Response accomplished as swiftly as reasonably consistent with exhaustion.

Force used against the aggressors and not the helpless foreign state if that state has not supported the terrorists.

Clear statement made that there is no intent to encroach on rights of the foreign state.

Reasonable means taken to prevent harm to innocent lives.

There are no impediments to using force on either legal or moral grounds. The impediment has been domestic and international reluctance to act for fear of retaliation to retaliation. The United States is learning, however, that whether it does nothing, as after Iran, whether it negotiates privately and is publicly silent, as with the kidnapped Americans, or whether it screams outrage and negotiates privately, as with flight 847, it does not stop terrorist attacks. That being the case, it must be prepared to add other tools.

The legal and moral arguments should not inhibit the United States in adding force as one of those tools. The debate in each case should center only on whether force will work. It is imperative that Congress support the use of force as an option because, without congressional consensus, the executive branch will be reluctant to act for fear of a repeat of Church committee investigations into the conduct of the CIA.

All future terrorists should know that the United States has a comprehensive counterterrorism plan, which includes an ability to strike back. No terrorist should ever kidnap or kill again without having to consider seriously whether one of the responses will be force.

Notes

1. *The Great Quotations*, comp. George Seddes (New York: Pocket Books, 1967), p. 800.

2. The captives and dates of kidnappings are William Buckley, diplomat, March 16, 1984; Benjamin Weir, minister, May 8, 1984; Peter Kilburn, American University Beirut (AUB) librarian, November 30, 1984; Father Lawrence Jenko, Catholic Relief Services, January 8, 1985; Terry Anderson, Associated Press, March 16, 1985; Dave Jacobsen, AUB hospital administrator, May 28, 1985; Thomas Sutherland, AUB dean of agriculture, June 10, 1985. An eighth American, Cable News Network journalist Jeremy Levin was captured March 7, 1984, but escaped February 14, 1985.

3. *Washington Post*, March 6, 1985.

4. Ibid., May 12, 1985.

5. Ibid.

6. Robert C. McFarlane, "Terrorism and the Future of Free Society" (Speech delivered to the National Strategy Information Center, March 25, 1985).

7. *Washington Post*, May 12, 1985.

8. *Great Quotations*, p. 566.

9. Ian Brownlie, *International Law and the Activities of Armed Bands*, 7 Int'l & Comp. L.Q. (1958) 712, 731.

10. M. Garcia-Mora, *International Responsibility for Hostile Acts of Private Persons against Foreign States* (1962) 118–120.

11. Q. Wright, "The Prevention of Aggression," *American Journal of International Law* 50(1956):514, 529.

12. Barry Levinfeld, *Israel's Counter-Fedayeen Tactics in Lebanon: Self-Defense and Reprisal Under Modern International Law*, 21 Columbia J. of Transnat'l Law

1(1982):17. Levinfeld uses the term *fedayeen* to refer to "Palestinian armed elements" to attempt a neutral description of groups rather than using *terrorists, guerrillas,* or *freedom fighters.*

13. Id, at p. 6.

14. *United States v. Arjona,* 120 U.S. 479, 484 (1887).

15. Levinfeld, at p. 6; see also H. Kelsen, *Principles of International Law* (1952) 120–21.

16. Levenfeld, "Israel's Counter-Fedayeen Tactics," p. 7.

17. Ibid., p. 10.

18. Ibid., p. 27.

19. John Bassett Moore, *A Digest of International Law* 2:409.

20. Ibid., p. 410.

21. Ibid., pp. 411–412.

22. John Bassett Moore, *A Digest of International Law,* (Washington, D.C., U.S. Government Printing Office, 1906), vol. II, p. 409.

23. Ibid.

24. Ibid., p. 404.

25. Hackworth, *Digest of International Law,* (1941) 2:282–91.

26. Ibid., p. 291.

27. Ibid., p. 293.

28. Green Haywood Hackworth, *Digest of International Law,* (Washington, D.C., U.S. Government Printing Office, 1941), vol. II, pp. 282–91.

29. (No. 83-1035), — U.S. — (1985).

30. Ibid. slip opinion at p. 10.

31. *Great Quotations,* pp. 561, 564.

32. Tennessee v. Garner, (No. 83-1035) US Supreme Court Slip Sheet (1985).

33. Id, at p. 10.

34. Ibid., p. 650.

35. Hugo Grotius, *The Law of War and Peace,* The Classics of International Law, ed. by James Brown Scott (Oxford: At the Clarendon Press London, Leslie B. Adams, 1984), introduction xxxix.

36. Ibid., p. 29.

37. Ibid., 38:62.

38. John Locke, in *Great Books of the Western World,* (Chicago, London, Toronto: William Benton, Encyclopedia Britannica, Inc. 1952), vol. 35, p. 28.

12

Using the Law to Combat Terrorism

Harry H. Almond, Jr.

T he challenge for legal control over the outbreaks of terrorism has bedeviled governments throughout the world. Embraced in this challenge is a widespread belief that there are major gaps in the law enabling the terrorists or the organized groups of which they are part to escape punishment or even encouraging them to conduct their activities. The challenge, however, goes deeper. Some believe that we may have to shift to a new perspective about terrorism and treat it as a kind of warfare. Others believe it to be a form of guerrilla warfare and, having adopted that perspective, would treat the terrorists as outlaw bands, calling for both global support and wide-ranging consent to crossing state lines to search out and destroy the terrorists, even in the territories of other states.

By the way of introduction to this increasingly complex problem, recent communiqués of the NATO (North Atlantic Treaty Organization) economic summit conferences (in which Japan also participates) and several of the statements of public figures might first be appraised. Although these do not establish law to fill the gaps, they express a growing consensus in policy, and policy clarification and articulation is critical in the development of law.

The London Economic Summit Conference held by the heads of the NATO states and Japan on June 7–9, 1984, raised the question of gaps in the law with regard to regulating the conduct of terrorists. The communiqué issued at the close of that conference declared that while hijacking and kidnapping had declined since the declarations of the previous economic summits at Bonn (1978), Venice (1980), and Ottawa (1981), the signatories expressed their resolve to counter "by every possible means" the problems of international terrorism and its techniques "developed sometimes in association with traffic in drugs":

This chapter contains the views of the author. The comments and positions taken should not be attributed to the U.S. government or to Georgetown University.

They viewed with serious concern the increasing involvement of states and governments in acts of terrorism, including the abuse of diplomatic immunity. [Proposals that found support in the discussion included]: Scrutiny by each country of gaps in its national legislation which might be exploited by terrorists; action by each country to review the sale of weapons to states supporting terrorism. Consultation and as far as possible cooperation over the expulsion or exclusion from their countries of known terrorists including persons of diplomatic status involved in terrorism.[1]

In the earlier communiqué at the fourth economic summit held at Bonn, July 16–17, 1978, the same countries had reached consensus on countering acts of terrorism involved in aircraft hijacking. That communiqué declared that where a country refuses the extradition or prosecution of "those who have hijacked an aircraft and/or does not return such aircraft," their governments will take action to cease all flights to that country.

These two communiqués, although expressed in relatively informal language rather than by treaty, express a shared policy of the NATO countries and Japan. In addition to expressing a concern over lacunae in the law and the legal processes, they extend to the policy factors: the claims relating to states that support terrorism or those that give asylum to persons or groups involved in the aircraft offenses. They call for cooperation and consultation, essential steps in moving toward shaping law to be enforced.

Legal controls over terrorism by independent or autonomous groups is one thing. A far more complex issue for controls arises when states sponsor, directly or indirectly, the terrorists themselves or the groups that invoke terrorism. The Soviet Union, for example, does not claim to support terrorism, but it supports "wars of liberation" under Article 28 of its constitution. It identifies this support in the larger context of that article of "safeguarding the state interests of the Soviet Union" and of "consolidating the positions of world socialism." Moreover, it insists that such support and such efforts as "safeguarding" its interests are part of "implementing the principle of peaceful coexistence." In other declarations and official pronouncements, all of these notions of support to peoples fighting for their rights and claims against colonial powers are identified as part of the legitimate support of the claims of self-determination.

The Soviet Union and states with policies that are similar to its have enjoyed substantial success in promoting this proposition. That success commenced, after the World War II, particularly in the language used in the Declaration on Principles of International Law Concerning Friendly Relations and Cooperation among States in Accordance with the Charter of the United Nations. There, and in subsequent resolutions relating to aggression, self-determination itself was first raised, and the claims of peoples using violence in these claims were released from the stigma of aggression. These developments have led recently to special privileges for those involved in such wars under the Geneva Protocols of 1977, supplementing the Geneva Conventions of 1947, relating to the protections of persons during time of armed conflict.

Other themes cause confusion in establishing effective legal regulation, particularly with respect to the democratic nations. Legal controls in those countries, unlike the controls imposed in the totalitarian countries such as those in the Communist bloc, must take into account the rights of the individual: rights of due process, rights against unreasonable search and seizure, rights regarding the application of force when directed against them, and so on. But expanded to a global context, these issues cause confusion regarding support given by the democratic states to authoritarian regimes—that is, states that have not reached the stage of totalitarian controls identified with the Communist states, and, in any event, states that can be shaped into democratic policies that will respect human rights. Much of the democratic change in Latin American states can be identified with the change that could be induced by outside pressures on authoritarian regimes in those states that would have been entirely ineffective in the totalitarian states.

Henry Kissinger has noted the significance of this perspective in the policy sense, and the implications of this larger policy issue on the formulation of legal controls are evident. We must not expect all the gaps in legal controls to be resolved quickly where major policy issues must first be resolved. "In the comtemporary world," says Kissinger, "it is the totalitarian systems which have managed the most systematic and massive repression of human rights":

> We must therefore maintain the moral distinction between aggressive totalitarianism and other governments which with all their imperfections are trying to resist foreign pressures or subversion and which thereby help preserve the balance of power in behalf of all free peoples. . . . The ultimate irony would be a posture of resignation toward totalitarian states and harassment of those who would be our friends and who have every prospect of evolving in a more humane direction.[2]

Secretary of State George Shultz observes that "terrorism these days is becoming less an isolated phenomenon of local fanatics, and increasingly part of a new international strategy resorted to by the enemies of freedom." Links, he pointed out, extend between terrorism and international drug trafficking. Defense against terrorism is part of the broader problem of "the defense of our interests and the relevance of our power as the backstop to our diplomacy":

> A counterstrategy for combatting terrorism . . . must encompass many things. We and our allies must work still harder to improve security, share information, coordinate police efforts and collaborate in other ways. We in

this country must also think hard about the moral stakes involved. If we truly believe in our democratic values and our way of life, we must be willing to defend them. Passive measures are unlikely to suffice; means of more active defense and deterrence must be considered and given the necessary political support.[3]

Accordingly, he concluded, "While working tirelessly to deny terrorists their opportunities and means, we can—and must—be absolutely firm in denying them their goals."

Although there are gaps in the law as formulated with regard to the control of terrorism, terrorism clearly has many faces. Controls in the domestic setting are relatively easily applied because the criminal law of the United States is ample for meeting the threat or responding to the social outrage for the acts of terrorism that occur within the nation. Transnational terrorism—terrorism in which groups of terrorists plot or plan their actions in one country, gain support or assistance from one or more other countries, and carry out their acts against individuals or property in still another country—raises, depending on the extent of the terrorist enterprise, the laws of all of the countries involved. Here the gaps arise because the countries involved have differing laws, and this means differing policies as to the conduct involved within those countries. International terrorism, when more closely defined as conduct in which states on a regional or even global basis have condemned that conduct through treaty or international agreement or even through customary international law, provides gaps that arise as to state policy itself. States that sponsor terrorism or groups invoking terrorism are clearly insisting that such conduct is only legitimated violence for legitimate ends—an exception to international law in general or to the undertakings relating to aggression.

Assessment of the Legal Framework

The gaps relating to the legal control of terrorism, regardless of how it appears, arise from either difficulties in clarification of social policy or, where several states are concerned, in clarification and formulation of a shared policy that will be applied among them.

Definitions of Terrorism

A common complaint is that there are no definitions of terrorism, and without a definition, the development of effective legal controls is thwarted. Some have attempted definitions, and some of the definitions have been very broad, compelling the entities making their determinations to fill in the gaps on a case-by-case basis. Other definitions have been detailed in terms of the activities to be condemned, individuals to be protected, property to be safeguarded, and so on. However, as experience with definitions of international crimes—including those associated with terrorism such as are appearing in the crimes against or within aircraft in the Tokyo, Montreal, and the Hague conventions—has shown, some elements involved in definitions cannot be resolved by language alone.

Although these treaties and agreements are able to identify the prohibited conduct with substantial precision, the policy or political question is simply shifted to a differing stage. The judicial procedures may allow for introduction of a political defense; the processes relating to evidence may provide for special protections to the evidence adduced by the terrorists; the punishment or sentencing may enable the court to introduce the political concern of the particular state in which that court is located, and so on.

The Foreign Intelligence Surveillance Act contains the following definition of international terrorism that can be used to illustrate the intrusion of policy elements. International terrorism is an activity that

1. Involve[s] violent acts or acts dangerous to human life that are a violation of the criminal laws of the United States [or of any state, or that would be a criminal violation if committed within the jurisdiction of the United States or any state];

2. Appear[s] *to be intended*

   A. To intimidate or coerce a civilian population.

   B. To influence the policy of the government by intimidation or coercion; or

   C. To effect the conduct of a government by assassination or kidnapping; and,

3. Occur[s] totally outside the United States or transcend[s] national boundaries in terms of the means by which they are accomplished, the person they appear intended to coerce or intimidate, or the locale in which their perpetrators operate or seek asylum.[4]

This definition has been adopted not for the purposes of indicting individuals or groups for crimes but exclusively for the purpose of issuing warrants permitting surveillance activites pursuant to the limitations imposed by the act. There have been recent bills and proposals seeking to adopt the same definition for a federal crime of terrorism, but the arguments against the definition in that context appear in the constitutional issues that are raised. Constitutional issues such as those raising due process of law, Fourth Amendment protections against unlawful search and seizure, First Amendment protections against interference with the freedom of speech, and the substantial body of constitutional law in the United States establishing around these rights a detailed national policy for protection do not provide gaps in the law as such but reflect the balancing out of policy objectives.

From the standpoint of criminal law, it is evident that the burdens are on the state to prove the crime. But a critical element in the crime is the proof of intention, and the definition cannot fill this gap. The language of the definition must not be vague or so general as to be void for vagueness under the due process of law standards of the Constitution. But such language as intimidating or coercing "a civilian population" suggests that freedom of speech may be engaged—that the law if so adopted for criminal purposes would be addressing conduct recognized as permissible under the Constitution, therefore creating unconstitutional violations.

A related issue under the general principles of law recognized in the United States and other nations is also raised in the definition. This standard, expressed in the Latin as *nullum crimen nulla poena sine lege,* declares that no crime or punishment shall be established except by law. Therefore, gaps in the language used in formulating the crime of terrorism cannot be filled by recourse to some general concepts of law—or outrage—alone. The definition must be free of those language gaps and consistent with constitutional requirements. Under these standards, such terms as *intimidation* or *threats* may be suspect.

U.S. cases have shown a gradual strengthening of legal doctrine regarding the conduct of individuals identified as agents of hostile foreign governments or acting for their own purposes to use violence to overthrow the U.S. government. Mr. Justice Oliver Wendell Holmes in *Schenck* v. *United States* declared the "clear and present danger" rule:

> But the character of every act depends upon the circumstances in which it is done. The most stringent protection of free speech would not protect a man in falsely shouting fire in a theatre and causing a panic. The question in every case is whether the words used in such circumstances are of such a nature as to create a clear and present danger that they will bring about the substantive evils that Congress has a right to prevent. It is a question of proximity and degree.[5]

Mr. Justice Holmes is referring here to the need for courts to balance out the interests or equities of society and the individual. But he is also saying that rules or naked norms for prohibiting terrorism or complex criminal conduct identified with speech, no matter how they are drafted, will not provide the needed precision and must give way to a development of policy content through judicial practice.

Moving closer to the problem of taking action preempting the plans of terrorist groups, the Supreme Court in *Dennis* v. *United States* faced violations of the Smith Act for conspiracy to overthrow the government. The Supreme Court observed that an alleged right to overthrow dictatorial governments was inapplicable for a democratic government that provides "for peaceful and orderly change." As to the clear and present danger rule, the Court noted that the test is conditional: "overthrow of the Government by force and violence is certainly a substantial enough interest for the Government to limit speech":

> Obviously, the words cannot mean that before the Government may act, it must await until the putsch is about to be executed, the plans have been laid and the signal is awaited. If Government is aware that a group aiming at its overthrow is attempting to indoctrinate its members and to commit them to a course whereby they will strike when the leaders feel the circumstances permit, action by the Government is required.[6]

The Court establishes a basis for preemptive action, assuming that such action is consistent with law in the United States. Revolutionists, the Court then noted, strike not when there is "certainty of success" but "when they thought the time was ripe." If these constitute serious threats to society, the officials serving society for its security have the responsibility to limit, if not prevent, the damage that the threats will lead to damage.

Recent statements by Secretary of State Shultz for preemptive strikes against terrorists might be supported by such cases as this, assuming that constitutional protections are not impaired. But it is notable that judge-made doctrine has been gradually shaped in the cases and informed by enlightened public opinion concerning the acts and threats of groups engaged in terrorism. Furthermore, cases such as *Tennessee* v. *Garner* have in parallel actions upheld the constitutionality of state law providing that an enforcement officer can use "all necessary means" to arrest.[7] And where the threat posed by an escaping suspect is of serious physical harm, escape can be prevented by using deadly force.

Extradition

As with the other legal issues concerning the control of terrorism, extradition raises the policy question: the problem of the political offense and the traditional claims of states to refuse extradition on the basis of that offense. U.S. practice relating to extradition is largely conducted through law and the courts of law. The policy of the United States is to permit extradition only in pursuance of treaties or international agreements and the provisions set forth in those agreements.

According to the Harvard Draft Convention prepared by leading experts in 1933, "Extradition is the formal surrender of a person by a State to another State for prosecution or punishment."[8] The modern extradition treaties treat this difficult subject by a variety of provisions, however, that are aimed at reducing the political offense issue. The experts on the Harvard Draft were quick to point out that extradition processes relate to "the suppression of crime" and that the problems of extradition have "international dimensions . . . requiring cooperation." This becomes apparent when it is recognized that the extradition treaty must specify the crimes on which extradition is based, get a common understanding as to what those crimes cover, deal with procedural issues that might arise, and so on. The political offense is spelled out—frequently to include military, fiscal, religious, and other offenses—but then is qualified where provisions are added that the contracting states will extradite or prosecute, or where they have the responsibility to report to each other on action taken, or to punish according to laws of specified severity.

Some policies are shared among states to such an extent that we can expect that they will overcome their differences in the future concerning the grounds or terms for extradition. They expect reciprocal behavior from each other, and there are strong tendencies to cooperate over crimes that are abhorred universally. There are shared concerns over public transit: the hijacking and interference with air flights. The notions about asylum and sanctuary are changing where the terrorist has begun to lose his color of right and claims to unlicensed violence.

The practice relating to extradition in the United States might be compared with the practice concerning exclusion: that is, the legal measures taken to exclude undesirable aliens, but inapplicable to citizens, and deportation, another practice applicable only to aliens. Some aspects of the practice of the United States might be summarized, indicating the gaps that might arise through extradition policies.

The United States has refused to extradite on the basis of nationality alone. It has refused to extradite to Germany German seamen alleged to have murdered four officers on their ship on the high seas, where the German claim was based on nationality alone.

The U.S. practice adopts the principle of double criminality in its extradition treaties: crimes are extraditable only where the crime for which extradition is requested is the same crime in both states. For example, in a request for the extradition of Gerhart Eisler for false statements in a form for an exit permit required by the United States, the British, with custody of Eisler, refused extradition because perjury (the crime specified in the extradition treaty) is limited to false statements under oath "in judicial proceedings." Further problems arising here include the differing interpretations that might be made of the crimes even when specified; questions where the states have differing statutes of limitation; and the consensus on standards by which such statutes are "tolled" (suspended from running).

The U.S. practice adopts the principle of speciality: extradition is permitted by the United States only for the crime actually specified. Under this principle, the treaty states must assure themselves that each has adopted the same procedures for extradition—that where the individual to be extradited might have committed several crimes, the crime requested in the extradition demand is the crime specified in the treaty.

The United States has recognized jurisdiction over fugitives charged with crimes and within the jurisdiction of the court even if the fugitive may have been brought to the court's jurisdiction illegally. This has become the general rule in U.S. practice, subject only to due process of law exceptions, such as that which occurred in *United States* v. *Toscanino*.[10] There the fugitive, a narcotics law offender, claimed successfully that he had been kidnapped with the knowledge of U.S. officials, drugged, and subjected to physical violence and torture. The court, however, remanded this case, calling for Toscanino to provide "some credible supporting evidence, including specifically evidence that the action was taken by or at the direction of United States officials."[11]

U.S. practice following that of England but distinguished from the practice of other European states permits the extradition of its own nationals. It can modify this practice by its treaty provisions. The reason is that jurisdiction under the common law is territorial, not personal. The Supreme Court has required the executive branch to have congressional authority to extradite nationals.[12]

Following Article 33 of the Convention Relating to the Status of Refugees, the United States will not surrender a person sought if the requesting country is seeking extradition for the purpose of prosecuting or punishing him or her because of race, religion, nationality, or political opinion. Decisions on this exception are made by the secretary of state.

Gaps in the enforcement of extradition are reinforced through the judicial practice among nations. This practice differs widely under even the best of circumstances, but it arises in the courts in the United States because such courts are moving into unfamiliar areas, and many of the judges of the federal district courts lack the experience and background in foreign affairs or international law involved in such cases. The U.S. judicial practice pursuing the development of law through precedent commens with the broad test established in the English case of *In re Castioni*. The political offense according to that case is a crime tested by the standard of acts that are "incidental to and [have] formed a part of political disturbances."[13]

This broad standard led to a set of recent cases requiring the requesting state to overcome a difficult burden before extradition will be granted. Even the grossest misconduct—appearing in the killings of British military forces by the Irish Republican Army—was found to fall within the exception in such cases as *In re the Extradition of McMullen*,[14] *in re Extradition of Desmond Mackin*,[15] and *Quinn v Robinson*.[16]

This far-reaching set of cases is balanced somewhat by the opinion in *In re Extradition of Eain*,[17] where an alleged member of the Palestinian Liberation Organization (PLO) was charged with placing a bomb that led to the death of several children in Israel. The magistrate and the U.S. Court of Appeals found the political offense inapplicable because the bombing was not incidental to the political aims of the PLO and consisted solely of "anarchist-like activity." But even this court accepted the proposition that "acts that disrupt the political structure of a State, and not the social structure" would be exempt.[18]

The extradition treaty of the United States with the United Kingdom, a fairly typical treaty, does not provide a deciding rule for the political offense. Article V of the treaty states:

(1) Extradition shall not be granted if . . . (c)(i) the offense for which extradition is requested is regarded by the requested Party as one of a political character; or (ii) the person sought proves that the request for his extradition has in fact been made with a view to try or punish him for an offense of a political character.[19]

As one authority has noted:

We are not dealing with the substantive rights of a fugitive. The "political offense" exception, just as the concept of political asylum, is not a recognition of some inalienable right of the fugitive to commit crimes in another country, and escape extradition merely because the offenses were committed with a political purpose. The right involved is that of a state which has an interest in being able when the state deems it appropriate, to give political asylum for humanitarian reasons or simply to refuse to become involved in the political disputes of other states.[20]

Because this is judge-made law in large part, the opinion of the Irish Supreme Court in *McGlinchey* v. *Wren* allowing extradition is of interest as to the balancing test that must be used with such treaties as that between the United States and Britain:

The judicial authorities on the scope of such offenses have in many respects been rendered obsolete by the fact that modern terrorist violence, whether undertaken by military or paramilitary organisations or by individuals or groups of individuals, is often the antithesis of what could reasonably be regarded as political either in itself or in its connections. . . . Whether a contrary conclusion [as to extradition] would be reached in different circumstances must depend on the particular circumstances and on whether those particular circumstances showed that the person charged was at the relevant time engaged, either directly or indirectly, in what reasonable, civilized people would regard as political.[21]

This more effective balancing of the interests by the decision makers—whether courts or executive officers—was noted in the report of the American Bar Association, cited by Hannay:

There are limitations on the conduct of internal armed conflict and that revolutionary violence which transgresses these limitations is not tolerable under the political offenses exception. Moreover, every political disturbance does not provide justification for violent criminal acts.[22]

Use of Force to Counter Terrorism

The use of force under legal authority is an instrument that serves public order. Among nation-states competing about the future of global order, the use of force is also a strategic instrument projecting their policies toward their own policy goals. The competitive nature in these activities, often on the edge of hostilities, is widely known, but in that environment terrorism becomes an instrument for some states, appearing then as state-sponsored terrorism. States are perceived either as seeking to maintain the existing global order, and the values that it promotes, or of revolutionizing and replacing that global order and substituting a new system of values. In a competitive arena of this kind, terrorism is a use of force that such states will consciously seek to legitimize.

When states seek to counter terrorism or enforce measures against terrorism, they purport to act under legal authority. Enforcement measures then become the instruments of law. They serve to strengthen the existing law, and they in turn, through mobilizing public opinion, are strengthened by the support of law, or legal authority. One of the conclusions reached in this chapter is that actions under legal authority taken against terrorists are actions against parties who are attacking the public order and that the most effective support for enforcement, as well as for law and for public order, is to seek community support and community recognition that community policies and standards are being advanced.

The legal framework regarding enforcement measures or the use of force to control terrorism is designed to direct measures and policies consistent with law under which the measures are to be invoked. Such a framework has the characteristics of the rules of engagement for invoking force because those rules provide a legal standard against which force is to be used by the armed forces of the nation. The broader framework of the rules of engagement declares and assists in determining when force is to be used, for what missions, against what targets, subject to what limitations on the amount, duration, and arenas of use, and subject to what standards of law, to achieve or accomplish U.S. policy (or strategic) goals. The policy and legal implications underpinning such rules establish the fundamental limits. Variants of such rules appear wherever force is applied: with the use of force during wartime, in reprisals or retaliation, or, as here, in general. They also apply to the initial decisions to use force. They are intended to protect the innocent and confine the use of force to the legitimate targets and missions.

The legal framework also entails the balancing of interests by the decision processes involved with law; these include the executive and judicial branches of government. The balancing process puts demands on these processes under U.S. law and constitutional practice to ensure that balanced into the claims and interests of the society at large are the claims of the individuals in terms of his or her rights against abuse by officials and in terms of his or her rightful claims when the occasion legitimately appears to self-determination.

When this legal framework is applied to the acts of terrorism, operating principles are required. Moreover, it is evident that when the framework is one to be shared among states, it involves competing claims, so we must expect a challenge from the Soviet Union and its claims for the rights of peoples to rise up against the Western powers, while we must also expect to firm up our opposition to that challenge and the falsity of those claims.

The operating principles proposed by Robert C. McFarlane, assistant to the president for national security affairs, at the Defense Strategy Forum on March 25, 1985, are, in part, included in a presidential directive. They include the following elements:

> The practice of terrorism under all circumstances is a threat to the national security of the United States.
>
> The practice of international terrorism must be resisted by all legal means.
>
> State-sponsored terrorism consists of acts hostile to the United States and to global security and must "be resisted by all legal means."
>
> The United States has a responsibility to take protective measures whenever there is evidence that terrorism is about to be committed.

The threat of terrorism constitutes a form of aggression (see, for example, Article 2(4) of the U.N. Charter) and justifies acts of self-defense.

Measures must be taken to improve "the collection and assessment of information on groups and states involved in terrorism in order to prevent attacks" and provide warning to potential victims and targets.

Terrorism is a problem shared among democratic nations. Cooperative efforts with such countries will be needed to cope with it, but "non violent means to deal with legitimate grievances" must be explored.

Acts of state-sponsored terrorism and organized terrorism must be exposed and condemned before world opinion.

Wherever possible, the United States "should help those friendly nations suffering intimidation because of terrorist threats or activities and assist them with all means" available, including intelligence gathering, training assistance, and, when requested for self-defense, the use of force.

Expressed in a larger framework, it is evident that these principles reflect those that guide the development of rules of engagement under U.S. practice. Other principles proposed by Secretaries Caspar Weinberger and Shultz will assist in clarifying the larger legal framework in which U.S. enforcement measures must operate. But there is wide discretion in fashioning such measures and also an expectation that such discretion will be exercised by those with judgment meeting U.S. community standards.

Decisions to use force are identified among states as decisions either to engage in aggression or in self-defense against aggression. There are some uses of force not identified as self-defense but part of the larger perspective of self-help. Accordingly, if the force must be used against a state that has sponsored terrorism, the legal authority must show either self-help or self-defense clearly articulated for public support. These decisions are qualified by necessity, subjected in other words to a standard tht goes back to the *Caroline* case, where Secretary of State Daniel Webster declared that the standard for self-defense at least was "a necessity of self-defence, instant, overwhelming, leaving no choice of means, and no moment for deliberation" and then "limited by that necessity."[23] Modern weaponry and modern threats necessarily affect such a standard, changing to meet modern perceptions of those threats with the potential harm and the speech with which it might occur.

Using force—for example, using force or violence during wartime when, under law, it is licensed—raises other general legal rules, again requiring discretion and judgment but not detailed. These are the rules that unnecessary suffering—hence, unnecessary force—must be avoided, the use of excessive or indiscriminate force must be prohibited, and the use against illegitimate targets (the innocent) must be prohibited. These rules applied through the law of war find their counterpart in the rules of proportionality and necessity in general, applicable when countermeasures are used against terrorists. The use of force in the threat in May 1985 in Philadelphia of the MOVE group might be assessed against such standards, the necessity there of major destruction and the discretion that was clearly not exercised.

Terrorism during wartime is regulated through the laws of war, particularly through the Geneva Conventions of 1949 and the Geneva Protocols of 1977 (not ratified by the United States). Two things should be said about this. Terrorism itself during wartime is excessive or wrongful use of force occurring in situations where force itself is permitted. It is force unlawfully used in hostilities—in the methods of attack, weapons used, or targets selected—or abuse by officials and military forces with respect to individuals under their control. All of these forms of terrorism are condemned and should be subjected to prosecution and punishment during wartime by the belligerents, pursuant to the treaties. The second element is that of the Geneva Protocols of 1977. These protocols provide for Geneva protections to individuals engaged in "wars of liberation." Although such wars are defined under the protocols as those against "colonial domination and alien occupation and racist regimes," the individuals fighting them are given the special protections of the armed forces of the belligerents. It is evident that this provision affords legal status to such groups. It is also evident that it is confined to struggling against the West and does not include self-determination in general, applicable then to struggles against Communist and other totalitarian regimes.

The last framework relating to the use of force occurs in a threat framework. Little will be said about that here, except that it is the framework of arms control and disarmament. In such a framework, the threat shared by the participants involves the targeting for use, if necessity demands, of weapons of great speed and destructive force. The potential for causing major indiscriminate damage exists by the nature of these weapons. For the purposes of maintaining equilibrium against use, however, such a framework is tolerable. But the framework on the use of force would be in jeopardy if weapons of great destruction were to be used under conditions in which the line separating the innocent from the legitimate targets of war fighting could not be drawn. This would lead to the end of the law of war. In application to terrorists, the issue may arise if terrorists can threaten societies with such weapons. The use of counterforce as in wartime may then need to be considered primarily in terms of the possible damage to the innocent.

Some indication of further developments of the principles already mentioned appears in the proposals of Secretary of State Shultz calling for preemptive strikes, if necessity dictates, against terrorists. For this purpose, he would enlighten public opinion as to the matter of necessity. He would elaborate the nature of the threat and the possibility of major destruction and assure the public that such strikes would be subject to lawful authority and sound controls.

Secretary of Defense Weinberger, though indicating that he was not addressing the use of armed forces against terrorism, indicated that the use of force must be timely, the amount and duration appropriate to the goals, that there be well-established public support and high probability of success, and that such uses of force be a last resort (that is, after the exhaustion of all other nonforcible measures). The Weinberger and Shultz principles are expressed in general language, but they constitute policy proposals, readily adaptable to the legal framework.

On May 14, 1975, Robert A. Fearey, special assistant to the secretary of state at that time, provided a Senate committee with policy guidelines for dealing with terrorism involving international implications and for dealing with terrorism involving U.S. citizens abroad. These and other such guidelines are of a policy nature yet well within the broad, though ambiguous, frameworks of law that relate to this subject. The guidelines declare that the United States intends "to pursue legal remedies in dealing with terrorists and endeavors to influence other governments to do likewise." They also observe that "under principles of customary international law," the country where terrorism occurs has the responsibility of taking actions and providing protections. The guidelines also propose strengthening the law both in terms of extradition and with regard to political movements. As to the latter,

> While political motivations such as the achievement of self-determination or independence are cited by some individuals or groups to justify terrorism, the U.S. rejects terrorism in any circumstances. Political objectives should be addressed in appropriate forums rather than by resort to violence against innocent bystanders.[29]

These policy frameworks underscore the need to shape law in the future with regard to dealing with terrorism involving two or more states, the special attention to be given to extradition, cooperation, and assistance, and the intention of the United States not to pay ransom and to negotiate only through the host governments but reserving the right to counsel the host government "on all aspects of the rescue operation."

Accordingly, it must be concluded that with respect to the use of force, the loopholes in the law are not substantial. More difficult is the policy question: establishing community policy among states, state commitments to that policy, and support of states when force is used. Even in such situations as the Entebbe rescue mission, an operation involving self-help, there were many complaints among otherwise friendly states that such a mission was a form of aggression. Future such threats might best be managed through international agreement.

Conclusions

An inquiry in greater depth might explore current developments in the form of proposals for a federal law relating to terrorism. It might examine the possibilities of elaborating the international crimes with a view toward making terrorism a universal crime like genocide or piracy or the war crimes. The success of the conventions relating to crimes against aircraft or against the crew or passengers, and the conventions for the protection of diplomats might be considered in depth. It is apparent, however, that more can be expected from conventions that are limited to a region—such as the European Convention on the Suppression of Terrorism—because greater cooperation, critical in suppressing the terrorists, can then be expected. Resolutions of the U.N. General Assembly, treaties that are global in nature, attempts to promote the broader base of human rights through implementation of the Helsinki Accords, and so on have great symbolic value, but they do not promise early implementation that will benefit the victims or even the social order itself.

Several additional conclusions might be proposed. First, it will be essential to formulate, strengthen, clarify, and then support policy against terrorism through effective and widely understood enforcement measures. The relationship and interdependence between enforcement and the promotion of law are well known but require careful articulation to ensure public support. Second, it will be increasingly important to establish the policies of self-help and self-defense, particularly against the changing circumstances of threat. New weaponry, new delivery systems, the growing simplicity of small but highly destructive weapons, and the spread of the technical know-how to terrorist groups must be introduced into the processes that balance out the claims leading to policy. The Webster formula relating to necessity and self-defense needs to be reexamined against these changing conditions.

Third, it will be increasingly important to find the means to determine when terrorism shifts from the conduct of a small number of individuals on a relatively random or irregular basis and becomes the systematic use of violence associated with a form of low-intensity warfare. This is important because with this shift the enforcement measures also shift from those that engage a relatively simple police action to one that demands the use of organized force capabilities, appropriately designed, again by the necessity, to counter terrorism that invokes modern weaponry and logistics.

Fourth, renewed attention must be given to the matter of human rights and to the rightful or legitimate claims of individuals and groups for self-determination, to countering the claims of the Communist states that self-determination will be limited exclusively to the claims against the Western states and their democratic forms of government, and to insist that self-determination will not be appraised by artibrary standards such as Marxist or

Leninist doctrine. This assessment is important because the terrorist is too often identified as an individual or group engaged in the rightful use of violence for just grievances against a social order or an individual who has been deprived of "human rights" by an oppressive or brutal society.

Terrorism is not a form of warfare for legal purposes because warfare presupposes a regulatory law of war, and that law presupposes equality under law of the belligerents. Moreover, that law presupposes that the belligerents can and are able to carry out the requirements imposed under law and to be subject to the full weight of that law for misconduct. Even organized resistance groups were not afforded the protections of the law of war unless such groups were, pursuant to the language now embodied in the Geneva Conventions of 1949, "belonging to a Party to the conflict." In addition they also had to meet the standards of international law: awareness of that law and the capability to fulfill it.

One possibility that might be explored for U.S. practice is the establishment of a special federal district court for matters relating to international terrorism and extradition. Such a court can be domiciled in the District of Columbia, or its judges might be sent on circuit to sit on federal courts throughout the United States, to be present where the case might otherwise be tried. Such judges would be chosen from individuals qualified to adjudicate such issues, including requests for extradition. They would not try cases concerned with domestic terrorism as such; such cases would be treated, as in the past, as crimes in the federal or state courts.

The purpose in establishing such a court would be to have qualified judges; the objective would be to have opinions consistent with the overall foreign policy of the nation or made with a high degree of awareness of the significance of that policy regarding the decisions relating to extradition. The court would draw on other departments of the government for help, assisted by an appropriate and expert staff, and be authorized to hear from other experts outside the government through advisory opinions.

This proposal might also consider the possibility of a special prosecutor for such cases. It might determine whether a three-judge court would be advisable, with a third judge from the federal district court and the other two from the special judges for such cases. This would enable the court to provide the generality of broader experience.

The proposal offers the possibility of a jurisprudence constante: a means to develop the law and the policy associated with law relating to international terrorism and extradition against a set of precedents, conforming to the law or measuring it against the main foreign policy themes and commitments of the United States. It would offer an opportunity for the nation to be served by judges more qualified in working with a changing set of circumstances affecting its security and even its public order while preserving the full protections of the federal court system.

Notes

1. Keesings, Contemporary Archives 30(1984):33072.

2. Henry A. Kissinger, "Continuity and Change in American Foreign Policy," *Society* 15(1977):97, 101–102.

3. George Shultz, "Shaping American Foreign Policy," *Foreign Affairs* (Spring 1985):705, 717.

4. 50 U.S.C., sec. 1801.

5. 249 U.S. 47, 1919.

6. 341 U.S. 494, 1951.

7. No. 83-1035, U.S. Supreme Court Slipsheet, 1985.

8. Research in International Law, section entitled "Extradition," 29 *American Journal of International Law*, 66, 1935.

9. *Digest of United States Practice in International Law* (Washington, D.C.: Government Printing Office, 1976), p. 177.

10. 500 F.2d 267, CCA-2, 1974.

11. Cf. also *United States ex rel. Lujan v. Gengler*, 510 F.2d 62, CCA-2; c.d. 421 U.S. 1000 (1975).

12. See *Charlton* v. *Kelly*, 229 U.S. 447, 1913; *Valentine* v. *United States ex rel. Neidecker*, 299 U.S. 5, 1936.

13. *In re Castioni* [1898], 1 Q.B. 149.

14. No. 37-81 099 MG N.D. Cal., Filed May 31, 1979.

15. No. 80 Cr. Misc. 1. S.D. N.Y., filed August 13, 1981.

16. No. C-82-6688, slip. op. N.D. Cal., filed October 3, 1983.

17. Magis No. 79 M 175 N.D. Ill., filed December 18, 1979.

18. 641 F.2d 504, 520 CCA-7, 1982.

19. U.S.T. 227; T.I.A.S. No. 8468.

20. William M. Hannay, "Legislative Reform of U.S. Extradition Statutes: Plugging the Terrorist's Loophole," *Journal of International Law* 13 (Fall 1983):53, 73.

21. 1982 Irish Reports 154.

22. Hannay, *op. cit.*

23. Webster to Fox, April 24, 1841, 29 B. & F.S.P., 1138; see also Jennings, "The Caroline and McLeod Cases," 32 *American Journal of International Law* (1938) 82-99; cf. Moore, *Digest of International Law*, 2:409–414.

24. Eleanor C. McDowell, Guidelines in *Digest of United States Practice in International Law*, (Washington, D.C.: Government Printing Office, 1976), pp. 195–197.

13
Rewriting the Rules of Engagement

Terrell E. Arnold

I am your king. You are a Frenchman. There is the enemy. Charge!
—Henry IV of France, at the Battle of Ivry, March 14, 1590[1]

In the late afternoon of May 12, 1975, I was seated in my office in the U.S. embassy in Manila when the ambassador walked in and asked, "What do you know about a ship called the *Mayaguez*?" The ambassador had just received a message from the U.S. embassy in Jakarta, Indonesia, relaying a distress call from the vessel and giving coordinates that placed the *Mayaguez* in the Gulf of Thailand off Cambodia. Through shipping contacts in Manila, I determined that the *Mayaguez* was a container ship of U.S. registry and had an American crew of more than thirty people. In the next twenty-four hours, the world learned that the Cambodians had seized the *Mayaguez* on the open sea in an act of piracy, that the ship itself was at anchor alongside Tang Island near the Cambodian port of Kampong Sam, and that the crew was in Cambodian hands at some unknown location.

In the intense four days between May 12 and 15, 1975, the *Mayaguez* was the subject of an extraordinary example of crisis management.[2] From the White House—the Oval Office, the Cabinet Room, and the Situation Room—President Gerald Ford and his key national security aides directed a mission to rescue the *Mayaguez* and its crew. They ran a command post that was halfway around the world from the scene of battle. White House management of this crisis was so close that on the third day, in the midst of a National Security Council meeting, the president personally ordered U.S. pilots—at that moment strafing Cambodian fishing boats—to stop their attack. He took that action because of a report flashed to the White House Situation Room that one pilot saw "Caucasians" on the deck of a fishing boat during a strafing run and was concerned that these might be members of the *Mayaguez* crew.[3] That hunch was correct; the entire crew of the *Mayaguez* was on one boat, and had the attack continued, they might have been killed by U.S. pilots.

On the fourth day of the crisis, the *Mayaguez* and its crew were rescued in a multipronged military operation that brought the United States practically to a full-scale military alert, monopolized the time and decision-making attention of its top leadership for the better part of a week, and drew heavily on military resources that were prepositioned in at least two allied regional countries (Thailand and the Philippines). The victory itself was punctuated with charges of overreaction, excessive use of force, and too many casualties (fifteen marines were killed and over 50 wounded, mainly in ground fighting during the rescue).

The *Mayaguez* crisis came at an awkward time. The United States had just made, in the estimate of many Americans and foreigners alike, an ignominious retreat from Vietnam. Its credibility was at a worldwide low. The will of the United States, the leader of the non-Communist world, to respond to challenge appeared close to nil. Conscious of this situation, President Ford felt that in responding to the Cambodian seizure of the *Mayaguez*, he had to show resolve and demonstrate that the United States could act decisively. He decided to use force if necessary, but uncertain about how much force was needed and how it should be used, he chose to use enough power to ensure success.[4]

At about 6:20 on the morning of October 23, 1983, a large yellow Mercedes-Benz truck approached the gates of the U.S. Marine barracks at Beirut International Airport. Traveling more than 35 miles per hour, the truck "penetrated the perimeter barbed and concertina wire obstacle . . . , passed between guard posts 6 and 7 without being engaged, entered an open gate, passed around one sewer pipe and between two other pipes, flattened the Sergeant of the Guard's sand-bagged booth, entered the interior lobby of the building and exploded."[5] The marine barracks was totally destroyed. A similar blast shook the French Multinational Force Headquarters a short distance away. In the debris of these two explosions, 380 U.S. Marines and French soldiers lay dead and wounded.

The marine barracks bombing caught the United States again in an awkward stance. From its first days in office, the Reagan administration had promised decisive action against terrorists. On that day, almost three years into the administration and with three assassinations and two Beirut bombings in barely two years, there were no successes to report. Rather, there was increasingly strident debate in the United States over the marine presence in Lebanon, the obviously deteriorating security situation around Beirut, and the growing combativeness of U.S. forces in the eastern Mediterranean in the face of low-level attacks. Much in the way President Ford had struggled through the *Mayaguez* crisis, President Reagan was wrestling with a problem of how to show resolve and decisiveness.

But President Reagan was dealing with a shadowy enemy. Representatives of the Islamic Jihad (the so-called Holy War and self-proclaimed perpetrators of the Beirut bombings) surfaced only at the moment of an attack. Clearly the United States, and many other countries with interests in the Middle East, had acquired a deadly new enemy in the Beirut forms of terrorism, and confronting and engaging such an enemy posed a different problem for national leadership. In succeeding months, attacks in Kuwait and Jordan and plots uncovered in Western Europe suggested that the pattern was spreading, while evidence was increasing that three Middle East countries—Iran, Syria, and Libya—were deeply involved. Terrorism had grown acutely more violent in the previous three years and was increasingly an instrument of policy for certain states. Moreover, terrorist attacks had occurred in half the countries of the world in 1983 alone, well over 40 percent of the victims were Americans, and the problem now was how to fight back on such an undefined but global scale.

The *Mayaguez* and the marine barracks in Beirut, almost a decade apart and thousands of miles distant from each other, had several qualities in common: both represented intense, short duration, remote, small-scale violent attacks against Americans; they occurred in areas considered critical to long-term interests of the United States; and they were sensitive politically. Those characteristics run to the heart of the problem the United States faces in trying to fight back against terrorist attacks. The *Mayaguez* crisis gave U.S. leadership a clear glimpse of its post-Vietnam challenge: low-level warfare.

Before the debris of the marine barracks in Beirut had been fully searched for casualties, the U.S. public and the Congress began asking questions about the use of force by the marines in Beirut to defend themselves. As deputy director of the State Department Office for Combatting Terrorism, I was among the first people to be notified of the tragedy, and my immediate questions were whether the marines tried to stop the truck or whether they shot at it. Only days later did it emerge that probably no shots had been fired; the suicide bomber crashed into the barracks unopposed.

Secretary of Defense Caspar Weinberger asked a panel of senior military officers, under the chairmanship of Admiral Robert L. Long, to study the facts of the bombing and to suggest ways to avoid such disasters in the future.[6] The Long commission looked particularly into three questions, the answers to which were vital to explaining the immense terrorist success represented by this bombing: Did the marines know why they were in Beirut? Did they appreciate the rising hostility of the environment in Beirut? Did they understand their rules of engagement?

Rules of Engagement

Rules of engagement (the military term is ROE) sound like an arcane topic for debate by military scientists, but they are the very essence of warfare. ROE tell combat forces when to use deadly force and how much and what kind to use to engage the enemy. "Engagement means fighting," Carl von Clausewitz reminds us, and "The object of fighting is the destruction or defeat of the enemy."[7] President Ford had a rules of engagement problem when he was trying to decide how much and what kind of force to use to ensure the rescue of the *Mayaguez*. President Reagan faced a similar problem in deciding how many and what kind of forces to send into Grenada. When the Long commission asked whether the marines in Beirut understood their rules of engagement, the commission was asking whether the marines knew what they should do to protect themselves against a hostile threat. How far could they go?

Long commission findings on all three of its questions were mostly negative. Commission members felt that the basic mission of the Marine Multinational Force (USMNF) contingent—to keep the peace in Beirut—was accurately stated at the beginning, but neither Washington leadership nor higher-echelon military commands revised the mission statement, as the situation changed, to take account of the rising hostility to the marine presence, especially after the April 1983 bombing of the U.S. embassy. The marines did not appear to understand the risks that accumulated during 1983 in the Beirut environment, and the Long commission felt this was an intelligence failure. Intelligence analysts in Washington, however, believed that the problem was too much intelligence; the marines did not have enough staff to read and assess all the information they had. In effect, the growing combativeness of the situation had not been taken into account in this regard either, and inadequate resources therefore had been assigned to the intelligence function.

The most serious question for the Long commission investigators concerned the rules of engagement. According to commission findings, peacetime military rules of engagement were in force for the marines at the airport. The main elements of this guidance were as follows:

> Action taken by U.S. forces ashore in Lebanon would be for self-defense only. Reprisal or punitive measures would not be initiated. Commanders were to seek guidance from higher headquarters prior to using armed force, if time and situation allowed. If time or the situation did not allow the opportunity to request guidance from higher headquarters, commanders were authorized to use that degree of armed force necessary to protect their forces. Hostile ground forces which had infiltrated and violated USMNF lines by land, sea, or air would be warned that they could not proceed and were in a restricted area. If the intruder force failed to leave, the violation would be reported and guidance requested. Riot control agents would not be used unless authorized by the Secretary of Defense. Hostile forces would not be pursued. A "hostile act" was defined as an attack or use of force against the USMNF, or against MNF or LAF [Lebanese Armed Forces] units operating with the USMNF, that consisted of releasing, launching, or firing of missiles, bombs, individual weapons, rockets or any other weapon.[8]

These rules of engagement remained in effect for the USMNF in Beirut until after the October 23 bombing. Although the military commands responsible for the marine forces in Beirut believed that these rules were adequate to meet the October 23 attack, the Long commission concluded that the marines were uncertain about what those rules meant and how to apply them.[9]

Uncertainty about exactly when and how to use force constitutes a major barrier to an effective U.S. response to terrorism and other low-level violent attacks. As a matter of routine, combat troops usually are told what the rules of engagement are for any specific operation. Peacetime military rules of engagement spell out the general terms for using force against a conventional hostile military force, but peacetime rules, by their very nature, are not case specific. The October 23 bombing underscored this fact, showing all too graphically that conventional peacetime military rules of engagement, as commonly interpreted by forces, do not provide an effective posture of readiness to cope with the types of hostile situations U.S. forces and many other official Americans are facing abroad.

In the case of terrorist attack, a mismatch of the rules to the engagement is probably inevitable because terrorism is not a battlefield kind of target. Terrorist attacks usually are carried out by groups and individuals who are secretive about their membership, locations, and plans. Gathering tactical intelligence on their operations is difficult because the groups tend to be small, closely knit, and lacking in distinguishing marks such as uniforms. Terrorists often attack in the midst of otherwise peaceful urban settings, and any forceful action against the terrorists has a high risk of harm to innocent bystanders. During hostage situations particularly, the terrorists deliberately arrange to maximize the risk of harm to bystanders. Terrorist groups configure themselves for specific types of operations; a hijacking is different from a bombing, and organization, dress, demeanor, and points of vulnerability to attack will differ depending on which operation is planned. Terrorist attacks in general tend to be directed against particular physical targets, single individuals, or small groups. The attacks themselves are of short duration and highly localized. The tactics are hit and run. In both scale and nature of attacks, terrorism most often requires civil-police-level decisions about the use of deadly force, although many terrorist attacks are quite large events on a civil police scale of violence.

The terrorists make their own rules of engagement; the targeted victims and governments can only react. The times, locations, targets, weapons, and objectives are all set by the terrorists.

This pattern must be reversed. Essential steps in doing that are to spell out the principles that will underlie future uses of force against terrorists and then to define the basic rules of engagement for use in those cases where the decision is made to use force.

Principles for Using Force

Recent speeches of leading Reagan administration officials show a good deal of progress toward formulating the principles needed to decide when to use force. During an October 25, 1984, talk at the Park Avenue Synagogue in New York, Secretary of State George P. Shultz spelled out the main factors the public needs to consider in any decision to use force.[10] The national security adviser, Robert C. McFarlane, in a March 25, 1985, talk at the National Security Information Center in Washington, D.C., also stated several principles for deciding when to employ force in dealing with terrorist attacks.[11] Moreover, Secretary of Defense Weinberger has suggested principles he says need to be used in deciding whether to engage U.S. combat forces abroad, including against terrorists.[12] Taken together, these statements suggest that the administration is working toward the following principles for employing force against terrorism:

> If a country or group persists in mounting terrorist attacks against U.S. citizens and facilities or its friends and allies, the United States may use force.

> If the United States uses force, it will not use more than the case requires and will seek to limit casualties, military or civilian.

> Before using force, the United States will discuss the matter as fully as possible with other countries at interest, but it may be necessary to act before all the facts are at hand.

> The aim will be to stop terrorist attacks, and any use of force would be confined to pursuit of that objective.

> Force will be used only as a last resort, but it will be used if no other option proves workable.

These are rigorous force employment principles, and they appear accurately to reflect the administration's thinking, but there is as yet no apparent agreement in the administration to use military force regularly or systematically against terrorist targets. Neither specific targets nor the rules of engagement appear to have been decided.

The thinking of military officers regarding the use of military force in the post-Vietnam era against terrorist targets strongly accords with Weinberger's views. Military officers among my students at the National War College during the past five years constantly have said that they would like to know before forces are committed to any engagement that the public fully supports that decision, that the probabilities of success are high, that the objectives of the attack directly serve vital U.S. interests, and that the rules of engagement for any combat situation are set and known to the forces who will carry out the attack.

As military officers see them, such prior judgments about the use of force are insurance against having the armed forces pick up the tab for failed political judgment, as they feel they did in the case of Vietnam. The most frustrating form of that political judgment, as experienced Vietnam officers describe it, was that they were given rules of engagement that prevented them from fighting to win. In the future, they therefore would like to see findings on such issues as outlined by Weinberger before forces are employed in any engagement, and they would prefer to have them made before any forces are deployed to avoid situations in which deployment may snowball into the use of such forces without any further examination of the choices.

Such operating-level attitudes, strongly bolstered by the Weinberger principles, have led to a sort of chicken-and-egg hesitation about deploying forces, and this hesitancy has extended to prepositioning forces only potentially to deal with a terrorist threat. Senior Pentagon officials have resisted the deployment of actual fighting teams, as distinct from survey or advisory missions, because they could not foresee when or how a fighting team might be used. Some would say that is all right because it keeps them out of trouble, but the other side of the coin is that the failure to deploy in a timely manner effectively preempts the opportunity to use force in any way, including an appropriate and effective one.

While cautious on commitments to their use, military officers generally agree that the United States has the special forces needed to do the counterterrorism job: the small-scale military operation against a terrorist training camp, the hideout of the terrorist group, or a group's logistical support. These forces are kept in a regularly trained and exercised condition, on standby and equipped to move if ordered. In a number of specific cases the United States also has the intelligence needed to make an operation reasonably surgical and effective. What it lacks is public confidence in its ability to use such force effectively. Military officers think that lack of confidence needs to be tackled through persuading the public that the principles for force employment and the rules of engagement make sense in terms of the country's needs and values.

Rewriting the Rules

The rules of engagement problem is not a simple one of merely telling the troops whom and when to attack in the manner of Henry IV of France. Rules of engagement have at least two primary purposes. The first is to put forces on notice as to the manner and circumstances in which they may use deadly force. The second is to put the potential enemy and the public on notice as to what those circumstances are. It has two purposes: one object of a public affairs effort is to gain support, but a key purpose of such advertising is to gain as much deterrent value as possible from maintaining counterterrorism forces.

To get that deterrent value, there needs to be a change in mind-set about current peacetime conditions, especially about the uses terrorists and others are making of low-level violence. These conditions require that counterterrorist forces be equipped to match skills, be able to anticipate moves, and be able to adapt tactics to hostile situations that lie somewhere between urban guerrilla warfare and civil police actions. Largely the numbers, equipment, training, and operating tactics of the counterterrorism forces needed fall in the special operations category but usually on a microscale compared to the norms of special operations.

The microscale and the brief duration of most terrorist attacks place an exceptional premium on preparedness to apply the rules of engagement. There is no time to consult before using force once an attack begins. As shown in the marine barracks bombing, if a security guard waits long enough to decide whether a move is hostile, it may already be too late. Waiting until the terrorist initiates the attack puts the advantage inevitably with the terrorist. Once an attack begins, the terrorist will use any device or tactic thought necessary to succeed. The attack will not be constrained in either its force or its targeting by the rules of warfare. Rules of engagement for an active defense against a terrorist attack must take all of these factors into account.

Such easily noted characteristics of a terrorist attack raise important philosophical problems that inhibit including terrorism in the military rules of engagement. Although the aggregate effect of international terrorist attacks is a form of low-level warfare, the individual attacks usually are ordinary crimes, not acts of war. Military forces engaged in combat are restrained by the rules of armed conflict. But terrorists engaged in an attack are committing a crime; they are not restrained by the rules of armed conflict or by the criminal laws of the countries where they attack. For this reason, a number of Pentagon officials say that terrorism should not be made to appear legitimate by treating it as normal combat under rules of engagement or by giving terrorism status through permitting it to creep in under the heading of guerrilla warfare in the protocols to the Geneva Convention.

In part that is a valid concern. One of the real dangers is that a national response to terrorism will be taken by the terrorists as a form of recognition. Negotiating directly with a terrorist group or working through another government to do so tends to convey a sort of diplomatic recognition. Even informal recognition of this type gives the terrorist group a status and may cause the group to be seen by interested people and governments as having graduated from terrorists to insurgents. If the group then continues to practice terrorism under the protective cover of insurgency, dealing with attacks by the group and coping with other countries associated with it become more complicated. Therefore the first rule of engagement against terrorists is to avoid treating them in any way that legitimates their activities. ,

Several other factors make the rules of engagement for international terrorism especially difficult to develop. First, the terrorists are likely to be operating in a foreign jurisdiction where the access of U.S. forces, if not met with hostility, is likely to require specific approval of another government. Second, the selection and equipping of forces to deal even with one specific type of terrorist incident will vary greatly with the locale, size and armament of the group, potential sources of support for the group or for the attackers in the vicinity of the incident, and other aspects of the case. The rules of engagement in these circumstances become incident-specific tactical matters. Third, the forces and equipment needed to deal with an incident or a threat may change radically as the situation develops, and where deployment times and distances are great, organizing and equipping a force for a wide range of attack modes may pose serious logistic, training, or rehearsal and other preparation problems. Moreover, the tactical or the political situation may change while forces are en route, causing the rules of engagement most appropriate for the case to shift as well.

Illustrating these problems, in 1983 a group of anti-Nimeiri dissidents in the Southern Sudan took five missionary workers hostage at a remote southern village, Boma. Even for the Sudanese armed forces, the problem of deploying a team to rescue the hostages was difficult, given distance and the primitive infrastructure of the region. The hostages were American, German, and Canadian. Had any of these governments attempted a rescue themselves, the logistical tails, the communications problems, and the management of any assault would have presented nearly insurmountable problems.

Packaging a team equipped to deal with the array of contingencies likely to arise in such a case is a major challenge and one that causes the military planner immense difficulties. In many instances, a force large enough to cover all the contingencies would be highly visible and probably would not be granted entry to the country where an incident is occurring. Operating at great distance would give the force a long and tenuous logistics tail unless intermediate basing could be arranged.

Strike Team Rules

Despite all the problems, rules of engagement have been developed for using force to resolve a terrorist incident, and in principle they work well. The major strike teams now maintained by various countries generally operate from the same concept: the attacking team is prepared to shoot anyone who resists, and the terrorists are expected to try to respond in kind. The rule of engagement is to eliminate all resistance as quickly as possible. Terrorism strike teams are trained to identify hostages or other noncombatants quickly and to direct their force against the terrorists. Such decisions are split-second, however, and a hostage who tried to intervene during an attack can easily be mistaken for a terrorist. Nonetheless, the basic rules of engagement for such a team cannot be improved very much, nor can they be tailored more precisely except in the circumstances of a specific case.

If the United States decides to undertake preemptive strikes or to retaliate against a terrorist attack, the basic rules of engagement for the forces used would have to be the strike force rules or similar ones. When a strike force is sent on such a mission, its rules of engagement must be clear and unequivocal: the object is to win, and the requirement is to be sure that enough force is used to succeed. President Ford saw this very clearly in the *Mayaguez* case, and the United States won. Somehow President Carter and the planners of the Tehran rescue mission did not see it, and the United States lost.

Rules for Static Security Situations

Ensuring adequate rules of engagement for forces deployed to the scene of a specific terrorist incident or target only meets one leg of the rules of engagement problem. In combating international terrorism, there are actually three separate tiers to the problem. The rules of engagement for U.S. special forces deployed to deal with a particular incident are likely to be clear, case specific, and unlikely to go stale. The Beirut bombings, however, demonstrated that the rules for security forces of U.S. diplomatic missions and military commands, the people coping with high threat but relatively static security conditions, must be reviewed and regularly updated and clearly explained to the forces using them. Moreover, some set of rules of engagement appears increasingly necessary for officials serving abroad.

As the bomb-laden vehicle approached U.S. Marine headquarters in Beirut on October 23, 1983, it is probable that the marines on watch hesitated because their rules of engagement permitted them to use deadly force only if attacked. The split-second judgment to be made by the guards at post 6 and 7 that morning was whether the truck actually represented an attack.

One study, undertaken in the Pentagon, concluded that the reaction of the marines in that situation was probably not atypical. Opinions vary widely among military personnel as to when the use of deadly force may be authorized. When not in combat, firing a weapon in any but authorized and controlled circumstances usually means an investigation. The word on this is so deeply drilled in that in the case of marines on watch in Beirut, the need to be absolutely sure was undoubtedly at the front of their minds.

The question here is, What kind of rules of engagement will protect the individual and the unit he serves in high-risk but noncombat situations. Security guards everywhere have the problem of deciding what their weapons normally are for. I recall being given a loaded rifle and sent out to patrol the Lake Michigan waterfront along Navy Pier Chicago during World War II. Quite aside from the fact that it was January and I was freezing, I could not think of any reason for being there or for carrying the rifle. When I went back inside and was shown by the petty officer of the watch that the cartridges were dummies (no powder, no primers), I relaxed and did my patrol on several successive nights without a thought to the rifle. My weapon, if it had any role, was to be seen, not heard.

Security guards often are under similar rules of engagement for the weapons they carry. Even in places with bad reputations like Beirut, if the quiet times go on long enough, weapons go back into their holsters and become showpieces. For both the individual and his unit, knowing when conditions have changed, when a potential threat may demand actual use of weapons under established rules of engagement, can mean the difference between warding off an attack or taking part in a disaster.

Ensuring Readiness

The key to this problem is not different rules of engagement but a different approach to readiness. In many places abroad, the psychology of a mission can intervene and undermine the preparedness of a security force. In a diplomatic mission, the U.S. Information Service libraries, consular and commercial sections, agricultural offices, and Agency for International Development missions thrive on being public places. They still are designed to be public places despite the rising threat levels in many countries. At many military bases and facilities abroad, off-base living arrangements and the efforts of base commanders to maintain good community relations have similarly erosive effects on security discipline. Unless there is a more or less constant reiteration of the danger, the members of such organizations will agitate for reductions in security to meet their public access needs. Moreover, military base commanders and ambassadors and deputy chiefs of mission become nervous about possible accidental discharge of weapons, possible excessive shows of force, and possible adverse public reactions. USMNF marines in Beirut indicated that they were regularly cautioned against any accidental firing of a weapon, and only in the rules of engagement spelled out after the embassy bombing were there explicit instructions to carry weapons loaded.[13] The more the quiet intervals go on, the more such factors will intervene, and the more the security posture of a unit, military or civilian, will be compromised.

Rules for Embassy Security Guards

Providing good rules of engagement for U.S. Marine security guards at diplomatic and consular posts abroad poses special problems. Historically the marines' mission was to protect classified information and systems, but increasingly the mission of these security details has moved over to protecting people and facilities. With rare exceptions, even so, the marines have no security functions outside a few designated buildings in a diplomatic or consular post. These usually include the embassy chancery, any annexes that contain key mission elements, and possibly the ambassador's residence. Rules of engagement are defensive in purpose, and they do not apply outside the boundaries of diplomatic properties. Firing shots into public streets or buildings—the kind of shooting that occurred at the Libyan People's Bureau in London in 1984—is not in the rules. Usually the rules do not apply outside the designated buildings. The marines can use force to defend themselves. They can use force to repel boarders or avert forcible entry. They can use nonlethal force, such as tear gas, to break up a threatening situation but normally only after a group or threatening individual has gotten inside the diplomatic compound, and in some cases inside the building, being protected.

A hardening of these rules worldwide could be useful to the marines in doing their jobs and to embassy leadership in providing appropriate guidance. Moreover, as the Long commission found in its investigation of the Beirut bombing, the rules of engagement for embassy marines and for the security forces of U.S. military facilities and bases need to be reexamined to ensure that both adequately reflect threat conditions and that there are no potentially dangerous inconsistencies. In the Beirut case, the embassy marines had one set of rules of engagement and the USMNF marines another. The way the USMNF marines interpreted their rules caused them to operate under much tighter constraints than embassy marines on use of firearms.[14]

Rules for the Threatened Individual

Specific rules of engagement are an increasing requirement for individuals at overseas diplomatic posts and in military units. More and more individuals, some without asking for official approval, are carrying handguns, Mace pens, and other protective devices. One ambassador in a high-threat post used to travel to and from his office with a handgun on his lap and a heavier weapon at his feet. So far as is known, his rules of engagement were entirely personal. The question of what might have happened had he been caught in a shootout on the street did not have to be answered, but security threat conditions are poor enough in a number of foreign capital cities for that situation to arise sooner or later.

The most practical rule of engagement for these cases is similar to the civil police rule: the individual can be told that use of a weapon is authorized only in actual, life-threatening hostile situations where police protection is not available. According to military officers who have looked at this problem, enforcing that kind of a rule may take care of itself because the most natural frame of mind for someone who regularly carries a weapon seems to be to see it as a personal defensive tool. Even many security officers come to view their weapons as personal defense.

Finding a Home for Terrorism Rules of Engagement

Where do the rules of engagement for dealing with terrorism cases most naturally fit? Shortly after the Beirut bombings, a Pentagon study of this issue seemed to conclude that the rules for preemptive or retaliatory moves against terrorists should not go into the military rules of engagement. Rather, although recognizing a need for rules for such engagements, military officers appear to favor keeping them out of the military rules that apply in warfare. Their strongest reason for this preference relates to the fact that terrorist situations tend to require one-shot exercises of police power.

Here the real question is where terrorism fits in the pattern of challenges to national security. Terrorism is not in any common sense a military challenge. Although it is dangerous as an insidious kind of attack on democratic values and institutions, the question reasonably can be asked whether that challenge is greater than the one presented by ordinary crime or whether the challenge is basically different from crime.

One of the major points of difference between the United States and other governments during the Reagan administration has related to whether terrorism should be considered a police or military matter. Generally European governments consider terrorism a civil police matter, and they are postured mostly to deal with it through exercises of civil authority. Inside the United States, the same perspective applies: terrorist attacks generally are viewed as challenges to civil authority. The Federal Bureau of Investigation (FBI) has lead agency responsibility in the federal government for dealing with most attacks inside U.S. territory, except for aircraft in flight.[15]

Any U.S. problem of deciding who is responsible seems to exist only with respect to international terrorist attacks. Lead responsibility rests with the State Department, but the Central Intelligence Agency, Defense, Treasury, the Federal Aviation Administration, the FBI, the Energy Department, the National Security Council, and the Office of the Vice-President have roles in dealing with international terrorism. Even so, whether the United States might use force in preempting or retaliating for a terrorist attack abroad is the only context in which use of the armed forces has arisen.

Who is in charge affects the choices on rules of engagement. For a terrorist attack inside U.S. territory, military forces would be used only if the president made a specific decision to use them and set aside the provisions of *posse comitatus* rules against use of military forces in enforcing civil law. Military forces were used in many capacities related to providing security for the 1984 Olympics in Los Angeles, but the issue of their possible use in a hostile situation did not arise. Had there been a need to use force, the most likely rules would have been civil police ones.

Civil Police Rules of Engagement

The distance between military and civil police rules of engagement is substantial. Military rules are designed to meet the primary purpose of the engagement, usually to defeat the enemy. Police rules, on the other hand, have as their primary objective resolution of an incident without loss of life if possible and without harm to participants or bystanders. Police officers can use deadly force to meet a threat to their own lives or to others, but use of force in other circumstances appears increasingly limited.[16] Similar rules apply to federal agents of the FBI, Treasury, and the Drug Enforcement Agency (DEA). The official U.S. government policy of no concessions to terrorists contrasts sharply with the habit of most civil police agencies, which is to talk and make the minimum concessions needed to resolve an incident.

Much of the problem of choice between civil and military arises in international terrorism cases because the only forces the United States has to project abroad are military. The CIA does not maintain forces for military or paramilitary operations. Only the Defense Department does. FBI and DEA personnel operating abroad do not fit the bill although DEA people in Mexico, Colombia, Bolivia, and other locations face some very warlike, hostile situations.

Conclusions

The issue finally is how much of the overall strategy for countering international terrorism depends on rules of engagement. In this connection, the most constant posture of security forces in an environment of high terrorism threats must be one of complete readiness to meet the unexpected. That state of readiness cannot be guaranteed if the rules of engagement are unclear or if the purposes of the rules are left in doubt by misleading signals from leadership.

The risks Secretary Shultz has said the government must face in deciding to use force to preempt or retaliate against a terrorist attack also apply to static defense situations. To keep security personnel ready at their posts to meet an attack, we must be prepared to have them make a few mistakes, to shoot in a few cases where the actual intent may not be hostile but the approach appears nonetheless threatening. To posture security forces in that way is perhaps to risk a public hue and cry every time a security guard makes a mistake that results in bodily harm, but the alternative seems to be leaving Americans vulnerable to the Beirut type of attack.

The rules of engagement problem for dealing with terrorism comes down to two pieces of insurance. First, the rules of engagement must permit an effective response if rigorously followed. The personnel covered by those rules must be kept fully alert and able to react immediately to certain types of situations. Second, security personnel must know what to expect. The exact scenarios for terrorist attacks cannot be predicted, but personnel must be aware of several possibilities, any one of which would justify their invoking the rules of engagement to respond to a hostile move. There are several fairly common modes of attack, and there is a good deal of copy-catting. Thus security personnel should be made aware of the common forms of attack. They should be regularly rehearsed in dealing with such situations so that their movements in the event are cool and calculated. They should be put through drills that constantly force them to deal with the unexpected, even in the working out of a commonplace attack scenario.

Rules of engagement for terrorist situations are highly dynamic and case specific. The challenge is to design generic rules that will ensure an effective response to specific attacks only generally covered in the rules. Moreover, the kinds of political sensitivity connected with both the *Mayaguez* and Beirut bombing incidents can be expected to enter into every terrorist or other low-level warfare situation likely to invoke a rules of engagement problem. Rules of engagement for terrorism thus are likely always to be cautious and restrictive, authorizing the use of force but rarely, if ever, encouraging it.

These considerations put the emphasis most clearly where it belongs, on readiness, and on a knowledgeable reading of the threat environment. That means training and rehearsal, and it means constant collection and assessment of intelligence. Without those, the rules of engagement cannot come effectively into play.

Notes

1. H.L. Mencken, *A New Dictionary of Quotations* (New York: Alfred A. Knopf, 1952), p. 71.
2. The events occurred during Sunday to Wednesday, May 11–14 Washington time due to the international date line.

3. Roy Rowen, *The Four Days of Mayaguez* (New York: W.W. Norton, 1975), pp. 140–144.

4. Ibid.

5. U.S. Department of Defense, "Report of the DOD Commission on Beirut International Airport Terrorist Act, October 23, 1983" (Washington, D.C., December 20, 1983). This document is commonly referred to as the Long Commission Report.

6. Ibid.

7. Carl von Clausewitz, *On War*, ed. and trans. Michael Howard and Peter Paret (Princeton, N.J.: Princeton University Press, 1976), p. 227.

8. Long Commission Report, p. II.

9. Ibid.

10. George P. Shultz, The Scherr Lecture, Park Avenue Synagogue, New York, Oct. 25, 1984.

11. Robert C. McFarlane, "Terrorism and the Future of Free Society" (speech delivered at the National Strategy Information Center, Washington, D.C., March 25, 1985).

12. Caspar Weinberger (speech delivered at the National Press Club, Washington, D.C., November 28, 1984).

13. Long Commission Report, p. II.

14. Ibid.

15. Under national security decision directives issued during the Reagan administration, lead agency responsibility for international terrorist incidents is assigned to the Department of State; lead agency responsibility for domestic incidents is assigned to the FBI, except that the Federal Aviation Administration has lead responsibility for a hijacked aircraft in flight.

16. The Supreme Court decided in early 1985 (*Tennessee* v. *Garner*) that deadly force could not be used to stop a fleeing suspect "unless necessary to prevent the escape and the officer has probable cause to believe that the suspect poses a significant threat of death or serious physical injury to the officer or others." In rendering this opinion, the Court argued that the common law rule allowing the use of whatever force was necessary to stop a fleeing felon had been "distorted beyond all recognition" by changes in technology that have greatly increased the range and the deadlines of weapons and changes in law that have reduced the number of offenses that constitute capital crimes. It remains to be seen what impact this decision will have on the rules of engagement for civil police officers, but the direction is clearly toward a more restrictive policy on the use of force than now applies.

14

Moral Response to Terrorism

James Tunstead Burtchael

Nearly thirty years ago, shortly after the Soviet invasion of Budapest, the European Communists were asked to relieve some of the international pressure on Moscow by condemning the use of gas by the United States in the Korean conflict. According to reports, the gas acted as a disabler, rendering soldiers listless and virtually unconscious, so that they could be picked up and taken prisoner without combat. I was a student in Rome then and attended a noontime rally in the Piazza del Risorgimento, where I listened with curiosity to an impassioned party leader attack this immoral new form of U.S. destruction. Her voice rose to an angry shout as she reviled the inhumane gas that would render soldiers senseless. I distinctly recall my bewilderment at her implied invitation to think of shrapnel and bullets as humane by comparison. Personally, I would have preferred to have been doped than shot and was stupefied at her denunciation of the new gas. But I realized then that it was war, not this or that weapon, that was inhumane.

There is a sense in which every accusation that some new weapon of armed conflict is immoral distracts us from the fundamental ethical issues about warfare itself. There is ample documentation that the introduction of every new deadly armament has aroused questions as to its moral acceptability. The Second Lateran Council in 1139 anathematized the crossbow and the longbow and forbade their use against Christians and Catholics.[1] Comparable outrage met the introduction of gunpowder.[2] Submarines, torpedoes, liquid fire, dumdum bullets, biological and chemical agents, and poison gas have been the subjects of intense ethical debate in the last two centuries.

U.S. positions taken at the Hague Conference and the Washington Conference surrounding World War I elicited three quite diverse positions. One condemned the new armaments as immoral. In this vein, one editorial commented, "America's influence at the [Washington] Conference should be thrown against the weapons that are directed against non-combatants—the submarine and poison gas." "Since a gas attack is uncontrollable, chemical warfare falls into the well-poisoning class."[3] A second position accepted the fearsome new tactical devices precisely because they would serve to deter nations from warfare: "Chemical warfare with its unlimited choice of weapons and its unlimited methods of making war intolerable, will make warfare universal, and better than any other means will bring war home to its makers. . . . Knowing that the war of the future will be brought home to every individual, the effort will be made to avoid it at all costs."[4] The third position was that the evolution of more devastating weaponry was simply the natural unfolding of warfare and that they ought be evaluated by the classical criteria of morality in war, just as they ought to provoke new consideration of what warfare had always been.[5] Those conversant with the ethical debate surrounding nuclear weapons in our time and with the renewed discussion of biological and chemical weapons will find these moral judgments quite familiar.

There is a sense in which this moral concern is very nearsighted. It dwells uniquely on armaments that directly inflict bodily harm or death. Yet cryptography, radar, sonar, missile delivery, laser directional systems, and satellite photography have escalated the body count in warfare without falling subject to any similar moral condemnation before the forum of public sentiment.

Ethical challenge to new weapons eventually subsides in one of three ways. The new weapon may become available to all parties in conflict, in which case no one will complain of it any more. Or it may be met by a newly developed form of defense and will no longer seem so frightening. Or it may be so catastrophically destructive that no nation wishes to court retaliation in kind, and thus it goes unused. What this suggests is that ethical discourse regarding methods of warfare may not be all that profoundly principled. What appears to be moral alarm over a new and deadly weapon is often merely a tactical and temporary disequilibrium on the battlefield. Once balance is restored, the devices are either accepted as a legitimate part of conventional weaponry or they are proscribed, not so much by moral condemnation as by fear of facing them.

There is a fourth alternative. Occasionally a people will reject the use of some form of force that is available because they do not wish to undergo the moral change that affects those who take it up and use it. One thinks of Gandhi, the Christian Zulu leaders, and the Arab insurgents against the Turks. This is a truly moral stand, but it is rare and carries a heavy military risk. That risk is undergone because of a perceived moral penalty that a people of uncommon integrity may be unwilling to accept: a disintegration of character that would invalidate their cause and make them the principal victims of their own use of force.

In general, however, what passes for moral judgment is the acceptance of convention. Moral judgment pretty much corresponds to self-justification.

I am willing to forgo moral condemnation of my enemy for any action that I myself am prepared to perform, and I am prepared to do virtually everything my enemy can do. Thus most of what is ordinarily presented as the refined moral estimate of battle practices—a moral code of warfare—is little more than a description of what we are all willing to do and to face.[6] The sign that one has encountered one of those rare warriors who exercises true moral judgment is when that belligerent is purposely willing to face actions to which he or she is unwilling to resort.

Since World War II there have been very few declared wars yet a plethora of armed conflicts involving national military forces. At first, the military were bewildered about how to address insurgency and guerrilla hostilities. Unconventional insurgency was denounced at the outset as immoral and as a defiance of the humane conventions of warfare. But in time the international legal community began to have increased sympathy for the notion that there was after all a commonalty between guerrilla warfare and conventional conflict. Even in the period of the Korean struggle, this was gaining credence within formal military circles.[7]

As this was happening, insurgents began to adopt some of the forms and usages of the military. Thus the Khmer Rouge, like the Vietcong, used a characteristic bandanna to qualify as military insignia and organized themselves, as had the Chinese Communists before them, in units and echelons of command. Although neither the Geneva Convention nor the later protocols unambiguously acknowledge guerrilla insurgency as a variant upon traditional warfare and although in many areas (such as Northern Ireland) the civil power refuses to consider insurgents as anything but domestic criminals, the international trend has been progressively to acknowledge that armed guerrilla resistance is but a modern adaptation on warfare and is to be conducted increasingly within the norms of conventional armed conflict.[8] Once again, the gravitational field of conventional warfare has proved irresistible to a new form of armed strategy and has pulled the new form of belligerency into its ancient toleration.[9]

These issues of history suggest that it would perhaps be misleading to address the ethics of terrorism and response to terrorism by accepting without question the fashionable presumption that terrorism is a development so discontinuous with the traditions of warfare that it deserves unconventional moral scrutiny. On the contrary, terrorism, like the many enlargements of savagery before it, is a lineal descendant of traditional warfare. It can best be understood and evaluated by analogy with conventional conflict. And I am increasingly of the opinion that it raises not old questions about new kinds of combat but new questions about all the old forms of war. It is warfare's newest and most sobering progeny.[10]

An Attempt to Clarify What Terrorism Is:
Inter bellum et pacem nihil est medium

No sooner had guerrilla fighting been accommodated within the conventions of warfare than terrorism presented a similar challenge. Terrorists characteristically choose symbolic targets rather than those of narrowly military significance. They purposely ignore the conventional distinction between combatants and noncombatants, often choosing to kill or injure civilians. Their purpose is political: to terrorize, to intimidate, to dispirit a government or a people through audacious and brutal aggression. Their actions are the work either of a government that accepts no public responsibility or of a dissident group that has no political standing. There is no declaration of war, no professional military adversary, no willingness by the perpetrators to abide by conventional military constraints.

Getting a definitional clasp on terrorism is difficult. At the present time *terrorism* is so negative, so despised a term that it is frequently used as an epithet without any consistent sense of what it really is. Used in this propagandistic fashion, *terrorist* means your enemy, who is "fanatic," "radical," a "goon." This is the sort of language abuse that produces, for instance, an amusing headline that appeared recently in a Chicago newspaper: "South Africa to Crack Down on Violence."[11]

Some attempts at definition are more serious but still quite self-serving.

Terrorism is "the unlawful use or threatened use of force or violence by a revolutionary organization against individuals or property, with the intention of coercing or intimidating governments or societies, often for political or ideological purposes" (Department of Defense).[12] This definition leaves no room for state terrorism directed either to its own population or to another state.

"Terrorism is defined as the unlawful use of force or violence against persons or property to intimidate or coerce a government, the civilian population or any segment thereof, in furtherance of political or social objectives" (Federal Bureau of Investigation).[13] Identifying terrorism as unlawful force creates a bias in favor of unjust governments that encounter no difficulty in passing laws that authorize intimidation by force. Apartheid, for example, is perfectly lawful.

It is a tactic of indiscriminate violence used against innocent bystanders for political effect—and it must be distinguished from the selective use of violence against the symbols and institutions of a contested power, which is unfortunately a norm of international life" (William E. Colby).[14] According to this norm, a police officer standing on duty at an airport would be fair game for shooting by insurgents because, unlike a civilian, he or she is for them a symbol of a repressive government. This raises questions about the traditional but unreflective assumption that civilians are innocent, while police and military are not.

Terrorism would be "acts committed in time of peace that, if committed by a soldier in time of war, would be war crimes" (International Law Association).[15] On this view of the matter, it would not be a terrorist act for a uniformed soldier to walk into a private home and shoot its owner dead, provided that occupant were an enemy of the state. That is, after all, exactly what soldiers do in war without being accused of war crimes, but that does not prevent such violence from being terrorist.

"One man's terrorist is everyone's terrorist. Terrorism is best defined by the quality of the acts, not by the identity of the perpetrators or the nature of their cause. All terrorist acts are crimes" (Brian Jenkins).[16] But if the act, most bluntly defined, consists of homicide, arson, or house arrest, surely it makes a moral difference who is doing it and why.

Terrorism is the use or threatened use of violence for a political purpose to create a state of fear which will aid in extorting, coercing, intimidating or causing individuals and groups to alter their behavior. A terrorist group does not need a defined territorial base or specific organizational structure. Its goals need not relate to any one country. It does not require nor necessarily seek a popular base of support. Its operations, organization and movements are secret. Its activities do not conform to rules of law or warfare. Its targets are civilians, noncombatants, bystanders or symbolic persons and places. Its victims generally have no role in either causing or correcting the grievance of the terrorists. Its methods are hostage-taking, aircraft piracy or sabotage, assassination, threats, hoaxes, and indiscriminate bombings or shootings (a working definition much used in government today). This definition goes far to distinguish terrorism from insurgency, but it makes it quite difficult to recognize terrorism when it is a policy of a state against its own citizens.

Most definitions seem to lack an adequately large context. If one simply notices the acts themselves that we call terrorist, one thinks of abduction, extortion, mutilation, assassination, massacre, bombing, and the like. The word evokes religious fanaticism, ethnic hatred, class struggle, and a readiness to sacrifice the innocent and the uninvolved. Yet the word *terrorism*, indiscriminately pointed at these acts, can obscure the fact that the ventures we call by that name are really quite diverse politically and morally.

Some terrorism is perpetrated by an ethnic and/or religious (and usually economic) minority that demands self-governance: Basques in Spain, Catholics in Ulster, Huks in the Philippines. Some expresses the nihilist rage of small doctrinal groups that fail to rally public support. Examples might be the Red Brigades, the Weather Underground, and the Armed Forces of Puerto Rican National Liberation (FALN). Some is undertaken by governments threatened by majority dissent, such as in Haiti, Chile, Rhodesia. Some is the venture of a national minority that aspires to control the government. The National Socialists made it a strategy in Weimar Germany; the Zionists employed it in Palestine under the Mandate; the Phalange has been using it to reclaim its lost hegemony in Lebanon. Some emanates from a popular majority that has been disenfranchised. The Mau-Mau movement in Kenya, the FNLA in Mozambique, and some Indian uprisings against Britain could be so described. Some is the policy of a despotic or occupying power beleaguered by a resentful populace. Amritsar, Lidice, and the Ardeatine Caves are memorial names for this sort of terrorism. Some bears down on a victim group on behalf of an antagonized national majority. The Biharis in Bangladesh, the ethnic Chinese in Indonesia, and the Ndebele in Zimbabwe have been its targets. Some is practiced as a combat strategy of armed forces at war. Rotterdam, Dresden, and Hiroshima are a few reminders. And some terrorism is sponsored by governments to discredit, destabilize, and displace the government of another, uncooperative nation it wishes as an ally or as a client. The United States did this in Nicaragua, South Africa did it in Mozambique, and the Soviet Union did it in Hungary, Poland, and Czechoslovakia.

A firebombing is a firebombing; people die the same no matter who threw the torch. Yet in framing a response to an arson incident—an ethically reflective response—there is an enormous difference whether the perpetrators are an unpopular splinter group with no practical agenda, the agents of a tyrannical government, or an oppressed and outraged population that has specific grievances. The phenomenon may be outwardly identical: same explosion, same toll in lives and goods. But there are significant moral, political, and even military differences if one is to understand and respond to the phenomenon. The bombing may be morally reprehensible whoever does it. But for whoever must respond morally to the terrorist act, it surely makes a difference whether it is the work of a tyrant or the tyrant's victims. Even at the level of military responsibility, a commander must know whether he or she is sent to cope with an unpopular clutch of mercenaries or with an aroused national people.

I am not arguing that there is moral and immoral terrorism.[17] What I am arguing is that the background, identity, and purposes of terrorists must be known if one is to frame a moral response to them.[18]

Political Judgment before Moral Assessment:
Inter arma silent leges

An adequate response to terrorism requires a broad perspective: moral, political, strategic, and tactical. One may not restrict one's inquiry and judgment to the narrow, tactical realities. One must have political insight before framing an ethical judgment, no matter what the level of one's responsibility. This is no less true for military and police personnel who have to cope directly with terrorism. Terrorism cannot be addressed as a merely military or criminal phenomenon, for it is also defined by its political context. If a military person is to be a moral person in confronting terrorism, he or she must view it at every level. Even to describe an act as terrorist is to make a political assessment.[19]

There is a hierarchy of perspective and discourse: moral, political, strategic, and tactical. Just as a line officer needs a sophisticated understanding of the strategy before devising appropriate tactical options, the flag officer requires a discriminating grasp of political objectives in order to frame serviceable strategy. And both must be able to evaluate what they are told and what they decide in moral terms. The highest level of consideration—the moral level—requires competence on all intermediate levels, including the political.

By law and by conviction in the United States, military strategy and tactics are subordinated to civilian policy. It is likely to remain that way, for Americans will not accept a military government. Nevertheless, military leaders must frame their strategic and tactical plans in good conscience. And no moral evaluation is possible without some critical judgment of the political significance of the actions that military leaders are directed to confront or undertake.

Military action must remain subject to civilian policy. But both strategy and reality will require a military commander to operate with an educated political perspective comparable with that of the government officials who give the military their orders. Americans want no military junta running the country, but neither do they want Eichmanns serving their rulers.

An illustration of this necessity is afforded by the way the military understood the bombing of the U.S. Marine emplacement at Beirut airport on October 23, 1983. In his testimony before Congress one week later, General Paul Kelley, commandant of the marine corps, explicitly said that his remarks would "avoid discussion of the political or diplomatic considerations of our presence in Lebanon. It is not the place of a Marine to discuss those imperatives for military employment." He then proceeded to describe the marine presence as "conducive to the stability of Lebanon . . . we were guests of a friendly nation—not on occupation duty! . . . The Marines were warmly greeted by the Lebanese people." In that light, he interpreted the bombing: "This unprecedented, massive 'kamikaze' attack was not against young Marines, sailors, and soldiers—it was a vicious, surprise attack against the United States of America and all we stand for in the free world."[20] The general saw it as an act of terrorism. Despite his disclaimer, he was making statements that in every way made political assumptions and judgments.

The Long commission convened by the Department of Defense to investigate the Beirut bombing was even more explicit in its report submitted several months later. The words *terrorist* and *terrorism* occur 178 times in the document. The original portrayal is here amplified. The marines entered Lebanon to a warm reception by the populace, especially as they went about disarming dangerous ordnance left by the fighting of the Israeli invasion. "It was anticipated that the [marines] would be perceived by various factions as evenhanded and neutral." Only later, when they good-naturedly assisted the Lebanese army in its efforts to subdue several villages, did the U.S. military unwittingly incur local displeasure. "Although [U.S.] actions could properly be classified as self-defense and not 'engaging in combat,' the environment could no longer be characterized as peaceful. The image of the [forces], in the eyes of the factional militias, had become pro-Israel, pro-Phalange, and anti-Muslim."[21]

This report betrays the most primitive political and historical understanding. To the Palestinians still in the area, the Americans were the chief client and support of the Israelis who had seized their homeland and driven them out twenty-five years earlier as refugees without hope. To the Shiite Muslims, the United States was the guarantor of a three-decade regime of exploitation and repression by the shah of Iran. To the Sunni Muslims, the United States was the prime obstacle preventing them from displacing the Christians who continued to dominate their country as a violent minority. To the Christians, the United States was the displacer of the Palestinian refugees who had been dumped in their country to ally themselves with the growing Muslim majority with whom they, the Christians, were unwilling to share power. And to every Lebanese, the United States was the funder and protector of the invading Israeli army and air force that had destroyed Beirut and every other city that had fallen beneath their path.

No one who had enough familiarity with the peoples of the region could possibly imagine that the bumbling fantasy of the United States of landing in Lebanon as peacekeeper would be reciprocated with anything but hatred. To them the United States has for nearly four decades been the principal destabilizer of the Middle East. Instead of vilifying the driver of the explosive-laden truck as a crazed, fanatic terrorist, we should rather try to understand what long train of frustration and rejection would make that man—and any number of others ready to do the same—ready to count his life cheap. Thus, to describe his act as terrorist in the hope of degrading it morally or justifying possible reprisals is frivolous. No reliable moral estimate would be possible until one gained enough political savvy to see how the United States has come to be regarded as the major terrorist of the region.[22] The chief of naval operations, Admiral James D. Watkins, has made this same point candidly: "Any moral framework for a response to terrorism cannot be applied in a vacuum, but must be placed in context with the political, military and other realities which necessarily impinge upon the decision making process."[23]

An Understanding of Violence, Innocence, Solidarity:
Aquila non captat muscas

There are still other reasons why Americans must possess a sophistication that is not only political but also historical in order to make a moral response to terrorism.

The U.S. government now has a Department of Defense, whereas for the longest part of its history, it had a Department of War. The change of title reflects the universal human belief that the other nation is always the aggressor, and that the United States is simply trying to restore the peace. For the Allies, World War II began at the Polish border in 1939; for the Germans, hostilities dated back to Versailles. Your military operation is an attack; mine is a retaliation. No one ever claims to have fired a first shot.

Like virtually all other belligerency, terrorism is not perceived by its agents to be a first strike. It is intended as a reprisal. No one will ever comprehend or cope with it without reconstructing the sense of the past that the terrorists harbor.

It is important to the moral claims of the United States to assume the role of injured defender who is intent on restoring a violated peace. The use of the word *terrorist* can be used in this same sort of self-serving way, and military people especially run this risk. When we call people terrorists, we are usually implying that they have breached the peace, that they have initiated a stream of aggressive violence. But usually the stream of violence is an unbroken one, and the people we rush to suppress may themselves be breaking out of a long and gruesome time of violence we had overlooked because it had been imposed under governmental auspices.[24]

Aleksandr Solzhenitsyn has written:

> The opposition of "peace and war" contains a logical error. . . . War is a massive, dense, loud and vivid phenomenon, but it is far from being the only manifestation of the never-ceasing, all-encompassing world-wide violence. The only opposition that is logically equivalent and morally true is: Peace and Violence. . . .
>
> Any spontaneous mass guerilla movement that is genuine, in the sense of not being directed from abroad, may be caused by constant, forcible and unlawful decisions of a government, by systematic violence of the state.
>
> It is this form of established, permanent violence of the state, which has managed to assume all the "juridical" forms through decades of rule, to codify thick compilations of violence-ridden "laws" and to throw the mantle over the shoulders of its "judges," it is this violence that represents the most frightening danger to the peace, although few realize it.
>
> Such violence does not require the planting of explosives or the throwing of bombs. It operates in total silence, rarely broken by the last outcries of those it suffocates.[25]

We must beware of treating terrorist adversaries as violators of the peace if they were roused to rage in the first place by an injustice that had tormented them for years, an injustice of which we were reasonably seen to be the patron and guarantor. If a man has seen his children die from malnutrition because of medical aid withheld, his village ravished by industry that underpaid and sickened the workers, his voice stifled by a dictatorship that tortured patriots, his priests shot for preaching justice, and his wife raped by a plain-clothes death squad—if, after all this, he takes up arms in rage and bombs the vehicle of a government official with the official's innocent family inside, who has broken the peace? And can we, by military reprisal, restore the peace? Or will our reprisal only justify the rightness of his rage in his neighbors' minds and raise up ten more in his place?[26]

Apropos of those innocent family members, Americans must give thought to the peculiarity of their notion that any nation is divided into "innocent" bystanders and "guilty" militants who wear uniforms. Most of humanity throughout most of history has understood families and peoples to cohere in soldarity in ways that are incomprehensible to the rather recent Western views of the individual that date back to the Enlightenment.

Twenty years back, when a band of Africans raided a white man's Rhodesian farm and slaughtered his wife and children, the Western world was filled with loathing at this outrageous violation of the innocent and uninvolved. From the Africans' viewpoint, however, there was no uninvolvement. Those gentle children had been washed, dressed, schooled, and conveyed abroad and entertained and cultivated by dint of the occupation of *their* land and the low-paid labor of *their* backs and the deprivation and humiliation of *their* children. It had been the white children's father's rifle that violated them and their homeland, but it was his family that lived good-naturedly on his violence. How could he be guilty and they be innocent?

Westerners have been similarly chagrined at the practice by insurgents and terrorists of lodging their militants in the midst of an inhabited and sympathetic civilian area. Some of their opponents have complained that they could not attack them there because of danger to civilians; others have gone ahead and attacked on the ground that the civilians forwent their immunity by harboring militants. Westerners might ponder instead the reality that they are really facing an entire people, not just their militant members, and ask themselves what difference this makes for their response.

There are, then, three realities that terrorism introduces into the field of belligerency that move beyond the well-staked battleground of conventional warfare:

1. Terrorism is the warfare of the desperate.
2. Terrorism is a warfare of solidarity: a people against a whole people.
3. Terrorism is a warfare of selective targeting.

These three aspects are present in two remarkably different ways. Some terrorism is the work of a group that lacks public support and sympathy and is flinging itself upon the representatives of an intractable people. Such would be the spoiled, bourgeois adolescents of the Weathermen or the radicalized Baader-Meinhof gang. Their terrorism is desperate because they have so little claim to authority. Their assaults are on anyone in sight because there is hardly anyone whom they can claim as their partisan. The targets they select are symbolic, for their rage is bent upon desecration.

It is otherwise when the agents of terror are a mass of people that has been denied its rightful claim to political influence. Such would be the Ulster Catholics or the blacks of South Africa. Their terrorism is desperate because they have suffered long outrage. Their terrorism is one of solidarity because there is no one in the privileged minority that has not fattened by seizing their nourishment. And their targets are chosen to frighten their oppressors into receding before their massive, yet frustrated, force.

What has been said of peoples can also be said of nation-states that turn to terrorism as a desperate measure against other states and peoples. Terrorism is always the gesture of those who feel themselves at a disadvantage. But it makes a considerable difference whether the terrorizing nation is one that is trying to subdue its rivals or one that is trying to break free of oppression.

Lest anyone imagine that the rise of terrorism has drastically altered the relative advantages in the world of conflict, it should be noted that the cybernetic revolution has made available to both governments and technologically astute dissidents new and potent access to information-based power. Although it is true that terrorism hits the most powerful nations in their soft and vulnerable underbelly, those governments are possessed of even more advantageous means for identifying, pursuing, and neutralizing their enemies, especially if they consider themselves bound by no restraints of law or morality.

The need to see all such matters in context is a moral one. It is for that reason also a practical one: to repress the terrorism of an unpopular and audacious splinter group is one thing; to deny the normal aspirations of an entire people is drastically more difficult and much harder to justify.

A Moral Estimate of Terrorism as Warfare: *Nemo me impune lacessit*

Now let us follow up the proposal that terrorism is in fact not a rejection of warfare but the resort to new and disconcerting measures that are the direct offspring of what we had previously grown familiar with as conventional warfare. To put the thesis to the test, let us see what results if we attempt to apply the traditional ethical doctrine on conventional warfare to the response to terrorism.

The tradition distinguished between the right to go to war (*jus in bellum*) and rightful conduct in war (*jus in bello*). Much of what has passed as moral discrimination between armaments and tactics in war, as defined by treaties, laws, and military codes of discipline, is little more than convention. It simply states what most warring nations agree not to do in order not to risk the same in return. We do not butcher prisoners because we want ours to survive. This is a convention, and indeed a desirable convention. But it is not a canon of morality, as if there would be clear reasons why it would be moral to protect prisoners but also moral to shoot active combatants.

This concentrates the fullest weight of moral inquiry and decision making on the *jus in bellum*: what justifies going to war in the first place? According to the Western tradition of justified warfare, there are five principal requisites for a war to be morally undertaken:

1. Action by a legitimate national authority.
2. A just grievance.
3. The exhaustion of other alternatives.
4. A reasonable likelihood of success.
5. More good foreseen than evil.

Let us see whether these criteria can be applied to counterterrorism.[27]

Action by a Legitimate National Authority

The issue here is not whether a government faced by terrorists is such an authority but whether its adversaries are. The international convention is that nations declare war only on other nations. We are brought to ask, however, whether this need necessarily be so.

A problem presented by terrorism is that while it is in fact an act of armed belligerency—an act of war—it is treated legally as if it were instead an act of crime. While the terrorizing group is acting in solidarity, the nation that is the object of its belligerency acts on the fiction that it faces only individual miscreants and restricts itself to dealing with those persons who can be convicted of actual crimes. International law may need to supply a new category or, better, an extended category of warfare. If a whole people is in fact actively mounting hostilities against a nation (think of the Kurds against Iran, Iraq, and Turkey, or the Mafia against Italy, or the French connection against the United States), then the target nation ought have some deliberative and formalized way of declaring the terrorist group as a whole its adversary.[26] Thus, for instance, the Irish Republican Army Provos as a group might be declared by Great Britain to be its adversary at war. Any member of the belligerent group, not just one who was convictable of violent acts of terrorism, would be at risk of capture.

In the international legal community, the first moves have already begun to accommodate terrorism and its opposition within the conventions of warfare, just as had been done years before for insurgency. But in the meantime sovereign nations are left relatively free to decide whether to acknowledge terrorist enemies as formal belligerents. To date few have been willing to do this.[29]

Furthermore, since terrorism is often undertaken by peoples who are in arms precisely because they have been denied the opportunity for national self-determination, they cannot be represented by a recognized government. The nations they oppose use this as an excuse to deny them legitimate recognition as conventional belligerents, but this is often a self-serving exercise of political self-interest. That way, the dissidents can be classified as criminals instead of as belligerents. Israel, for example, consistently refuses to acknowledge the Palestine Liberation Organization (PLO) as a legitimate representative of the Palestinian people, though Israeli polls have consistently shown that more than 90 percent of the Palestinians resident in the homeland consider the PLO their rightful representative: a degree of support probably greater than what Charles de Gaulle's government in exile in London enjoyed from the French during World War II and twice as strong as any Israeli party has enjoyed from its people since 1948.

It is the legal convention among nations that we recognize established governments as representing the national populace. But there are some countries where this is not true. Is our first obligation of fellowship to the unpopular government or to the people? Are there ways in which we can render the government its formal due while also supporting the people's just claims on our aid? And if this is impossible, then should we not on occasion withdraw our recognition of a government and establish our links of fellowship with other, more credible representatives of the people? If a government is our terrorist adversary, could we not declare war on that government without declaring war on the population? For that matter, could we not declare war on a nonnational group that has in effect entered into systematic hostilities against us? These are possibilites worth considering.

Current moral inquiry on the subject of terrorism has been puzzling over the acceptability of preemption. This may not be the best way of approaching the question. It is only by regarding terrorist activities as distinct acts of criminal violence that we could speak of preemption. The criminal law does not easily permit authorities to move against persons who are contemplating a crime. But if a group is described and declared to be at war, then an action to fend off their intended strike is not preemption but part of a continuing campaign. Once again, the ethical picture depends on the model one chooses to use. If terrorism is merely a crime, then it must be dealt with by according due process to individual persons for individual actions. If it is a state of belligerency, then it must be dealt with by warfare and by the restraints appropriate to warfare.

For any response to a terrorist group to be ethical, then, a nation must acknowledge popular leadership in its adversaries as pragmatically as it recognizes de facto governments after coups, and it must consider the group as a whole as its true challenger.

A Just Grievance

As in the criterion of legitimate authority, the question here is not so much whether a government has a just grievance in defending itself against terrorists but what grievances the terrorists are wanting to redress.

The criminal law gives little sympathy to grievances behind violent acts. It need not be so between warring parties. Before taking action against terrorists, a government must satisfy its conscience about what motivates its adversaries. What is the grievance that has roused them to a violence that is often costly and risky to themselves? Is their cause just though their method wrong? If so, should our response be a redress of their grievances instead of a reprisal? We have no easy way of acceding gracefully to criminals. Still, we must learn to yield to belligerents who are rising against injustice and oppression.[30]

Patience and magnanimity are peacekeeping virtues. They are required to pursue the norms of a just war. The vice that defeats these norms is hubris. It is an act of hubris to refuse to visualize the character, motivation, and popular constituency of one's adversary.

When we can bring ourselves to recognize no fair grievance, then we are obliged to suppress a terrorist movement. The discernment of justice will be sensitive to whether the terrorists are a group that attempts to manipulate a larger people or a group that has been manhandled. A military junta and a national population would not have the same benefit of doubt. A dissident minority patronized by an imperial power would have grievances more suspect than the national population they opposed.

A nation that must address a terrorist adversary, then, has the highest moral obligation to discern what the terrorists have experienced and what are their complaints. That nation must, ironically, make a reflective moral appraisal of the grievances of its adversary before allowing itself to respond with the use of force. In the face of passion and anger, the offended and affronted government is morally compelled to use patience and dispassionate objectivity. Granted the heroic difficulty of such objectivity, it may be that nations should turn to detached, judicious outsiders to render their opinion before any decision is made. A moral decision to move into war against terrorists requires mighty patience and discernment of grievances.

Exhaustion of Other Alternatives

The first alternative always to be considered is the satisfaction of terrorists' demands, and nothing could be less agreeable to their target nation.

The natural instinct of all victims of terrorism is outrage and the desire to retaliate. But leaders of state and of the armed services, perhaps more than any other citizens, have the duty not to operate on instinct, especially this sort of instinct, for it is most likely to increase the force of the vortex of violence. Secretary of State George Shultz has given voice to the retaliatory instinct in its simplest form: "Our goal must be to prevent and deter future terrorist acts, and experience has taught us over the years that one of the best deterrents to terrorism is the certainty that swift and sure measures will be taken against those who engage in it."[31] The classic embodiment of this instinct is to be found in Israel, where retaliation has become, in the words of one former head of military intelligence, "a conditioned reflex."[32] Other senior Israeli personnel have privately admitted that the policy of instinctive, escalated reprisal has done nothing to stem the virulence of terrorism or to bring peace within their grasp, but it has become a habit from which they seem unable to free themselves. The history of the state of Israel is the world's best contemporary example of how incessant resistance to injustice cannot be repressed by reprisals.

The Allied bombing policy during World War II, in reprisal for the German bombing of English cities, was a similarly terrorist destruction of the German civilian population. The result of this reprisal was the increased conviction that they could not capitulate. The earlier German bombing of Rotterdam, in its turn in retaliation for the unexpected military defense by the Netherlands, simply motivated the creation of the Dutch resistance movement. Reprisal is so rarely an end to things and so often a renewal of the cycle of violence.

I am not making the case that terrorists should be given satisfaction simply because they have indulged in violence. My point is that terrorists should not be denied redress and satisfaction simply because they are terrorists. It is in the national interest not be blinded by outrage but to ascertain whether we are dealing with people who are themselves the victims of earlier, and possibly more grievous, injury: injury that we may have inflicted or conspired in or from which we can give them relief. To fail in this inquiry out of anger is to fail in one of the primary duties of patient statecraft.

When there is no justice in terrorist demands, then the next alternative is measured retaliation: purposefully restrained, with the promise of harsher reprisal to follow. Should that not stay the hand of terrorism, then is the time to declare that belligerency has begun. After that, the strategy is not to await further strikes in order to strike back but to move to capture or to destroy the terrorists. Nothing could be clearer at this point than the difference between a small band of destructive criminals, such as the Colombian drug network, and a great national populace, such as the combined peoples of Central America. It is conceivable that the former could be dispersed and destroyed. It is inconceivable that the latter could be and unthinkable that the United States should undertake it.

Reasonable Likelihood of Success

The only success is peace, and the only steady ground under peace is justice. A nation must ask whether a belligerent response to a terrorist attack will quench hostility or only foment more determined resistance and widespread sympathy.[33] Will it enlarge the conflict? Will it rupture the relations we now maintain with the sponsoring group? They may only be civil and formal, but even so they may offer an access to reconciliation that rupture would remove. Would a belligerent response lead to confrontation with a more formidable patron power?

Every nation must ask its people, especially its military and its police, to absorb outrage when no reasonable advantage is likely to accrue from a hostile response. It must be endured. Once again, one sees the difference between an adversary group of terrorist criminals and an adversary nation. The one group may much more easily be neutralized by armed response than the other, which ultimately cannot be either squelched or destroyed. It must be rendered peaceable, and this is not deftly done by belligerent response.

On the other hand, the principal service of war is to make people once again prefer peace. Not until the two peoples loathe the war more than the price they must pay for peace will they cease their hostilities. And there are some injustices so despicable that men and women will count their lives cheap in resisting them. It is this sort of readiness to sacrifice oneself that we must be noticing in our terrorist adversaries, especially if they are an entire people. There is little reasonable likelihood of success against such a people except by coming to terms.

More Good Foreseen Than Evil

The primary risk in responding to terrorism is the moral danger to the respondent: what brutalization of character do we incur if we enter into comparable hostilities or, on the other hand, if we stand idly by? By striking out at terrorists, one may seize the advantage. But by striking out intemperately, a nation may sacrifice the advantage of moral sympathy from other nations. The difficulty in applying this criterion for justified belligerency is that one must compare such incommensurables: human life with property, urgent needs of the moment with long-term values, individual welfare with the common good.

The ultimate good is the creation of peace. Every response to terrorism must have as its desired outcome that the terrorist people would eventually become allies. Thus we must measure how far we can go in destroying their dignity and driving them into insensate and irredeemable hostility.

When terrorism is an act of covert warfare initiated by another state and all parties know that, we face a severe conflict. Do we wish to suppress public mention of the true source of the violence in order not to exacerbate what remains of our public relationship, or is the crisis so acute and our opportunity to prevail so likely that we would choose a public showdown? What response is vigorous enough to maintain the respect that may discourage further attempts at terrorism yet not so headlong that we are entrapped into needless forfeiture of life and property? Is there a response available that might cope with the terrorist program itself but that, once introduced into accepted usage, would find us as an especially vulnerable and exposed potential victim?

The Goal: Peace Not Capitulation: *Opus justitiae pax*

Many conflicts come to apparent cloture through the capitulation of one party to another, yet peace is not really created, and a resentment is left to fester until another more violent day.

The criteria for rightful entry into belligerency against another power offer an array of challenges to those in public office who must determine how to respond to terrorism. The just war test meets the terrorist situation well: well enough to lead to the expectation that terrorism will eventually be seen not as an anomaly in international relations but as one more of the degenerate progeny of conventional warfare.

Weapons development early in this century had elicited three distinct reactions. Some thought the new devices were horrendous and therefore immoral. Others thought they were so horrendous that people would become more reluctant to engage in war. Still others thought that they were indeed horrendous but that they only brought out more clearly how horrendous all warfare had always been. The realities of terrorism may justify all three conclusions. Terrorism is indeed savage and inhumane. It is a moral quagmire into which a nation steps at its peril, for it may be as bottomless as quicksand. And yet it brings to the light the essential character of warfare, which, despite conventions and mutual restraints, is a form of inhumane savagery that threatens at any moment to break loose into uncontrollable destruction. Inquiry into the nature and ethical imperatives of terrorism is sound only if we do not imagine that it is inhumane by contrast with war, which is humane. Conventional warfare is conventionally inhumane.

There is a double paradox about peace being the desired outcome of belligerency. On the one hand, you may not be preserving the peace by refusing to fight. Thomas Jefferson, who had explicitly renounced any resort to warfare, eventually sent the navy to suppress the Barbary pirates. He explained, "Against such a banditti, war had become less ruinous than peace, for then peace was a war on one side only."[34] Yet on the other hand, armed intervention can destroy the possibility of peace when its target is a resolute group of men and women who believe themselves to be defending their families, their homes and homeland, their faith and their freedom: in short, the precious things people are willing to die for. Every decision to use force or to abstain from force can be justified only by its realistic claim to make peace more possible.

Notes

1. John Hewitt, *Ancient Armour and Weapons in Europe* (London: Henry and Parker, 1855), p. 158.

2. See, for instance, the passage where Hotspur quotes a dandy he disliked in Shakespeare's *1 Henry IV* 1, 3: 59–64.

> And that it was great pity, so it was,
> This villainous saltpetre should be digg'd
> Out of the bowels of the harmless earth,
> Which many a good tall fellow had destroyed
> So cowardly, and but for these vile guns
> He would himself have been a soldier.

3. *St. Louis Star* and *Norfolk Virginian-Pilot*, quoted in "Viper Weapons," *Literary Digest*, December 24, 1921, pp. 8–9. See also "The Herald of Gospel Liberty," quoted in "Christian Consciousness and Poison Gas," *Literary Digest*, January 8, 1921, p. 38: 'The whole 'gas' enterprise is only another leaf out of the book of militarism which has been written into the history of our nation just at the present time by those who make profit and gain out of war—but it is a page that ought to arouse every Christian conscience to a quick and defiant resentment in behalf of the honor and nobleness of America, against which it ought not for a moment be possible to bring even the suggestion of such inhuman practices, no matter what the rest of the nations of the world may do."

4. "Chemical Warfare," publication of the Chemical Warfare Service of the U.S. Army, quoted in "Viper Weapons."

5. One journal welcomed chemical warfare as possibly "making war humane. ... The real reason for the instinctive aversion manifested against any new art, or mode of attack is that it reveals to us the intrinsic horror of war. We naturally revolt against premeditated homicide, but we have become so accustomed to the sword and latterly to the rifle that they do not shock us as they ought when we think of what they are made for. "Fighting with Fumes—A Humane Innovation?" *Independent*, May 10, 1915, pp. 227–228.

6. All too often the law is accepted as possessed of intrinsic moral value rather than as a conventional norm that should, but may not, correspond to a moral imper-

ative. For instance, some define terrorism as immoral simply because it operates outside the law. "Terrorism, that is, international and politically motivated terrorism, is impermissible use of political violence. . . . It is impermissible morally because it is not restrained by the rule of law or the laws of war." Ernest W. Lefever, in "Terrorism: A National Issues Seminar," *World Affairs* 146 (Summer 1983): 104. This has been enunciated even more bluntly and crudely by C.E. Zoppo: "Custom is law, law is morality. . . . Politics basically defines what is moral." "The Moral Factor in Interstate Politics and International Terrorism," in David C. Rapoport and Yonah Alexander, eds., *The Rationalization of Terrorism* (Frederick, Md.: University Publications of America, 1982), pp. 137, 144. Leszek Kolakowski writes: "The worst atrocities committed by the Soviet government against its own people, including the genocide during Stalin's regime, have been for the most part entirely legal." *Harper's* 269 (October 1984): 46.

7. See *The Law of Land Warfare*, U.S. Department of the Army Field Manual 27-10 (Washington: Government Printing Office, 1956). This manual has enjoyed an extended existence and has been much cited in judicial proceedings.

8. The 1977 Geneva Protocols attempt to draw international irregular conflicts into the ordinary regulations of Geneva and even to extend these provisions (regarding prisoner of war status) to domestic belligerents. The language of the protocols remains hedged, however, and has left it up to signatory nations to decide whether to accord the status of belligerent to terrorists. Typically they will not. In some countries, however (Vietnam, Northern Ireland), captive insurgents have been in fact treated as prisoners of war or as political prisoners even though they may not have been awarded that status formally by the protocols or by the government. See the protocols in Dietrich Schindler and Jirit Toman, *The Laws of Armed Conflicts* (Geneva: Henry Dunant Institute, 1981).

9. My colleague Stanley Hauerwas is persuaded that the crossbow and longbow were outlawed because they constituted a new and formidable handicap to the way knights fought in battle. It was thus as much a class issue as a moral one since the newer forms of archery gave too much advantage to the peasants and threatened the entire order of chivalry. Even without this suggestion, one might observe that much of the outrage against guerrilla warfare, and subsequently against insurgent terrorism, has been turned by the affluent upon the poor.

10. See Harry G. Summers, Jr., "What Is War?" *Harper's* 268 (May 1984): 75–78.

11. For two splendidly opposed views of who are the terrorists in South Africa, see Paul Rich, "Insurgency, Terrorism and the Apartheid System in South Africa," *Political Studies* 32 (1984): 68–85; Keith Campbell, "Prospects for Terrorism in South Africa," *South Africa International* 14 (October 1983): 397–417.

12. DOD Directive 2000.12.

13. "Stuart Taylor, Jr., "When Is a Terrorist Not Necessarily a Terrorist?" *New York Times* December 12, 1984, p. 14Y.

14. William E. Colby, "Taking Steps to Contain Terrorism," *New York Times*, July 8, 1984, p. 21E.

15. See Alfred P. Rubin, letter to the editor, *New York Times*, July 28, 1984, p. 22Y.

16. Brian M. Jenkins, "Statements about Terrorism," *Annals of the American Academy of Political and Social Science* 463 (September 1982): 12.

17. There are, however, some intellectually serious moves in that direction. See, for example, Robert Young, "Revolutionary Terrorism, Crime and Morality," *Social Theory and Practice* 4(Fall 1977): 287–302; H. Odera Oruka, "Legal Terrorism and Human Rights," *Praxis International* (January 1982): 376–385.

18. Aleksandr Solzhenitsyn writes: "The great world organization of man was unable to bring forth even a moral condemnation of terrorism. A selfish majority in the United Nations countered such a condemnation with yet another effort at dubious distinction by asking whether any form of terrorism was in fact harmful. And what is the definition of terrorism, anyway? They might well have suggested in jest: 'when we are attacked, it's terrorism, but when we do the attacking, it's a guerilla movement of liberation.' But let's be serious. They refuse to regard as terrorism a treacherous attack in a peaceful setting, on peaceful people, by military men carrying concealed weapons and often dressed in plain clothes. They demand instead that we study the aims of terrorist groups, their bases of support and their ideology, and then perhaps acknowledge them to be sacred 'guerillas.' (The term 'urban guerillas' in South America almost approaches the humoristic level.)" "Peace and Violence," *New York Times*, September 15, 1973, p. 27M.

19. Arthur Wolffers observes, in the opposite direction, that a political or judicial understanding of terrorism implies moral judgments: "Philosophische Überlegungen zum Terrorismus," *Archiv für Rechts- und Sozialphilosophie* 66 (1980): 453–468.

20. White Letter No. 6-83, Headquarters U.S. Marine Corps, November 4, 1983.

21. Report of the DOD Commission on Beirut International Airport Terrorist Act, October 23, 1983 (December 20, 1983).

22. "We must recognize that the real problem facing the United States in the Middle East is not crazed terrorists driving stolen vans but the widening gulf between America and the Arabs." Augustus R. Norton, "The Climate for Mideast Terrorism," *New York Times*, September 26, 1984, p. 23A.

23. Admiral James D. Watkins, "Countering Terrorism: A New Challenge to Our National Conscience," *Sea Power* (November 1984): 37.

24. John F. McCamant gives an interesting illustration of how selective the public view can be of terrorism. "How far the antiseptic view of government permeates the U.S. culture was demonstrated by reports on the 1982 elections in El Salvador. Newspaper editorials waxed enthusiastic about the large turnout of voters and exclaimed what a wonderful example of democracy the elections were. President Ronald Reagan said that we in the United States should be inspired by the Salvadoran example. It had been public knowledge for some time that some 30,000 civilians had been killed for political reasons over the previous two years, mostly by government troops, and that six leaders of the opposition Revolutionary Democratic Front were dragged by government troops from their last meeting in San Salvador in November, 1980, and brutally murdered. Yet the 200 observers brought in for the occasion still reported that the elections were free and fair. The public imagination seemed incapable of putting human rights violations together with political processes." "Governance without Blood: Social Science's Antiseptic View of Rule: or, The Neglect of Political Repression," in Michael Stohl and George A Lopez, eds., *The State as Ter-*

rorist: The Dynamics of Governmental Violence and Repression, Contributions in Political Science 103 (Westport, Conn.: Greenwood Press, 1984), p. 12.

25. Solzhenitsyn, "Peace and Violence."

26. See William F. May, "Terrorism as Strategy and Ecstasy," *Social Research* (Summer 1974): 277–98.

27. This has been done, interestingly and competently, by Watkins, "Countering Terrorism," pp. 35–37. He had essayed the same argument earlier, in his commencement address that May (1984) at the U.S. Naval Academy.

28. Recent legislation against organized crime has moved somewhat in this direction by considering the entire enterprise as a conspiracy and thus under a criminal cloud from the start.

29. See Alfred P. Rubin, "Terrorism and the Laws of War," *Denver Journal of International Law and Policy* 12 (Spring 1983): 219–235.

30. For two differing partisan estimates of how the Carter and the Reagan administrations have related the defense of human rights with opposition to terrorism, see remarks by Elliott Abrams and Robert A. Blair in *World Affairs* 146 (Summer 1983): 69–78, 114–116. Walter Laqueur has some sobering conclusions on how little terrorism has actually abated even when attention has been given to its expressed grievances and also how little terrorism itself has accomplished. *Terrorism* (Boston: Little, Brown, 1977), pp. 215–226.

31. Address to the Park Avenue Synagogue, New York City, quoted in *New York Times,* October 26, 1984, p. 6Y.

32. Thomas L. Friedman, quoting Aharon Yariv, in "Israel Turns Terror Back on the Terrorists, But Finds No Political Solution," *New York Times,* December 4, 1984, p. 8Y.

33. For a study of the delicacy and weight of public opinion regarding terrorism, see Albert Legault, "La dynamique du terrorisme: Le cas des Brigades rouges," *Etudes Internationales* 14 (December 1983): 639–681.

34. Letter to John Wayles Eppes, September 11, 1813, In Paul L. Ford, ed., *The Writings of Thomas Jefferson* (New York: G.P. Putnam's Sons, 1898), 9:396. Jefferson is also remembered to have said that "an insult unpunished is the parent of others." See n. 31.

15
Terrorism and the Media Revolution

W.D. Livingstone

> It is no daring prophecy to say that knowledge of how to create
> consent will alter every political calculation and modify every po-
> litical premise.
>
> —Walter Lippmann, 1922

Satellites, microwave relays, and portable video cameras and recorders have radically altered the structure and content of television news broadcasting. Video cameras linked to satellites can instantly transport television viewers to the corners of the earth and beyond into space. The development of new technology has created a tidal wave of pictorial information and has even changed the definition of what is news.

In years past, television news programs relied on anchor people to read brief overviews of the day's events. News now means seeing pictures of an actual event. It means immediacy, going live to a reporter on the scene. To capture the attention of the viewers, the news above all must be punchy, colorful, and fast paced. If video pictures are unavailable, there is little chance the story will be reported unless it is of major consequence. The Afghan rebels' battle against the Soviet Army and the Iran-Iraq war receive attention only occasionally due to the unavailability of video pictures. By comparison, the military incursion by Israel into Lebanon in 1982 was broadcast nightly on news programs since camera crews were able to document the shelling of Beirut and the fighting in the war-torn streets.

In the same way that the technological evolution in television is responsible for changing the dynamics of news broadcasting, it is now altering the strategy and the methods terrorists employ to gain access to the media and thus communicate their grievances and demands to the general public. It used to be that professional video cameras were owned and operated only by the major television stations. Few could afford $80,000 for a camera or had the required knowledge in electronics to operate the sophisticated machinery. Recent advances in the development of video technology, however, have made electronic communication affordable and accessible to the lay public. Compact and easy to operate professional cameras can be purchased for less than $6,000. Home video cameras cost much less. Thus terrorists can easily get their hands on portable video cameras and recorders. Such a development forebodes a new era in terrorism and is likely to kindle serious problems for the media and government officials. The opportunities to manipulate the media through video communication present a new threat to the Western world and could lead to a crisis in the First Amendment and the free flow of information because of its unique power to transmit horror and provocations.

Already there have been scattered incidences where terrorists have utilized video technology to record material for distribution on television stations. In January 1985, for instance, a terrorist group believed to be in Lebanon relied on videotape to disclose to the world that U.S. diplomat William Buckley and other kidnapped Americans were still alive. In a 56 second videotape, Buckley was recorded making a plea for help to the U.S. government. Visnews. an international television news service, played back the videotape to reporters and made the recording available to NBC, which broadcast an excerpt on the evening news.[1]

In another recent incident, a quasi-terrorist group identifying themselves as the Animal Liberation Front (ALF) produced a ¾ inch videotape showing several members of the organization breaking into an experimental animal laboratory at the University of California in Riverside.[2] According to the People for the Ethical Treatment of Animals (PETA), which is based in Washington D.C., the ALF offered NBC the videotape for its exclusive use. Four days after the break-in, NBC broadcast a story on the evening news about experiments on animals, incorporating video pictures provided by the ALF.

Finally, in a suicide bombing to protest the Israeli occupation of Lebanon, a seventeen-year-old Shiite Muslim girl drove a Peugeot car loaded with 440 pounds of explosive into an Israeli convoy, killing two soldiers. What makes this incident especially noteworthy is the fact that a videotape of the girl, Sana Mhaydali, was produced prior to the bombing. Sitting behind a desk, wearing a camouflage uniform and a red beret, Mhaydali explained why she was willing to sacrifice her life and urged other young girls in her country to join in the National Resistance Front to drive Israel out of Lebanon. In a matter of weeks after her death, Mhaydali achieved martyrdom, due in large part to the production of the videotape and its effective distribution throughout the region.[3]

In each instance, terrorists were able to communicate their message vividly and forcefully to the public because of the advantages of video recordings. Seeing is believing. Producing the material on videotape created theater and increased the likelihood that the terrorists' stories would be broadcast by major television networks.

Targeting the Media

"The media are the terrorist's best friend," Walter Laqueur, a noted expert on terrorism, explains. "The terrorist's act by itself is nothing; publicity is all."[4]

Given the need for terrorists to publicize their acts widely on the world stage, one would expect that they would be masters of communication. Fortunately for modern society, this has not proved to be the case. For the most part, terrorists have failed to exploit fully the channels of communication. They have been content to attack targets and then let the media almost singlehandedly communicate the stories to the general public. Given the growing sophistication of terrorism, along with the necessity to provide video pictures, however, it can be only a matter of time before terrorists realize that their acts of violence can be amplified a thousandfold by taking the time to understand and accommodate the technical requirements of producing news for mass media.

Terrorists who simply distribute printed material to the media detailing their political demands have learned that there is little chance that their views will be reported by local newspapers and radio stations, much less by the national media. Hence, they rely on violence. They know that journalists will report when and where an attack occurred, the extent of the damage, who is responsible, and why the attack was instigated. Blood and guts is news. Terrorists hope that stories by the press covering such incidents will emphasize their message.

For fifteen years, insurgents in Angola, Mozambique, and French Guinea conducted rural guerrilla warfare with little effect or public notice. When a similar number of Palestinians moved their battleground from the West Bank to the cities of Europe, their grievances quickly became front-page news around the world. Gaining access to the mass media, they understood, magnified their voice and was responsible for exerting pressure on Western governments to seek a resolution to the conflict.[5]

While violence in and of itself usually is newsworthy, past events demonstrate that it can also overshadow the communiqués terrorists hope to bring to the attention of the public. The Palestinians successfully achieved international acclaim following their spate of bombings. But in the process, they forfeited a level of respect and credibility because of their attacks on innocent people. Instead of the media discussing the reasons behind their violent attacks, the Palestinians themselves became the issue.

This double-edged sword of violence has led many terrorist groups to employ innovative techniques to ensure their messages are broadcast over the airwaves or printed in newspapers. In Uruguay during the early 1970s, the Tupamaros briefly took control of various radio stations in order to broadcast their political views directly over the air.[6] In another incident, a group of terrorists shot their way into an OPEC meeting and held the oil ministers hostage, demanding that the Austrian government transmit over the radio a declaration calling on the Arab world to rise against Israel.[7] In 1975, Croatian nationalists hijacked a TWA jetliner and demanded that the *Washington Post*, the *New York Times*, the *Chicago Tribune*, and the *International Herald Tribune* print two documents, which the papers agreed to do reluctantly.[8]

In each of these hit-and-run attacks, the terrorists were able to communicate through the mass media an unedited message to the general public. But the success of their techniques still did not guarantee that the public would accept their point of view. Gaining direct access to the various media for terrorists often is more a matter of symbolism than substance. Broadcasting a message over the airwaves or having it printed in a newspaper one time only, terrorists realize, proves little and persuades almost no one. Still, given the current trends of terrorism, it can be expected that terrorists will increasingly embrace more elaborate and complex techniques to communicate their grievances that will use violence sparingly, while maximizing the distribution of their message. As Brian Jenkins points out, "Terrorists want a lot of people watching and a lot of people listening, not a lot of people dead."[9]

Attempting to limit the number of innocent deaths in attacks for terrorists may seem clear-cut, but it poses a catch-22. Violence provides the battering ram terrorists need to gain access to the mass media, yet at the same time it discredits the message they might hope to communicate. To resolve these conflicting goals, it is inevitable that many terrorists will begin to publicize a single attack or kidnapping as widely as possible. In this way they can attenuate negative reactions to the use of violence. Carrying out a series of violent attacks that are not widely publicized will yield an equal amount of media coverage as of a single attack that is widely publicized.

Terrorists have only begun to examine the possibilities for manipulating the media to communicate their messages. To understand the potential threat to society of television terrorism, consider how television reporters usually cover a story on terrorism. There is a bombing somewhere. Cameramen from local and national television stations scramble to the scene of the attack. All is confusion. Rubble litters the ground. Amid flashing lights and ambulances speeding to hospitals, medics attend to the wounded, while the police comb the area for clues to the crime. Television cameras document the aftermath of the attack on videotape while reporters begin piecing together the news story. The most dramatic element of the attack—the explosion—must be recounted by eyewitnesses. Only the wreckage is communicated by pictures. In other words, the public is told about the bombing, whereas they actually see the damage caused by the explosion.

The visual impact of the destruction alone is enough to cause widespread concern among the public and government officials. Terrorists are trying to capture the public's attention, yet the most vivid and shocking aspect of their crime—the visual explosion and subsequent death of innocent people—is never communicated. It is not possible for terrorists to alert journalists of an impending attaack or kidnapping without compromising their objectives. Still terrorists may soon begin to compensate for this missing element. Just as public relations firms now assist the media when they cover news events, the threat exists that terrorists will begin to assist reporters assigned to cover terrorist attacks by recording on film or videotape their bombings or hostage incidents to strengthen the impact.

Having already demonstrated a familiarity with video equipment, terrorists cannot but notice its advantage over other means of communication. Consequently it can only be a matter of time before they also begin to experiment with the possibilities of video communication. From atop a building or through a darkened window in Beirut, the day may soon come when a terrorist group will focus a portable video camera equipped with a telephoto lens on a car bomb several blocks away. At the appropriate time, the terrorist will turn on a video recorder to document the destruction and then distribute the tape to the media.

To date, the ALF has employed some of the most sophisticated techniques in video terrorism. Instead of just taking clinical photographs of experimental animals to document their allegations that they are inhumanely treated, the quasi-terrorists have recorded hooded AFL members breaking into a laboratory using a hand-held camera. Such cinema verité images add drama to the pictures. It strengthened their visual impact and increased the likelihood that they would be used on national television.

The threat of television terrorism using portable video cameras and recorders is only the beginning. In addition to providing video recordings to television stations, the possibility exists that terrorists may also apply similar techniques to increase their coverage on radio stations and in newspapers. Just as the public has yet to see actual pictures of a terrorist bombing from beginning to end on television, they have not seen similar photographs in a newspaper or heard the sound effects of a bombing on the radio. As terrorists learn to produce specific media to manipulate television, they will in all probability adopt the same ideas in order to gain access to the airways and the front pages of newspapers. If the ALF had used a 35 mm photographic camera instead of a video camera to take pictures of their break-in and the distraught animals, in all probability they would have generated numerous stories in newspapers in the same manner as they generated stories on television. The same process can also be applied to radio stations. The sound of a bombing or, for that matter, the voice of diplomat William Buckley making a plea to the U.S. government for help can be as dramatic and powerful for radio audiences as pictures recorded by a video camera.

There is no limit to the creative opportunities—and danger to the society—for terrorists to dramatize and cajole the press to use their material.

Reuven Frank, the producer for NBC's "Huntley-Brinkley Report," observed in 1963 that the "highest power of television journalism is not in the transmission of information, but in transmission of experience . . . joy, sorrow, shock, fear." This he said, "was the stuff of news."[10] As terrorists begin to communicate directly their acts of terror, it will inevitably call into question the growing threat of television terrorism and the need to limit or censor such media ploys.

Media Morality

Once terrorists regularly distribute to the media recordings or photographs to illustrate in detail their attacks and demands, an ethical question arises: will the media use the material in their news stories, or will they shun such obvious manipulation and not play into the terrorists' hands? Reaction to this threat varies among journalists. Louise Schiavone, the Associated Press Radio correspondent for the U.S. Senate, said that she is undecided on what she would do if she received an audio recording supplied by terrorists. "As a news reporter," she explained, "you have the responsibility to report the news. And in the electronic media, you have the responsibility to illustrate it with whatever means you have available to you."[11] She remarked that it would be "tantalizing" to use material of an actual attack even though it was recorded by terrorists. But she quickly added that if she did incorporate such material in a broadcast, she would "naturally have to qualify it and say the tape was produced by terrorists, and supplied to [her] by terrorists."[12]

John Dancy, a top television news correspondent for NBC, said when queried about this ominous possibility that he believes his network would not broadcast a videotape of a bombing provided by terrorists. "Obviously, your first reaction is to use it," he said. "But I think we have a larger responsibility to say, are we going to accept and thereby foster that sort of thing."[13] Still, Dancy admitted that if someone had provided a videotape of the attack on the marine barracks in Beirut—even if it were produced by terrorists—it would have been broadcast. Dancy makes a moral judgment between videotape recordings produced by terrorists of a bombing and of a hostage held by terrorists. NBC broadcast pictures of U.S. diplomat William Buckley earlier this year. In this case, Dancy reasoned, "There was a certain public interest to be gained [by showing the videotape on television] because the victim was shown alive and well at a fixed point in time."[14]

The more media having access to video and audio recordings of a terrorist attack, the greater the likelihood that they will be tempted to use the material. If television and radio stations know that their competition have videotapes of a terrorist attack, that newspapers have photographs, can the media individually afford to hold back and not distribute the information?

Jody Powell, President Carter's press secretary, sees competition among the media to achieve high ratings as the driving force behind most decisions. The excesses in journalism during the Iran crisis and the hijacking of TWA flight 847, Powell believes, are a product of competition "for ratings and circulation between newspapers and networks and for personal advancement within a given news organization."[15]

If the major radio and television stations stand resolute and refuse to broadcast terrorist-produced material, terrorists may be tempted to distribute videotapes and recordings to smaller markets. According to some journalists, small markets are less sophisticated and would be more inclined to broadcast such material. But the fact that the major media stations refrain from showing videotapes produced by terrorists in itself is a story, further kindling pressure on networks to broadcast the pictures. Once a code of silence is broken, news tends to spread quickly. When the *Washington Post* broke a story about a defense satellite aboard one of the space shuttles, the networks, which originally had declined to broadcast the story because it was supposedly classified information, quickly changed their mind and followed the *Post*'s lead. This same pattern of events could unfold if the large media markets initially decline to show terrorist-produced material, while smaller media markets make no such agreements.

Media Mirrors

If the media ultimately decide not to censor videotapes and recordings produced by terrorists, this decision may dangerously offer terrorists unlimited opportunities for manipulating the media. Gone will be the fine line between illusion and reality. The possibility exists that terrorists will no longer have to initiate an attack every time they want to get their statements distributed to the general public. The threat exists that terrorists will begin producing videotapes in order to get their messages communicated.

If a terrorist organization detonates a bomb or kidnaps an official, a degree of credibility is established, and any subsequent threat terrorists may make must be taken seriously by law enforcement officials, the media, and the public. Imagine a videotape of a terrorist clad in black garb leaning up against a wall holding a machine gun. A single light overhead casts shadows across the terrorist's face, hidden from view by a ski mask. As the camera slowly zooms in, the terrorist, in a gruff voice scrambled to protect his identity, sets forth a series of demands and threatens to detonate another bomb or kidnap another official if the demands are not met.

If such a tape were distributed, the media would be faced with a deepening quagmire: use the material or refrain from such extortion? Not mentioning the threatened attack could endanger the public's safety. But if they report the threat, will they encourage a contagious spread of such terroristic techniques? A camera is a tool limited only by the imagination. If terrorists produce videotapes and audio recordings the media will broadcast, there is no end to the scenarios terrorists can create to terrorize the public.

Supposing that the media can be blackmailed to broadcast the video images, it is even possible for terrorists, using techniques designed for motion picture production, to create false scenarios. In the movies, a plastic pouch of blood combined with a small explosive charge are placed beneath an actor's clothing to simulate a gunshot. When the charge is set off, it rips a hole in the clothing, and blood pours out of the pouch, simulating a bullet wound. If terrorists were to use this technique during a mock assassination, creating the impression that a kidnapped victim was killed, it would surely generate an emotional public outcry. The next day, in another videotape, terrorists could expose the ruse, showing the victim alive, again possibly gaining access to the mass media. In the end, if the hostage were released, it would minimize the public's indignation over the use of violence.

In each scenario, the threat exists that a video recording could create a powerful dramatic effect sufficient to captivate both the media's and the public's attention.

Public's Right to Know

When a terrorist incident occurs, the journalist's job is to report it. But journalists must face the inevitable question: Are they being played by terrorists "like a violin"?[16]

In 1977, a storm of protest was ignited by the media following their coverage of two events: the Anthony Kiritsis case in Indianapolis and the Hanafi Muslim siege in Washington, D.C. Anthony Kiritsis believed that a mortgage company had cheated him in a deal to build a small shopping center. He kidnapped an executive of the company, Richard Hall, and attached a sawed-off shotgun to his neck. Over the next four days, Indianapolis television stations broadcast live reports on each development of the crisis, often interrupting their regular programming. The possibility existed at any moment that Hall would be murdered. Kiritsis held a 23 minute press conference, which was carried live by two television stations, and several times telephoned a radio station to present his case directly to the public. In the end, the police were successful in negotiating a peaceful resolution to the crisis. The shotgun was removed, and Kiritsis was taken into custody. After the incident, the media questioned whether they should have provided so much media coverage, especially when considering that Kiritsis was distraught and seeking publicity.

One month later, a dozen Hanafi Muslims stormed three buildings in

Washington, D.C., taking 130 hostages. Television reporters, dispatched to the scene of the attack, almost immediately began to broadcast live reports. Journalists, in hot pursuit of a story, directly interviewed the terrorists, tying up telephone lines, and in one case, they nearly foiled an attempt by law enforcement officials to rescue a group of hostages. NBC-TV alone assigned eighteen camera crews to cover the crisis. Over three nights, NBC allocated nearly 36 minutes of air time to report on the story, ABC 26 minutes, and ABC about 22 minutes.[17]

The media were severely criticized as a result of their interference and the intensity of their reporting. As a result, in the months following, numerous seminars were organized by the media to discuss the problems associated with covering a terrorist incident. Journalists sought to answer questions about the proper role of the media and probed for ways to prevent such mistakes from occurring again. If the media failed to regulate their reporting on terrorist incidences, many feared the government would be tempted to try to restrict or regulate their actions in the future.

Guidelines subsequently drafted by CBS—and many other television stations and newspapers—stated that they would try to work more closely with law enforcement officials to avoid any interference. Although CBS said it would continue to report the demands made by terrorists since this was an essential component of a story, officials did state they would restrict live coverage of terrorist kidnappers except in the "most compelling circumstances." But CBS remained adamant in protecting its rights under the First Amendment. William Small, then senior vice-president for CBS News, emphasized that the media "should never agree not to cover a news story such as a terrorist attack."[18] Small argued that CBS, as well as the press in general, had an obligation to the public: "The moment we begin to suppress anything, everyone who listens to us in broadcasting or reads you in the print has the right to say, 'If he's going to suppress that story, what else is he hiding from us?'"[19]

While CBS willingly established broad guidelines to assist journalist when covering terrorist attacks, the *Washington Post* has consistently expressed opposition to any such restrictions. Leonard Downie, Jr., assistant managing editor, flatly stated at a seminar after the Hanafi Muslim seige, "We abhor written guidelines . . . and have not committed ourselves to any."[20] The *New York Times* also is on record opposing any guidelines. "The last thing in the world I want [are] guidelines," A.M. Rosenthal, executive editor, emphasized in 1976. "I don't want any from professional organizations or anyone else. The strength of the press is diversity. As soon as by start imposing guidelines, they become peer-group pressures and then quasi-legal restrictions."[21]

Many journalists who participated in the seminars readily agreed there was a danger in becoming accomplices to terrorism by aiding and abetting terrorists' objectives. Yet they resolutely challenged any proposition to restrict a priori their ability to cover a news story concerning terrorism.

While the U.S. government has not tried to intervene and restrict the media's coverage of a terrorist attack, other governments have passed such laws. France, Italy, and the United Kingdom have resorted to limited censorship to, in their opinion, help control the level of terrorism.[22] In the United States, views widely differ. In 1977, Ambassador Andrew Young suggested that federal laws should be enacted to restrict press coverage of terrorist incidents.[23] Representative Lee H. Hamilton, on the other hand, acknowledges the contagious effect caused by the publicity surrounding a terrorist act. Still, he argues, "to restrict the coverage of such events by law raises the question of censorship: Who is to be trusted with the power to censor and when should it be applied?"[24]

In the United States, freedom of speech is not absolute. According to an opinion written by Justice Holmes for a unanimous Court decision, freedom of speech "depends upon the circumstances in which it is done. The more stringent protection of free speech," he explained, "would not protect a man falsely shouting fire in a theater and causing panic,"[25] Holmes argued that the test for freedom of speech is based largely on the concept of clear and present danger. "The question in every case," he said, "is whether the words used are used in such circumstances and are of such a nature as to create a clear and present danger that they will bring about the substantive evils that Congress has the right to prevent."[26]

The guide for determining the basis of freedom of speech today is still the clear and present danger test. "Thus, despite the strong presumption of unconstitutionality," M. Cherif Bassiouni, professor of law at De Paul University, states, "prior restraints may be consitutionally permissible where specific harm of a grave nature would surely result from media dissemination of certain information."[27]

Although the U.S. government may have legal grounds to limit the broadcast and publication of material by the media, Yonah Alexander points out that censorship is not an effective or desirable weapon against terrorism. "Any attempts to impose media blackouts," he posits, "are likely to force terrorists to escalate the level of violence in order to attract more attention."[28] If terrorists raise the stakes by increasing the number of violent attacks, he says, the government, not the terrorists, will be blamed for limiting the public's right to know.

Whether the media should be restricted from using material produced by terrorists comes down to the long-term interests of freedom of the press and the perceived national interests to protect the public. Walter Jeahnig, assistant professor at the University of Indiana, describes the problem as follows: "Can the news media assume adversarial roles in relation to public authority when the social order, its tenets and values are endangered? How can the public's right to know be fulfilled when the publication [or broadcast] of specific material could cause direct harm to members of the public or support for its enemies?"[29]

Mobilizing the Media

During the civil rights demonstrations in the 1960s, the media were severely reprimanded for some of their initial news coverage. The probing eye of the television camera panning across depressed neighborhoods filled with unrest, it was charged, irresponsibly created a contagious effect, inflaming the public to demonstrate in other cites. Within a short time, however, networks established guidelines to deal with the problem. During the Watts riots, John Dancy recalls, "stations and networks were very irresponsible in using the words 'mobs' and 'riots.' But very quickly—in thirty to sixty days—guidelines evolved." At NBC for example, Dancy explained, "We would not use the word 'riot' until the police use the word 'riot.' And until they used the word 'mob,' we would not call a disorderly crowd a 'mob.'"[30]

Following the widespread debate triggered by the media coverage of the Hanafi Muslim seige and the Anthony Kiritsis kidnapping, the media again responded by establishing guidelines to help prevent journalists from interfering with the police or providing terrorists with unlimited access to the media.

In both cases, the media proved they were not indifferent to the problems they caused by their frenetic reporting. Still when the next terrorist incident occurred, they seemed unable to restrain their level of reporting. Just two years after the Hanafi incident, the media were again in the limelight because of their disproportionate coverage of the captured Americans in Iran. According to David Altheide, "More media attention was given to the hostages in Iran than any single event in history, including the Vietnam War."[31] The considerable media hype given to the incident was blamed for unnecessarily fueling public opinion and political pressures. When the crisis finally came to an end, the common refrain for self-examination and further guidelines was sounded again.

Most recently, the media have come under attack for their "sensationalized," "exploitive," and "excessive" news coverage of the June 1985 TWA flight 847 hijacking. Over a period of two weeks, every angle of the story was exhausted. Not a day passed without the media's interviewing a distressed relative of a hostage, a terrorist expert's analysis of the options and vulnerabilities, or a comparison to President Jimmy Carter's handling of the Iranian crisis. Critics again questioned the role of the media. Are they just covering the news, pundits asked, or are they also making it? Did the surfeit of television news make the crisis worse? "With four large networks scrambling for exclusives and higher ratings," Eleanor Randolph opined, "the call for restraint is one that seems mostly to be recognized as important, then dismissed as impossible."[32] An editorial by Edwin M. Yoder Jr., chastised the media for their lack of restraint. "Television is about as capable of self-discipline in its chase after good footage," he wrote, "as a dog is in chasing a rabbit."[33]

In defense of the media, NBC's John Chancellor questioned whether there would have been a quick resolution to the hostage crisis had they not made the story an international event (massive media coverage did not force a quick resolution of the Iranian crisis). While criticizing the media "for excesses in taste" and some "mindless moments," the *Washington Post* in an editorial assessed the media's overall role as basically neutral: "We do not see that the ordeal of the hostages was extended or the price of their return bid up by the presence or conduct of television."[34]

The explosion of pent-up violence in the 1960s, the Kiritsis kidnapping, the Hanafi Muslim seige, the Iranian hostage crisis, and the hijacking of TWA 847: in each case, the messengers of ill tidings—the media—were severely criticized for their excessive reporting and the atmosphere they created. Although the media did not cause the acts of terrorism, some believe muzzling the press will prevent or at least inhibit future incidences of violence by terrorist organizations. Repeatedly backed into a corner, the media have responsibly responded by establishing general guidelines while calling for greater self-discipline and higher journalistic integrity and professionalism. In each instance, the media were clearly observers, providing exhaustive—and some would say pernicious—analysis and information. But it is a matter of degree and not whether they should have reported the incidences in the first place.

Many of the excesses of the media in the past can be traced to changing technology. The way journalists report the news is an evolving process. The development of lightweight portable video cameras replaced motion picture cameras, which used photographic film that had to be chemically developed, a time-consuming process. When the Hanafi Muslims raided the B'nai B'rith headquarters in Washington, D.C., television stations responded by reporting the crisis with the tools they had available to cover the story. Because journalists earlier had not had the opportunity to report on a similar terrorist attack using minicams and portable microwave transmitters, they were unprepared to deal with many of the problems that arose.

About the Iranian crisis, many of the difficulties created by the media can be attributed to the rise of international electronic mass communications, according to Don Oberdorfer. After the incident he wrote, "We are witnessing the enormous power of something new under the sun: the ability of human beings to bounce fragments of experience off satellites in space and transmit them widely and instantaneously across the country of across the globe to millions of people."[35]

Technology is once again altering the way the media are able to report on terrorist attacks. The next battle on the horizon is television terrorism. It promises, however, to be ladened with a far more difficult and dangerous challenge to the media. Television terrorism is fundamentally different from the earlier incidents because of the terrorists' obvious strategy of manipulation. The emotional titillation and engaging possibilities offered by videotape will undoubtedly entice the media to broadcast and print the material. The question is, Will the media be able to refrain from showing the terrorist-produced material, or will they become accomplices to the terroristic designs? Broadcasting the material will directly play into the hands of terrorists. It will obviously fan the flames of terrorism and cannot be justified or condoned under any circumstances.

To date, the media have not focused on the threat of television terrorism. If the past is a prologue to the future, they will probably make some mistakes as they come to grips with the problem. But the media can also be expected to take corrective actions if and when the threat worsens. When asked about video material produced by terrorists, John Dancy said he did not think NBC had any guidelines. But if terrorists begin to produce videotapes in order to gain access to the media, he predicted guidelines would quickly evolve.

Instead of waiting for the problem of television terrorism to develop into a crisis before they react, the media should consider holding seminars as soon as possible to discuss the potential threat. If some guidelines can be established before the problem gets out of hand, errors made in the past can be avoided. In 1977, Wayne Vriesman, then president of the Radio and Television News Directors Association, wrote a prophetic column following the Kiritsis kidnapping. He urged broadcast journalists to set guidelines immediately. "Don't wait for the event to happen," he warned, "because probably [you] won't have time enough to give all the ramifications proper perspectives."[36]

A parallel situation exists today. If the media would announce guidelines restricting the use of material produced by terrorists—though such material may better illustrate a story—the incentive for terrorists to produce videotapes could be eliminated. Terrorism is a dynamic process. Since the media are integral to the success of terroristic designs, they should regularly appraise the changing techniques employed by terrorists, the increasing threats posed to the society, and their responsibilities when reporting on terrorist attacks.

To help balance the pressures of competition for ratings, the media should also consider establishing independent task forces with members drawn from the general public and stock holders. General shareholders may be more inclined to forfeit a small portion of their dividends due to a fractional drop in ratings if they believe it will prevent an escalation in terrorism. Finally, the media should consider providing ample air time for programming to communicate the threat posed by terrorism and its relationship to the integrity of the media. If the media make public statements on record of their positions and their efforts to control terrorism, it will be far more difficult for them to explode later in an orgy of media coverage following a major terrorist incident.

Marshall McLuhan commented that "the pen daily becomes mightier than the sword."[37] Television is a 10 ton pen. Concomitant to the growing influence of television to shape the today's events is a growing responsibility. Unless the media take actions to prevent the evolution of television terrorism, there will be a revolution in the power terrorists will wield.

Postscript: On July 4, 1985, NBC broadcast a videotape produced by terrorists showing a suicide car bomber in southern Lebanon near Tyre crashing into an Israel convoy, exploding in a ball of flames. The videotape was recorded on February 5 with a home video camera from atop a building several blocks away. The fact that the videotape was broadcast five months after the bombing is testament to the omnipotence of video terrorism and its potential threat and ability to gain access on national channels of communication.

Notes

1. Kathy Sawyer, "U.S. Hostage Urges 'Action,'" *Washington Post,* January 29, 1985.

2. Pr Newswire, April 22, 1985.

3. "Girl Suicide Bomber Hailed as National Heroine," Reuter News, April 9, 1985.

4. Walter Laqueur, "The Futility of Terrorism," *Harper's* (March 1976): 104.

5. "Terror and Television," *TV Guide,* July 31, 1976.

6. Arturo C. Porzecanski, *Uruguay's Tupamaros* (New York: Praeger, n.d.), p. 43.

7. "Terrorists Kill Three, Take Seventy Hostages at OPEC Meeting," *Arkansas Gazette,* December 22, 1975.

8. *Washington Post,* September 12, 1976.

9. "International Terrorism: A Balance Sheet," *Survival* (July–August 1975): 158.

10. Frederic B. Hill, "Media Diplomacy," *Washington Journalism Review* (May 1981): 27.

11. Interview with Louise Schiavone, AP Radio correspondent for the U.S. Senate, April 19, 1985.

12. Ibid.

13. Interview with John Dancy, NBC correspondent for the U.S. Senate, April 19, 1985.

14. Ibid.

15. Jody Powell, "Ratings, Ratings, Ratings," *Washington Post,* July 30, 1985.

16. Interview with Louise Schiavone, AP correspondent for the U.S. Senate, April 19, 1985.

17. Herbert A. Terry, "Television and Terrorism: Professionalism Not Quite the Answer," *Indiana Law Journal* 53(1978) 754.

18. "The Media and Terrorism," Seminar Sponsored by the *Chicago Sun-Times* and the *Chicago Daily News,* April 1977, p. 13.

19. Ibid.

20. Ibid., p. 17.

21. David Shaw, "Editors Face Terrorist Demand Dilemma," *Los Angeles Times,* September 15, 1976, p. 14.

22. Jourdan Paust, "International Law and Control of the Media: Terror, Repression and the Alternatives," *Indiana Law Journal* 53 (1978): 654.

23. *New York Times,* March 15, 1977, p. 16 (quoting White House press secretary Jody Powell).

24. Lee H. Hamilton, "Terrorism," *Congressional Record,* April 7, 1977.

25. *Schenck* v. *United States,* 249 U.S. 49 (1919).

26. Ibid.

27. M. Cherif Bassiouni, "Terrorism, Law Enforcement, and Mass Media: Perspectives, Problems, Proposals," *Journal on Criminal Law and Criminology* 72, no. 1 (19??): 40.

28. Yonah Alexander, "Terrorism, the Media, and the Police," *Journal of International Affairs* 32, no. 1 (Spring–Summer 1978): 109.

29. Walter B. Jeahnig, "Journalists and Terrorism: Captives of the Libertarian Tradition," *Indiana Law Journal* 53 (19??): 720.

30. Interview with Dancy.

31. David Altheid, "Network News: Oversimplified and Underexplained," *Washington Journalism Review* (May 1981): 28.

32. Eleanor Randolph, "Networks Turn Eye on Themselves," *Washington Post,* June 30, 1985, p. A25.

33. Edwin M. Yoder, Jr., "The Press Shouldn't Play Censor," *Washington Post,* June 30, 1985, p. C8.

34. "The Media and Beirut," *Washington Post,* July 4, 1985.

35. Don Oberdorfer, "Now That It's Over . . . : The Press Needs to Reflect on Its Role," *Washington Journalism Review* (May 1981): 38.

36. Wayne Vriesman, "Vriesman, the Last Word . . . ," *RTNDA Communicator* (March 1977): 16.

37. Marshall McLuhan, *Understanding Media* (New York: McGraw-Hill, 1964), p. 294.

16
Fighting Back

Terrell E. Arnold
Neil C. Livingstone

Complex problems rarely admit simple solutions, and the challenge posed by international terrorism is no exception. Terrorism is a dynamic phenomenon, and its sprawling, multinational character and the involvement of states complicate the task of the policymaker who looks for neat, all-encompassing solutions. In 1984 alone, there were more than 650 terrorist attacks around the globe, involving bombings, assassinations, arson, kidnappings, hijackings, and other forms of mayhem. These attacks occurred in more than one-half of the 154 countries in the world and were directed against literally dozens of different kinds of targets: individuals, aircraft, embassies, military bases, office buildings, pipelines, bridges, hydroelectric plants, computers, ships, consumer products, refineries, and government buildings, to name only a few. In the 1980s, attack profiles ranged from a lone Cuban hijacker threatening a planeload of passengers with a cigarette lighter and a detergent bottle full of gasoline to a North Korean government–orchestrated bombing in Burma that killed four South Korean cabinet ministers and other high officials of that government. The motives behind the attacks range from personal grievances to reasons of state.

Thus, the task of designing and implementing effective national policies to deal with terrorism is overwhelming in its scope and permutations and argues less for a general all-embracing strategy to address the problem than a multitude of less-ambitious component strategies, which in sum provide an overall framework for controlling and suppressing terrorism on a global scale. As Field Marshall Helmuth von Moltke once observed, all strategy is a system of makeshifts, and in this spirit it is fair to suggest that there is an improvised, even jerry-built, quality to the strategies that have evolved to date in the Western democracies for combating terrorism. Moreover, despite the best efforts and intentions of policymakers in the United States and abroad, it is perhaps inevitable that this situation will persist for the indefinite future. The choices now before the United States and the other countries seriously challenged by international terrorism involve the selection of a mix of strategies tailored to their specific threat environments, political realities, moral and legal traditions, and the human and physical resources available. The component strategies currently being employed or seriously explored by the United States at the present time are as follows:

Improving physical security.

Training U.S. diplomatic and military personnel in personal security habits and to appreciate the terrorist threat.

Working closely with other governments to ensure that they meet their responsibilities for the protection of U.S. diplomatic and military personnel and facilities abroad.

Providing security to foreign diplomats and dignitaries in the United States.

Training foreign government officials in security and antiterrorist programs.

Working closely with other governments to collect, assess, and share intelligence.

Improving the legal framework to enable better investigation and prosecution for terrorist offenses.

Improving the framework for international cooperation to deal with terrorism.

Increasing and sharing antiterrorism technology.

Exposing the involvement of states in sponsoring or carrying out acts of terrorism in every possible forum.

Cooperating with other countries to persuade or force terrorism-sponsoring states to end such activities.

Using force in a judicious manner to prevent or respond to terrorist attacks and to deter future attacks.

Searching for appropriate ways of solving legitimate grievances by nonviolent means.

While the component elements, or options, of the overall strategy seem simple, their application and implementation are far more difficult. Each depends on the existence or creation of certain instrumentalities, structures, and agreements or understandings, for without creating the means to realize its objectives, any strategy, however well conceived, is reduced to bluster and hot air, and any country that embraces such a strategy runs the risk of being perceived as a paper tiger in the event a situation arises where it must act.

As Secretary of State George Shultz noted in an appearance before the House Foreign Affairs Committee in August 1984, an effective response to terrorism requires a fairly large kit of tools. Indeed, from the perspective of the policymaker, the worst possible dilemma is to have too few options for addressing a particular problem or crisis and therefore be forced to employ an innappropriate or inadequate tool and hope for the best. There is a story that former Secretary of State Henry Kissinger was once presented by a young assistant a decision paper laying out the various options for dealing with a problem. Kissinger reportedly sniffed at the decision paper and threw it back across his desk. The assistant inquired timidly as to what was wrong, and the secretary informed him that he had left out several important options. The assistant scratched his head and said that he had spent hours on the decision paper and could not imagine what options he had neglected. Kissinger coldly responded that the options of nuclear war and surrender had both been left off the list. The startled aide responded that had not considered either to be an option. "Everything is an option," Kissinger allegedly shot back. "Everything."

Whether apocryphal or not, the story illustrates an important point. Everything must be considered a potential option by policymakers as they assemble a tool kit to combat terrorism, even if some of the possible tools, like assassination, must necessarily be discarded as inappropriate or prohibited at the present time.

Improved Intelligence

The first line of defense against terrorism is good intelligence. Terrorists preparing to shoot down civilian airliners in Rome and Nairobi were apprehended before they could carry out their deeds because of timely intelligence. Terrorists can choose the time, place, and method of their attacks, and without prior knowledge those on the defensive are forced to be constantly vigilant, perpared for anything and everything. They have only to let down their guard once for a worst-case scenario to occur. As the Irish Republican Army vowed after narrowly missing British Prime Minister Margaret Thatcher in a bomb attack on her Brighton hotel, "Today we were unlucky. But remember, we have only to be lucky once. You will have to be lucky always."

Timely intelligence has permitted U.S. security officials to move diplomats and other targets out of range, to warn other government officials of plots against them, and to expose the intentions of various terrorist groups to friendly governments. Not only can a well-developed intelligence capability provide authorities with advance information about an upcoming terrorist operation, permitting them to take steps to avert the incident or at least minimize the damage, but it also aids them in tracking down suspected terrorists and identifying support from patron states.

Terrorism is a new kind of intelligence target. It has more in common with police work than traditional intelligence collection and therefore requires new tools and capabilities. Instead of the tradecraft of master spies, it requires the foot-slogging patience and streetwise savvy of big city cops, who also need a good deal of luck as well as skill to ferret out individuals and small groups of terrorists in urban centers. The Central Intelligence Agency (CIA) and the various U.S. military intelligence agencies are only now beginning to acquire the skills and personnel needed to succeed in this new intelligence arena.

This new intelligence requirement comes at an inopportune time, moreover, inasmuch as U.S. capabilities to collect and assess intelligence have been severely reduced in the aftermath of Vietnam, Watergate, and the investigations into CIA wrongdoing during the 1970s. The CIA's paramilitary capability was disbanded and excessive reliance placed on electronic forms of intelligence gathering. Humint (human intelligence) was regarded in many circles as unreliable and disappointing in terms of results, and opponents of humint pointed out that agents going off the reservation had been the source of many of the agency's public embarrassments. Although various forms of electronic intelligence gathering are vital to monitoring and understanding Soviet moves and intentions, such methods are generally of little value in collecting hard information about terrorists and their planned activities. Members of the Islamic Jihad, mindful of electronic surveillance methods, have all but abandoned the use of the telephone, telex, and even radio transmitters for their communications and have instead resorted to communicating by old-fashioned methods like messengers and notes scribbled on pieces of paper.

Following the bombings in the Middle East, numerous U.S. public officials called for a stepped-up effort to infiltrate terrorist organizations. Experience, however, suggests that such activities are extremely difficult and represent an even greater magnitude of difficulty than efforts by the largely white and clean-cut agents of the Federal Bureau of Investigation (FBI) to infiltrate the Black Panthers during the 1960s. Most terrorist organizations in the Middle East are composed of men and women who differ from the average American in nearly every conceivable respect in terms of language, religion, ethnic heritage, and life experiences. Each prospective terrorist is generally well known to others in the organization long before his or her recruitment, and often complex tests—including murder—are required before a recruit becomes a full-fledged member of the terrorist group.

Not only is it extremely difficult to infiltrate terrorist organizations, but it takes years, even generations, to assemble and put in place networks of agents in troubled areas like Lebanon. The agent networks lost or dismantled during the 1970s cannot easily be restored. While the task has begun, it will take a good deal of time, and therefore little relief can be expected in the short term from the violence emanating from the Middle East as a result of improved intelligence. In the meantime, the United States will have to rely on cooperation with various allied intelligence organizations for help in the Middle East and attempt to use rewards and various forms of coercion to turn identified terrorists and their sympathizers into U.S. agents.

Increased Physical Security

The absence of first-rate intelligence puts a premium on upgraded physical security at U.S. embassies and other installations. Indeed, if there had been a question before, the devastating vehicle bomb attacks in 1983 and 1984 left little doubt that the era of open diplomatic, political, cultural, and trade relations between nations was coming to an end. In addition to the Middle East attacks, terrorist incidents and threats directed against U.S targets in Rome, Paris, London, Bogotá, San Salvador, and other cities made it clear that significant changes were necessary with respect to the conduct of U.S. overseas relations and that it was essential that U.S. facilities abroad be hardened to the maximum degree feasible. This realization, however, was slow in coming, largely because it was difficult to believe that Americans could come under attack simultaneously in so many parts of the world. Particular resistance came from those in the U.S. Department of State, who felt that diplomatic missions, by their very nature, require daily contacts with the people of foreign nations and that elaborate security precautions pose both physical and psychological barriers to such contacts. There was also an understandable reluctance to adopt a fortress mentality, and many diplomatic personnel clung to the notion that "it can't happen here."

In the wake of the 1983–1984 bombings in Beirut and Kuwait, it was evident that if effective steps had been taken to secure the four target buildings, the resulting deaths, injuries, and damages could have been drastically reduced.[1] Perhaps most important, the attacks underscored the need to have U.S. missions and facilities abroad located some distance from the street, both to provide greater reaction time for security personnel and to allot enough distance for explosive energy to disperse without serious harm. In response to the attacks, Congress voted substantial increases in the fiscal year 1985 State Department budget to provide for physical security improvement programs. Major projects to improve security were initiated at thirty-nine U.S. diplomatic missions. The outright replacement of thirteen U.S. embassies was also undertaken because the structures were deemed too vulnerable to be adequately upgraded from a security standpoint.

Greater physical security for all U.S. missions and overseas facilities is now essential, and there is no country in the world where improved security is not a consideration. But it would be wrong to believe that the improvements now being undertaken, when completed, represent a final solution to the problem. Terrorists will always seek to discover weaknesses in any security system and with enough time and resources are likely to succeed in finding chinks in the armor. Security systems therefore must be constantly audited and upgraded to ensure that a high state of readiness is maintained and that new vulnerabilities are quickly addressed.

Other factors, including luck, also suggest that the problem of physical security is neither simple nor straightforward. Had the U.S. embassy in Kuwait been better equipped to halt the bomb-laden truck at the perimeter gate, the explosion that occurred would have severely damaged the chancery instead of the administration building and taken an even larger toll in lives and injuries. The chancery was probably the terrorists' real target, but they mistakenly focused on the less-important administration building.

Aside from procuring armored vehicles and providing security personnel to accompany key U.S. officials traveling between their homes and offices, the physical security steps a diplomatic mission can take are limited to areas inside the boundary perimeters of the diplomatic property. Even within its own boundaries, there are limitations as to what a diplomatic mission can do to secure its personnel and property, limitations set by the host government. Indeed, many countries have established limits on the sizes, locations, heights, communications systems, and appearances of diplomatic mission structures. The United States works with host governments to sensitize them, when necessary, to the security needs of U.S. missions, but often the process is difficult. In one country, the U.S. security adviser recommended the installation of a high chain-link fence around the U.S. ambassador's residence, which was located in a parklike area. City fathers rejected the idea on aesthetic grounds. In another capital city, the U.S. embassy is exposed to surveillance and sniper attack from an ancient aqueduct, but it has not been possible thus far to win the cooperation of the host government in controlling access to the aqueduct. For months prior to the 1983 attack on the U.S. embassy in Kuwait, the embassy security office had tried to persuade Kuwaiti authorities to close the street in front of the chancery to all vehicle traffic. Due to the presence of a major hotel and other businesses located on the street, Kuwaiti officials were reluctant to comply with the request; the December bombing was the ultimate result. Finally, most nations are unlikely to view with favor any effort to install defenses such as standoff weapons or surface-to-air missiles to protect a diplomatic mission, viewing such weaponry as indicative of a lack of confidence in the host government and a usurpation of its sovereign authority.

The involvement of states changes the dynamics as well as the practical utility of many actions required to combat terrorism from a physical security approach. Physical security measures at U.S. embassies, for example, are not as vital if the host government is positive and helpful and observes its obligations, so far as possible, to provide a secure and threat-free environment. Physical defenses can be rapidly subverted, however, if a host government assists a terrorist group in collecting intelligence about a particular embassy or facility and helps it formulate its plan of attack. Nevertheless, improved physical security at U.S. embassies and military installations abroad remains a top priority in combating terrorism because the lack of adequate security is simply to invite attack.

Training Personnel to Protect Themselves Better

Physical security systems must be augmented by security awareness and prudent behavior on the part of potentially threatened individuals. Whereas physical security systems are inherently static and therefore predictable and surmountable features of any security landscape, human behavior has the capacity to introduce continuing orders of uncertainty in the minds of any potential adversary. By varying habits, times, routes of travel, and staying out of potentially high-risk areas of the city and countryside, individuals can make it difficult, if not impossible, for terrorists to predict their movements and activities. Thus, they become far more difficult targets to hit when outside the sanctuary of their office or compound.

In many of the recent instances of assassination, assault, and kidnapping of individuals by terrorists, elementary security rules had been neglected or ignored by the victim. Some of the most commonplace errors were walking or driving to work over the same route every day, appearing at the same location at roughly the same hour on a routine basis, removing the ballistic glass from the windows of an armored car so that it would be more comfortable, and failing to check a personal vehicle for evidence of tampering. Such security lapses made the terrorist's job much easier, and although they heighten an individual's vulnerability in almost any locale, they are an invitation to disaster in a high-risk environment.

For several years, the U.S. Department of State has run a course, "Coping with Violence Abroad," which provides briefings to all personnel being assigned to overseas missions on how to deal with natural disasters, ordinary crime, riots and other civil disturbances, and, most important, terrorism. The course also focuses on how to cope with violence-related stress, such as being taken hostage, and includes instruction related to being a member of a hostage victim's family. In early 1984, President Reagan made such training mandatory for all U.S. government personnel going abroad. Since then, the State Department, with the cooperation of other U.S. government agencies, has begun to take its training program into the field, employing simulations and exercises to test a mission's crisis management planning and response capability.

Providing Security for Diplomats and Dignitaries

The United States is largely dependent on host governments for security at all of its overseas missions and facilities, and this is true of other governments when they send their diplomats and dignitaries to the United States. Providing security to diplomats and dignitaries, even when no specific threat is known to exist, has become a common problem to local and national authorities in capital cities and other urban centers throughout the world. Major governments traditionally have absorbed the costs associated with such protection as part of their normal political and internal security budgets, but as the international threat environment continues to grow, even the resources of some leading governments have been strained by such demands. The United States is no exception. In the fiscal year 1986 budget, the Reagan administration included a request for funding to reimburse various state and local authorities, particularly New York City, for the extraordinary costs involved in providing diplomats and dignitaries with adequate protection. The term *extraordinary costs* in the legislation refers to those costs over and above the ordinary maintenance of law and order for the community as a whole.[2] Reimbursements are in addition to the normal costs associated with the U.S. Secret Service and the State Department Office of Security, both of which have extensive diplomat and dignitary protection responsibilites. The assassination of the Turkish consul in Los Angeles and an attempt on the life of the Turkish consul in Boston, both by Armenian terrorists, are indicative of the threat climate that exists even in the United States.

A special case of diplomat and dignitary protection was presented by the 1984 summer Olympic games in Los Angeles. Cost figures for local, state, and federal security precautions are not yet in, but the Pentagon budget alone was $50 million for Olympic games security activites. The final figure is likely to exceed $200 million, or more than $2 million for every team represented in the games.

Not surprisingly, many small and relatively poor countries find that providing security to foreign diplomats and dignitaries is a disproportionately large item in their national budgets. During periods of fiscal austerity, some nations are hard pressed to justify such expenditures, especially when so many other needs are going unfulfilled. Increasingly obvious to the U.S. Department of State and other government agencies operating abroad has been recognition of the fact that the relatively small, undertrained, and underfunded police organizations in many countries can provide only minimal security to their own people, let alone foreign diplomats and dignitaries. As illustration, in one major West African nation, where both terrorism and crime are on the rise in the capital city, authorities asked the U.S. embassy to provide a vehicle and radios so that local police could mount a roving patrol at night in sections of the city where diplomats resided. Requests of this type have pressed home the point that to provide proper security for its diplomats, the United States needs to offer assistance and support to some host governments.

In 1983, Congress approved legislation permitting the Department of State to undertake a modest $5 million program to train foreign government officials in security practices and procedures.[3] Foreign police officials are exposed to the training normally offered by the FBI, the Federal Aviation Administration, the Immigration and Naturalization Service, and various local law enforcement organizations. Individually tailored training programs are subsequently developed to address specific gaps in the other government's own training and organization. To date, more than twenty foreign governments have participated in the initial program, generally sending groups of ten or more officals to the United States.

Cooperation with Other Governments

In view of the transnational character of terrorism and the fact that protection of U.S. citizens and property abroad is chiefly the responsibility of other governments, cooperation with those nations is crucial to any effective effort to control and suppress terrorism. The problem is that all governments are not alike, and some take a lax attitude with respect to preventing acts of terrorism. The hijacking of TWA flight 847 in June 1985 was made possible in large measure because of the permissive attitude displayed by the Greek government to international terrorism. Nevertheless, most governments readily cooperate in providing security to international travelers, and through a combination of counterpart agencies to the U.S. Federal Aviation Administration and the international air carriers themselves, a well-established network exists for sharing information on terrorist threats, targets, and tactics and various countermeasures and new technologies for thwarting hijackers. Reports of an attempt in 1984 to plant suitcase bombs on flights originating in several European cities, for example, resulted in widespread tightening of airport baggage and passenger screening in Europe and the Middle East.

Security-related exchanges and dialogue at the working level have continued even when relations have become strained between various nations because there is a general recognition by virtually all countries, with the possible exception of a few outlaw states like Iran, that an orderly international aviation system benefits everyone. Most of the constraints on such cooperation stem from government perceptions of the terrorist threat on any particular day, on what the traveling public will tolerate in the way of inconvenient security checks and passenger screening, on what costs airlines are willing to absorb, and on what governments are prepared to invest in security technology and personnel.

Although cooperation is often circumscribed by political considerations, the United States and other Western nations generally assist each other in the arrest and extradition of fugitive terrorists. In addition, the United States, Britain, West Germany, Israel, and several other countries maintain crack counterterrorist strike teams, which have been used to train counterpart organizations in friendly nations. Such training includes paramilitary attack procedures, the mastery of different firearms, hostage negotiation, explosive ordnance use and handling, communications skills, and various means of clandestine airborne and surface approach to the site of a terrorist incident. It is not uncommon, moreover, for representatives of allied counterterrorist commando units to be present as observers and consultants at major terrorist incidents. Representatives of the U.S. Delta force, for example, were among the observers at the standoff that developed in London at the Libyan People's Bureau following the murder of a British policewoman and the wounding of a number of anti-Qaddafi demonstrators by a gunman inside the building. Delta personnel have assisted in the resolution of a number of overseas terrorist incidents, at the request of friendly governments, including several hijackings in the Caribbean. U.S. explosives experts have lent their expertise to investigations by authorities in other countries of terrorist incidents such as the Brighton bombing that narrowly missed British Prime minister Margaret Thatcher. Similarly, elements of the French counterterrorist force GIGN (Groupe d'intervention de la gendarmerie nationale) were among the advisers sent to Saudi Arabia to help the Saudis recapture the Grand Mosque in Mecca from heavily armed terrorists.

One of the problems with this kind of training, whether provided by military or intelligence organizations, is the use another government may make of its counterterrorist force. In a few instances, this force has evolved into a palace or praetorian guard, essentially functioning as a security detail for a head of state. As was demonstrated by the attack on the life of Shiite leader, Mohammed Hussein Fadlallah, in Beirut in early May 1985, such a group can go off its own and carry out ill-considered and inept attacks that embarrass and discredit the power that conducted the training.

Economic, Diplomatic, and Political Pressure

Diplomatic pressure on terrorism-sponsoring states represents an option to the United States and its Western allies, but if diplomatic access is weak, as in the case of U.S.-Iran relations, little influence can be exerted through this channel. Third parties with influence on an offending state can be looked to for help, but the enthusiasm of such nations is often blunted by considerations of self-interest and fear of the potential risks inherent in becoming involved as an honest broker or go-between.

Political sanctions such as restrictions on travel and a curtailing of diplomatic relations help deliver a message, but if the offending state feels strongly or self-righteous about its actions, few tangible results can be expected. Concerted multilateral action, in the form of economic sanctions supported by numerous influential states, will carry more weight than the implementation of sanctions by a single nation, but such consensus and unity of action historically has been difficult to achieve.

Libya has been a testing ground for such premises, particularly with respect to economic and political sanctions, inasmuch as it has been the target of an extensive U.S. effort designed to restrain and temper the actions of the Qaddafi regime. Beginning in 1981, the United States launched a concerted program to inform the general public of Qaddafi's support of international terrorism. The United States terminated oil imports from Libya and discouraged the involvement of U.S. companies and citizens in Libyan oil production activities. New and more stringent controls were imposed on military and defense-related exports to Libya, and steps were taken to curtail financial transactions between the two countries. Not only was the Libyan People's Bureau in Washington closed, but severe restrictions were placed on the movements of officials from Libya's mission to the United Nations. U.S. passports were invalidated for travel to Libya. At the same time, the U.S. Sixth Fleet mounted shows of force in the Gulf of Sidra to challenge Qaddafi's assertion that the gulf was part of Libyan territorial waters.

With one exception, the campaign mounted by the United States to constrain the behavior of the Qaddafi regime seems to have had little lasting effect. Qaddafi, in fact, appears to have taken a kind of perverse satisfaction in being dealt with in this manner by such a powerful state, and judging from the reaction by other Third World countries, his personal image may even have been enhanced. Moreover, a significant number of Americans chose not to abide by U.S. restrictions on travel to Libya, and Qaddafi, in turn, disregarded the restrictions in U.S. passports and permitted U.S. citizens to enter the country and work there on various oil and other activities of interest to him. Unofficial estimates place the number of Americans now in Libya at 1,500 or more.

Efforts to enlist the aid of European countries also victimized by Qaddafi in applying trade sanctions to Libya have also been unsuccessful. Even in the wake of the shooting of a British policewoman by a gunman in the Libyan People's Bureau, the government of Prime Minister Margaret Thatcher was reluctant to take any meaningful action against Libya or to join in the U.S. sanctions. Libya made up for lost oil revenues in conjunction with its previous sales to the United States by developing new markets in Europe. The jobs previously held by U.S. oilfield technicians and engineers were assumed by British citizens and other Europeans.

Denied access to U.S. military hardware and spare parts, especially for its C-130 aircraft, Libya turned to arms brokers and dealers in Europe for replacement spares and to circumvent U.S. restrictions illegally. Qaddafi even went so far as to hire a series of lobbyists in Washington in an effort to win delivery of additional C-130 aircraft and spares. One lobbyist also served as a bagman for funding operations against Libyan dissidents in the United States, and he began to use an office he had been permitted to open in Arlington, Virginia, which liased with Libyans studying at American universities, as a sub rosa diplomatic and consular post.

In retrospect, all of the U.S. efforts to put pressure on Qaddafi by means of economic, diplomatic, and political means have failed. The only U.S. action that appears to have had any effect on the mercurial colonel was the shooting down of two Libyan warplanes in 1981 by U.S. F-14 interceptors in the Gulf of Sidra. The United States also reportedly assured Egypt in 1981 that it would provide a U.S. military umbrella against the Soviet Union if Egypt engaged in open hostilities with Libya. In addition, the United States and Egypt are said to have provided encouragement and covert assistance to anti-Qaddafi dissidents who have made several unsuccessful attempts to overthrow or assassinate the Libyan leader during the past twelve months. Judging, however, from Qaddafi's recent adventures in Chad, the Sudan, the United Kingdom, and elsewhere, the restraining influence of the Gulf of Sidra incident and the other anti-Qaddafi activities has been limited.

Elimination of Safe Havens

Western nations like the United States, France, Great Britain, Sweden, and Greece have traditionally granted asylum to political dissidents and refugees with the implicit understanding that such individuals comply with the laws of the host government and refrain from carrying out acts of political violence either in the country of safe haven or launched from its territory against third countries. Over the years, such understandings were generally observed by all concerned; however, recently, the pattern has begun to change. Some individuals and groups that qualified as political exiles have started to use the cover of asylum to escape punishment for terrorist crimes committed in other countries, establish contacts with other terrorist groups, recruit new members, raise funds and acquire weapons, and export their grievances to third countries. Even more serious has been the urge to violate the rules of safe haven and commit acts of terrorism in or against the host country. The Lebanese Armed Revolutionary Faction, long tolerated by the authorities in Paris, has been credited with at least four attacks in France since 1982, including the assassination of U.S. assistant military attaché Charles Ray and the killing of an Israeli diplomat. Similarly, Black June (Abu Nidal) has been implicated in attacks in France and at least two other European countries. France has become the battleground for terrorists from every corner of the globe, and as a result France, like many other Western nations, is reassessing its liberal asylum policy. Indeed, after Spanish death squads began crossing the border into France to strike back at Basque terrorists who had long used French territory as a safe haven, the Mitterand government took the unprecedented step of cracking down on illegal Basque activities rather than have French sovereignty violated by other states.

An even more difficult problem is that of states that provide safe haven to terrorists as a deliberate matter of national policy. Article 2, paragraph 4, of the U.N. Charter states that "every state has the duty to refrain from organizing, instigating, assisting or participating in acts of civil strife or terrorist acts in another state or acquiescing in organized activities within its territory directed towards the commission of such acts, when the acts referred to in the present paragraph invite the threat or use of force." Despite such prohibitions, Iran and Libya, among other nations, regularly provide safe havens to terrorists and often expect services from the terrorists in return. Most terrorist groups are happy to oblige since a protected base in a sponsoring state usually permits the terrorists to extend their geographic reach greatly and often to gain access to sophisticated weapons and military technologies by the host nation's military and intelligence establishment. In many cases, the host country will share intelligence data with the terrorist group, an extraordinary advantage in planning operations and anticipating threats to its own security.

The June 1985 hijacking of TWA flight 847 brought into sharp focus the problem of terrorist safe havens. It was the most elaborate hijacking in history and would have been impossible without safe havens where the terrorists in command of the hostage aircraft could seek refuge during the long and dramatic odyssey. In Lebanon, where there is no effective national government and Shiite Amal gunmen are in charge of the airport, the hijackers operated with relative impunity. According to some reports, one of the hijackers invited his brother aboard the aircraft for a look, and another hijacker spent the night in the city visiting relatives.

Without safe havens from which to plan, organize, and launch their attacks and to which terrorists can return during and after each incident, international terrorism would be a problem of far less magnitude. Diplomatic, economic, and military pressure must be stepped up against states that provide safe haven to terrorists. Victimized states might even consider legal action to recover damages against other states that permit their territory to be used to carry out attacks. In extreme cases, states that systematically provide safe haven to terrorists could be covertly destabilized or openly attacked.

New Legal Actions

Domestic terrorist attacks are clearly crimes, but terrorism was not explicitly addressed in U.S. law until recently. Terrorism is now treated in approximately thirty different sections of the U.S. Code; however, it is seldom defined, and when it is, as in the Foreign Intelligence Surveillance Act, the definition tends to be very broad. Until the passage of the omnibus crime bill in November 1984, it was not against U.S. law, for example, to conspire in the United States to assassinate a foreign head of state. It is now illegal, but there are still no laws prohibiting U.S. citizens from providing training, equipment, specialized electronics and explosives technology, logistical, and other kinds of assistance to terrorists.

Reagan administration efforts to plug some of the loopholes in U.S. law were only partially successful. Four bills were sent to Congress in April 1984, to (1) implement the Montreal Convention against aircraft sabotage, an international agreement the United had ratified but not fully implemented; (2) implement the U.N. convention against hostage taking, an agreement the United States had not ratified pending legislation; (3) provide for the payment of rewards by the Department of State for information on international terrorism cases; and (4) prohibit training and support for international terrorism by U.S. firms and individuals. The first three bills were passed in the last days of the session before Congress adjourned for the elections, but the fourth bill—to prohibit support for terrorists by Americans—was not so successful. The legislative issues raised by the training and support bill, as posed by opponents in the Congress and organizations such as the American Civil Liberties Union, were complex. Opponents raised concerns over any infringement of the legitimate right of political association, as well as confusion over the definition of what exactly constitutes terrorism. Some opponents even went so far as to maintain that the right of free association includes the right of Americans to be associated with groups like the Irish Republican Army, the African National Congress, and the Palestine Liberation Organization, despite the fact that such groups engage in direct acts of terrorism and receive some degree of state support for their violent activities. In view of such opposition, the Departments of State and Justice concluded in early 1985 that the most potentially rewarding domestic legal approach lies in combing existing statutes for language that can be specifically applied to terrorism cases.

With respect to new international agreements for combating terrorism, the prospect is even more dismal. Problems of definition, alliance relationships and patterns of friendship, trade relations, religious ties, and other factors have raised serious obstacles, which are likely to prevent any consensus among nations that could be embodied in new international agreements. Even among the relative handful of states that share similar values and outlooks with respect to terrorism, there is little agreement as to what might be feasible and effective remedies.

If they could be embodied in tightly drafted agreements with provision made for appropriate sanctions, many of the proposals currently being discussed by the Summit Seven nations are promising from the standpoint of combating international terrorism. These proposals include the following:

A tough policy of no concessions to terrorists.

Unified action against states that violate diplomatic immunity or abuse its privileges so as to carry out or support a serious terrorist attack on one of the signatories.

Mutual agreement to exclude persons, including diplomats, expelled from a signatory country for reasons connection with terrorism.

Controls on the export of arms widely used by terrorists.

Stricter controls on the admission of members to a diplomatic mission staff and more rigorous limitations on the size of diplomatic missions.

Reinforcement of the right of receiving states to insist on strict observance of the Vienna Convention respecting the uses of diplomatic mission premises.

Introduction, to the extent legal and practical, of measures to avoid improper use of diplomatic pouches.

Better information sharing on the foregoing and other matters related to the protection of embassies and to terrorist incident contingency planning.

Although the escalation of terrorist attacks during the past two years would, one might think, heighten prospects for concerted action on the part of the Western democracies, they nevertheless remain as divided and irresolute as ever. Discussions regarding terrorism during the May 1985 economic summit meetings in Bonn, Germany, failed to produce either a public statement pertaining to the problem or any agreement on future cooperation. Member nations like France still maintain that present patterns of international terrorism can be remedied by purely domestic actions on the part of the Summit Seven or by changes in their various foreign policies.

This does not mean that the United States should reduce its commitment to reaching new international agreements addressing the problem of terrorism; it is simply to argue for realistic expectations as to how little such efforts are likely to produce. Even existing agreements relating to air piracy and the protection of diplomats are rather thin gruel and regularly ignored by terrorists and their patrons.

Use of Force

In view of increase in state-sponsored terrorism and contemplating the all-too-limited kit of diplomatic, economic, and other tools available to deal with offending states like Iran, the United States must give new and serious consideration to the use of military force; however, the dispensing of small doses of force from a distance against terrorists located in other countries is a tricky business. In some instances, the United States lacks the proper instrumentalities or logistical assets to employ force effectively. In other instances, any limited use of force may escalate into a state of general conflict between the terrorist patron state and the nation seeking remedial action. Thus, any decision to resort to military force will have to be carefully calculated and prudently implemented in order to be effective.

Conclusion

Policymakers have a sufficient range of options to experiment with until they find the right mix for addressing any particular terrorist group or problem. This process will involve some trial and error, not to mention an inevitable amount of failure. Events will dictate the pace and momentum at which the United States and the other liberal democracies of the West proceed toward solutions. The war against terrorism will require, above all else, a significant measure of patience. There will always be a natural inclination to lash back at terrorists with force and rage in the aftermath of some especially grotesque or bloody incident such as the bombing of the U.S. Marine barracks in Beirut or the brutal murder of the young Seabee aboard hijacked TWA flight 847, but more is to be gained in the long run by forgoing precipitous action and not striking back until all is ready, forces are marshaled, the circumstances are right, and until most or all contingencies can be met. While a policy of patience may temporarily be bitter, its results are sure to be sweet.

If, as John Dryden once observed, one should "beware the fury of a patient man," so too should terrorists and their patrons fear the ultimate wrath of a patient nation. They are inviting U.S. retaliation,and it should soon grant them their wish.

Notes

1. In the wake of the September 20, 1984, bombing of the U.S. embassy annex in Beirut, once again there was a great deal of public talk by officials at the U.S. Department of State and elsewhere about how it is all but impossible to prevent determined terrorist attacks, especially those by suicide bombers. The most obvious problem, however, in conjunction with the bombing of the embassy annex as the location of the building in East Beirut. It was anything but isolated. Although various officials tried to explain that it was isolated because it was located in a quiet residential neighborhood in East Beirut, once the so-called Green Line dividing Christian East Beirut from Moslem West Beirut was reopened, any pretense of isolation quickly disappeared.

It was, moreover, a rather ordinary office building with large plate glass windows and situated close to the road. The embassy annex was a building that would have been difficult to protect under the best of circumstances, let alone in the midst of a civil war with an appalling legacy of violence. Ideally, a building set apart from its surroundings on a preserve or estate with a single access road would have been preferable. If such a structure was unavailable, a bunker-like embassy with narrow recessed windows, thick walls, and ringed with various security barriers should have been constructed. If neither option were feasible, serious consideration should have been given to pulling the U.S. diplomatic presence out of Lebanon until either its security could be guaranteed by the Lebanese government or an adequately secured site could be found or constructed for the embassy.

By contrast to those who bemoan funding limitations, good security measures can be improvised with relatively little money in a pinch. In lieu of tank traps or steel gates to block off a street, dump trucks filled with sand would have done the job or even steel cables stretched across the road. In the event that shatter-resistant glass and other kinds of window treatment to reduce the risk of flying glass were unavailable, ordinary masking tape on unprotected windows would have cut down the amount of flying glass. Even thick draperies would have provided some protection. Sandbags, grenade screens, tank traps, a reinforced wall, and a better trained and prepared guard force would have reduced the annex's vulnerability to terrorist attack and to the effects of such an attack once it had occurred. Finally, the security chief should have realized that the concrete barriers that formed the modified chicane were improperly placed to slow down a hostile vehicle adequately.

Americans seem to have an extraordinary capacity to be surprised. Yet there was no valid reason that another bombing attack on the U.S. embassy should have come as a surprise to anyone. The Islamic Jihad and other regional terrorist groups repeatedly had used vehicle bombs in their attacks. Nothing so symbolizes the long Lebanese civil war as the car bomb, with all of its impersonality and horror. Coupled with the fact that nearly one-half of all attacks on diplomats, on a global basis, at the time of the annex attack were bombings, there was no excuse for the building not to have been better defended from the standpoint of a suicide driver behind the wheel of a rolling bomb.

The most essential element in protecting a building like the U.S. embassy annex from a vehicle bomber is to keep all vehicles a safe distance away from the target structure. All explosives have impulse pressure. Even 75 yards away, the detonation of 3,000 pounds of explosive will potentially demolish the front of a large building. One inexpensive and relatively simple method of keeping trucks and vans from using a particular roadway adjacent to a target structure is to erect an I beam across the road at a desired height that will permit passage of autos underneath but not vans or larger vehicles.

The lack of permanent barriers at the embassy annex underscored the need to have a particularly alert and well-trained guard force, especially at the key checkpoints. In this connection, there appears to be little justification for replacing the ninety-man marine contingent assigned to provide security to the U.S. diplomatic mission in Beirut with eighty-five local militiamen. The suggestion by some officials that the marines represented such an inviting target to terrorists that they contributed more to the embassy's security by being withdrawn rather than left in place does not stand up to scrutiny. The decisions to remove the marines and to move into the new annex in East Beirut before security arrangements were completed apparently were taken by U.S. Ambassador Reginald Bartholomew. While the Joint Chiefs of Staff indicated their willingness to leave the marines in Beirut as long as they were needed, all but fourteen were shipped home, and Bartholomew hired the Lebanese contract guards. Not only was the Lebanese guard force inadequately trained and supervised, but their weapons were inadequate for the job of stopping the forward motion of a hostile vehicle.

In the aftermath of the attack, in a move representative of the lack of clear thought characteristic of efforts to secure the annex in the first place, a 106 mm recoilless gun was set up on the road traveled by the vehicle bomber, aimed at the checkpoint. This gun is not in the U.S. military inventory any more, and U.S. military personnel are not trained in its operation. It requires a spotter round to be fired first and takes too long to reload if the first shot misses its mark. If the round misses its target, moreover, and only a slight aiming error by the operator would produce a miss, there is no certainty where the round might actually hit given the range of the weapon. As one military man observed, "I would sure hate to live down range from that gun."

Any of the hand-held antitank missiles would probably be preferred weapons of choice to the 106 mm recoilless gun. The only problem with the U.S.-manufactured Dragon (M-47) system and many of its European-built counterparts is that they cannot be left for long periods of time in the ready-to-shoot configuration. A guard therefore could not snatch up the weapon and employ it on a split-second notice. The Soviet-made SA-7 is far more utilitarian, and given the ranges involved and the requirement for rapid traverse, a few captured SA-7s from U.S. stockpiles would have made the embassy far more secure than the recoilless gun.

Another solution—and perhaps the best—to the same problem would be a six-barreled 20 mm Vulcan machine gun mounted atop an armored vehicle positioned with a direct line of fire up the street. Like a Gatling gun with rotating chambers and bolts, the Vulcan has the firepower to stop virtually any hostile vehicle dead in its tracks. Unlike antitank missiles, it can be maintained constantly in the ready state.

2. The rationale for adopting the concept of extraordinary costs was to prevent local law enforcement from passing along to the federal government costs that should be borne by each locality as a normal part of the services they provide. In this connection, everyone, including visitors from foreign countries, is entitled to the normal

protections of the law; however, many local governments have found it necessary to provide an extraordinary degree of protection to diplomats and dignitiaries in view of the threat posed by terrorists.

3. A provision in the State Department authorization bill amended prohibitive language in the Foreign Assistance Act pertaining to the training of civil police authorities.

Afterword

Neil C. Livingstone
Terrell E. Arnold

The hijacking of TWA Flight 847 ended, not with the much-discussed reprisal, but with a release. After seventeen days in captivity, the thirty-nine American hostages returned to the United States to be greeted by President Reagan and more of the same media hoopla that had accompanied the incident from the outset. Then, within days, the hostages returned to the obscurity from which they had come prior to their ordeal, and the event began to recede from the public consciousness. Navy seabee Robert Stethem, who had been brutally beaten and then shot by the hijackers, remained the sole fatality of the affair, his death having something of the cruel irony that accompanies the distinction of being the last man to die in a war. As the weeks passed, Stethem's murder, instead of becoming the cause for strong U.S. action against those who perpetrated the attack, was looking more and more like just another terrorist statistic.

The final release of the hostages had been brokered by Syrian President Hafez Assad, who had long sought to impress on the United States Syria's pivotal role in the Middle East. Syria, one of the chief supporters of terrorism in the region and the Lebanese Shiite Amal's principal backer, emerged as one of the clear winners from the incident, a formidable power to be reckoned with in the future. The United States cautiously expressed its gratitude to Assad, and President Reagan, in a tough speech on July 8, 1985, left Syria's name off a list of state sponsors of terrorism. Syria's contribution to the disintegration of Lebanon and its patronage of Lebanese terrorist movements notwithstanding, administration officials spoke privately of their hope for a strengthened dialogue with Assad in the future and their belief that Syria's help would be needed to secure the release of the seven other Americans held hostage since before the TWA hijacking.

Lebanon, by contrast, was one of the losers in this incident, but then Lebanon had been losing for more than a decade, and if Beirut's international airport was closed down by U.S. military action or boycotted by international aviation, it was just one more hardship and humiliation to be endured by an already long-suffering population. Greece, where the hijacking originated, was also a loser, as the international spotlight focused on the Papandreou government's permissive attitude towards terrorism and the lax security procedures at the Athens airport. In the United States and Western Europe, thousands of fearful tourists, alarmed by a U.S. government travel advisory warning of the prospect of being hijacked, canceled summer vacations in Greece, adding new woes to that nation's mismanaged economy. Yet another loser was Israel, its leadership already reeling from criticism over the trade several weeks earlier of 1500 terrorists and captured Lebanese Moslem prisoners, mostly Shiites, for three Israeli soldiers. As part of the eventual understanding that resulted in the freedom of the TWA hostages, Israel was compelled to begin releasing some 700 other Lebanese prisoners. The irony was that Israel had been planning all along to repatriate these prisoners, but once the hijacking occurred its action—despite statements to the contrary—appeared to represent submission to terrorist blackmail and was hailed as a victory by Israel's enemies. The truth was that Israel had few options. If it refused to release the Lebanese prisoners, it would be held responsible for the failure to achieve the release of the hostage passengers from TWA Flight 847, and if it went ahead with their repatriation this action would be interpreted as a sign of weakness. As it was, a nationwide ABC News poll conducted in the United States during the hostage crisis showed a significant decline in the U.S. support for Israel, as 42 percent of those polled indicated the United States should distance itself more from Israel to reduce the threat of terrorist attacks against this country and its citizens.[1]

The jury is still out as to whether the other major protagonists in the hostage drama were winners or losers. The Hesbollah terrorist who initially commandeered the plane appeared to have gotten away with another brazen and successful attack against the United States without feeling the sting of retaliation. Nabih Berri, leader of the Shiite Amal in Lebanon, who had been thrust onto the world stage by the incident and given unprecedented exposure and a platform from which to expound on his grievances against the United States and Israel, was looking more and more like a winner, despite some half-hearted talk in the U.S. Congress of stripping him of his "green card," or U.S. resident alien status.

The biggest question mark concerned public perceptions of the performance of the Reagan administration. Most Americans approved of the president's handling of the crisis, and unlike the Iranian hostage episode which had lasted 444 days, Reagan had secured the release of the TWA hostages in just 17 days. Rather than negotiate directly with the terrorists, the U.S. government had gone to the source and, in behind-the-scenes diplomacy, used both veiled threats and persuasion to convince Syria's Assad that the safe release of the hostages was in his best interest. Reagan, unlike Carter five years earlier, had made clear his intention to use force if necessary, by arraying a large fleet of U.S. warships off the Lebanese coast and advancing a number of already-planned military exercises. Nevertheless, while the crisis had been successfully resolved, at the time of this writing the hijackers are still at large and the United States has not publicly taken any substantive retaliatory steps against those involved. The issue of using force against terrorists remains as clouded and elusive as ever. Despite the results achieved, critics noted that once again the administration engaged in tough talk but little action. During the crisis, President Reagan announced that the United States had reached "our limits" with respect to terrorism—maintaining that responses, "military and otherwise," were still under consideration.[2] In the aftermath of the crisis, he vowed that "[w]e will not forget" what was done to "Robbie" Stethem[3] and declared that, "Terrorists, be on notice: We will fight back against you in Lebanon and elsewhere. We will fight back against your cowardly attacks on American citizens and property."[4] However, instead of the "swift and effective retribution" promised by the President during his first term, Reagan administration officials indicated that the U.S. war on terrorism would remain primarily a defensive war, designed to preempt potential terrorist attacks and covertly disrupt their activities rather than going on the offensive against terrorists and their state supporters or punishing them in the aftermath of an attack. In what could only be anticipated as a futile gesture, Justice Department lawyers were instructed to prepare a case and seek extradition of the hijackers who had killed Stethem.

The Reagan administration had properly shown restraint once the hijackers had forced the pirated TWA aircraft to land in Lebanon a third time; a rescue operation would clearly have been too risky after the number of gunmen on board the plane was increased and some of the hostages had been taken off the aircraft and spirited away to other locations. But the exercise of continued restraint was very much open to question once the hijacking was resolved, with many observers arguing that the United States should carry out punitive raids against terrorist training camps in the Bekka Valley or against other suitable targets as a lesson to terrorists that they could not escape punishment for their actions. Others called for even sterner measures, including dispatching "hit" teams to assassinate those responsible for the hijacking and Stethem's murder. Such calls to action were countered by other observers who maintained that any retaliation would sign the death warrants of the seven remaining American hostages and likely irreparably harm U.S. interests in the Middle East and elsewhere. And on the question of assassination, critics argued that it was inconsistent with American traditions and that the damage the United States would suffer in the eyes of world opinion would far outweigh any gains that could be scored against international terrorists.

Thus, the debate over how the United States should respond to international terrorism remains just as inconclusive as ever. Public opinion, however, seems to be shifting in favor of strong action to combat terrorism, and even heretofore passive voices in the Congress and the media are beginning to call for a tougher stance on the part of the administration. The issue of using force against terrorists is no longer a question of "if" but rather of "when." And the matter of assassinating terrorists, once confined to whispered comments behind closed doors, has become an issue of open public debate. At the very least, the hijacking drama of TWA Flight 847 has given the public, together with lawmakers and opinion generators, new insights into the threat posed by international terrorism and new appreciation for both the complex issues and potential risks and gains associated with the use of force against terrorists.

Notes

1. *The Washington Post*, "Poll Finds Rising Sentiment for Distancing U.S. From Israel," June 26, 1985.

2. *The Washington Post*, "U.S. Has Reached 'Limits' on Terrorism, Reagan Says," June 21, 1985.

3. President Ronald Reagan, quoted in *The Washington Post*, "Relief, Pride and 'Promises to Be Kept'," July 3, 1985.

4. President Ronald Reagan, quoted in *The Washington Post*, "39 U.S. Hostages Freed After 17-Day Ordeal; Reagan Vows to 'Fight Back' at Terrorism," July 1, 1985.

Index

Abu Nidal, 19–20, 241
Accelerator rounds, 27
Acoustic barriers, 104
Acrylics, 105
Action directe, 1
Advance team, 99–100
Agent networks, 232–233
Aircraft hijacking: Air France (1983), 16; conventions, 9, 54, 85–86, 136, 158; FAA responsibilities for, 51; Iranian-supported, 16; Kuwait Airline (1984), 16, 21–22; TWA flight 847, 22, 223–224, 241
Alarms, panic, 102
Alexander, Yonah, 13, 122
ALF, 214, 217
Alliance, Western, erosion of, 5
Alternatives, lack of, 146–149, 205–206
Altheide, David, 223
Aluminum armor, 106
Aluminum oxide, 106
Ammonium nitrate, 43
Ammunition, 26–28
Anderson, Terry, 155 n.2
Angola, Portuguese, 120–121
Animal Liberation Front (ALF), 214, 217
Antitank rockets, 30
Anti-Terrorism Assistance Program, 54
Arafat, Yasir, 126
Arcane round, 27
Armed Forces of Popular Resistance, 46
Armed Forces of Puerto Rican National Liberation (FALN), 2
Armed Resistance Unit, 2

Armor, 105–106
Armor-piercing rounds, 26–27
Arms, small, 26–28
Assad, 19
Assassination, prohibition on, 137
Asylum, 5, 240–242
Attacks, nature of, 179, 182. *See also* Mechanics of violence; Vehicle bombs
Attorney general, 137
Audio surveillance, 102–104
Aukar embassy bombing, 61, 66–67, 74, 234, 245 n.1
Aung San bombing, 11–12
Authority, national, 202–204

Baader-Meinhof gang, 201
"Baby food bomber" case, 37–38
Bacterial agents, 31–32
Bag, diplomatic, 18, 87
Baltimore Sun, 115
Barbed tape, 102
Barbed wire, 102
Barriers, 29, 101, 102, 104
Basque Homeland and Liberty Movement (ETA), 13, 20
Bassiouni, M. Cherif, 222
Beirut: car bombings in, 41; embassy bombings, 19, 61, 66–67, 74–75, 234, 245 n.1; Iran and, 1–2. *See also* Marine barracks bombing (1983)
Betancourt, Romulo, 40
Biological agents, 31–32
Black June (Abu Nidal), 19–20, 241
Black September, 126
Black steel projectile, 27

Blacks, South African, 201
Blasting caps, 36
Bodyguards, 98–99
Bombacino, Louis, 37
Bombs, vehicle, 35–47, 245 n.1; in
    Beirut, 41; booby trapped, 46–47;
    checking for, 38; construction of,
    36–37; defenses against, 44–45;
    evolution of, 47; for killing
    occupants, 37–40; with large
    quantities of explosives, 42–45;
    methods of, 35–36; with multiple
    bombs, 45–46; with munition
    launching system, 42; popularity of,
    35; proxy, 40–42; remotely
    controlled, 40; uses of, 28–29
Bonn economic summits, 9, 54, 89, 90,
    158
Booby traps, 36, 46–47
Buckley, William, 16, 155 n.2, 214
Bulgaria, 21
Bullet-resistant materials, 105–106
Bullets, 26–28
Bureau of Alcohol, Tobacco and
    Firearms, 52
Bureaucracy: defined, 80 n.7; dilemmas
    within, 55–57; transient interest of,
    61. See also Government response;
    Policy(ies)
Bush, George, 115

Cabinet Committee to Combat
    Terrorism, 50–51
Calhoun, John, 150–151
Caltrops, 25–26
Capone, Al, 37
Caps, blasting, 36
Car bombs. See Vehicle bombs
Caroline incident, 150, 169
Carrier current detectors, 103–104
Carter, Jimmy, 4, 184
Casey, William, 15, 111, 119, 146
Catholics, Ulster, 201
CBS, 221
Censorship of the media, 222
Central America, suicide car bombings
    in, 72
Central Intelligence Agency (CIA), 51,
    112, 113–114, 232
Centralization issue, 55
Ceramics, 106

Chain link fence, 102
Chancellor, John, 224
Chemical warfare, 4, 31–32, 191–192,
    208 nn.3, 5
Cheysson, Claude, 63
Chouf Mountains, shelling of, 122
CIA, 51, 112, 113–114, 232
Cicero, 144, 152
Civil police rules of engagement, 188
Civil rights demonstrations (1960s),
    223
Clear and present danger rule, 162–
    163, 222
Cline, Ray, 13
Coast Guard, U.S., 52
Colby, William E., 194
Collective responsibility, 122
Colombia, drug traffickers-insurgents
    alliance in, 143–144
Command post, protective detail's, 99
Communication, technical security and,
    100–101
Communist Combatant Cells, 47
Communist Fighting Cells, 1
Constitutional law, definition of
    terrorism and, 161–162
Convention Relating to the Status of
    Refugees, 165
Convention on the Suppression of
    Terrorism (1977), 90
Convention to Prevent and Punish the
    Acts of Terrorism Taking the Form
    of Crimes against Persons and
    Related Extortion That Are of
    International Significance, 90
Convention, acceptance of, 192–193
Cooperation, international, 74,
    81 n.34, 88–89, 237–238. See also
    Diplomacy
"Coping with Violence Abroad"
    (course), 235–236
Correlation of forces concept, 80 n.16
Costs, extraordinary, concept of, 236,
    246 n.2
Council of Europe, 90
Court, federal, for dealing with
    terrorism, 173
Covert responses, 133–144; challenge
    of, 142–144; infiltration and, 138–
    139; legal parameters, 134–137;
    public response to, 143, 144; review

procedures for, 141–142; Rowe case, 139–141; societal values and, 142, 143, 144; training for, 146–147

Crime: organized, 37; terrorism as, 202–204

Criminality, double, 164

Customs Service, U.S., 52

Czar, counterterrorism, 55

Czechoslovakia, 21

Dancy, John, 218, 223, 225

Data collection phase of target study, 97

Deadly force, 191 n.16

Declaration on Principles of International Law Concerning Friendly Relations and Cooperation among States in Accordance with the Charter of the United Nations, 158–159

Defense Department: definition of terrorism, 194; jurisdiction of, 135; motivations of, 57; oversight of, 137; position of, 114; preparedness of, 77; role of, 51–52. *See also Report of the DOD Commission on the Beirut International Airport Terrorist Act*

Delta force, U.S., 238

Democracy, 1–10; destabilization of, 63; modern terrorism and, 3–5; paradox of, 8; strategies available to, 8–10; use of force and, 120; war against, 2–3

Dennis v. *United States,* 162–163

Detectors, 103–104

Deterrence, 53–54

Dignitaries, security for, 236–237

Diplomacy, 85–94; bilateral context of, 90–91; economic summits and, 89–90; efficacy of, 74; immunity, 116; impact on, 5; in Lebanon, 93; NATO and, 88–89; pressure from, 238–239; proactive responses and, 91–92, 115–117; sanctions, 92–93; termination of, 93; United Nations and, 85–87

Diplomatic bag, 18, 87

Diplomats: Libyan, 18; security for, 236–237; Vienna Declaration on protection of, 9

DOD directive 5148.11, 137

DOD Regulation 5240.1, 135

DOD report. *See Report of the DOD Commission on the Beirut International Airport Terrorist Act*

Dodge, David, 16, 19

Double criminality, principle of, 164

Downie, Leonard, Jr., 221

Dozier, James, 85, 88, 91

Drop transmitters, 104

Drug trafficking, 143–144, 159

Dryden, John, 244

"Duties, Of" (Cicero), 144

East Germany, 21

Economic sanctions, 74, 93, 239

Economic summit conferences, 9, 54, 89–90, 157–158, 243

Economic terrorism, 26

ECT, 51

Egypt, 240

Eisler, Gerhart, 164

Electronic inspection, 103

Elite paramilitary units, 126–128. *See also* Strike teams

Embassies, U.S.: Beirut annex, 61, 66–67, 74–75, 234, 245 n.1; rocket attacks on, 42; roles of, 117; security guards of, rules for, 186; suicide bombings of, 43–45, 61, 74; transformation of, 5

Encryption devices, 104

Energy Department, 52–53, 57

Engagement, rules of, 175–190; civil police, 188; defined, 177; for embassy guards, 186; Marines in Beirut and, 176, 177–179; *Mayaguez* crisis and, 175–177, 184; nature of terrorist attacks and, 179, 182; place of, 187–188; principles for using force, 180–181; purposes of, 181–182; rewriting, 181–183; for static security situations, 184–185; strike team, 183–184; for threatened individuals, 186–187. *See also* War(fare)

ETA, 13, 20

Ethics. *See* Morality

Evacuation, as threat response, 105
Exclusion practice, 164
Executive Committee on Terrorism (ECT), 51
Executive order 12333, 135, 137
Executive order 12334, 137
Executive protection, 95–107; initial assessment, 96–97; intelligence, 106; personnel for, 98–100; steps in, 95–96; technical security, 100–106
Exiles, political, 240–242
Explosives, 28–29, 104–105
Export Administration Act amendment, 20–21
Extradition, 163–167
Extraordinary costs, concept of, 236, 246 n.2

FAA, 51, 52
Fadlallah, Mohammed Hussein, 6, 146
FALN, 2
FBI. See Federal Bureau of Investigation
Fearey, Robert A., 171
Federal Aviation Administration (FAA), 51, 52
Federal Bureau of Investigation (FBI): definition of terrorism, 194; jurisdiction of, 51, 52, 137; lead agency responsibilities of, 187; Los Angeles Olympics security from, 112; Rowe case and, 139–141; success of, 91–92
Fence, chain link, 102
Fluoroscopic equipment, 104
Force, use of: arguments for, 149–152; community policy and, 171–172; deadly, 191 n.16; democracy and, 120; framework for, 167–170; human rights and, 168, 172–173; lack of remedies and, 146–149; legality of, 145–156, 167–171; morality of, 152–155; principles for, 180–181; public confidence in, 181; self-defense/self-help rationale for, 169, 172; threat framework and, 170; through U.S. military, 71–77; U.N. Charter on, 147, 149–150; viability of, 244; Vietnam legacy and, 180–181; correlation of,

80 n.16. See also Engagement, rules of
Ford, Gerald, 175–176, 178, 184
Foreign Intelligence Surveillance Act, 135, 161
Foreign policy. See Policy(ies)
France, 5, 17, 241
Frank, Reuven, 218
Free association, right of, 242
Fugitives, 165

Garfield, James, 147
Gas tank, 39–40
Gas, poison, 31–32
Geneva Convention, 86–87, 136, 170
Geneva Protocols (1977), 170, 209 n.8
German Red Army Faction, 13
Germany, East, 21
GIGN, 238
Glaser Safety Slug, 27–28
Glass reinforced plastics (GRP), 106
Gonzalez, Felipe, 13
Goren, Roberta, 13
Government response, 49–57; attention paid to terrorism and, 92; bureaucratic issues in, 55–57; current structure and policy, 53–54, 56; evolution of, 54–55; historical review of, 50–53. See also Bureaucracy; Policy(ies)
Grenada invasion, 82 n.45
Grievance, just, 204
Gromyko, Andre, 13
Grotius, Hugo, 153
Groupe d'intervention de la gendarmerie nationale (GIGN), 238
GRP, 106
Guerrilla Resistance Movement, 2
Guerrilla warfare, 193
Gulf of Sidra incident, 240
Gurr, Ted Robert, 12

Hague Conference, 191
Hague Convention (1970), 136
Haig, Alexander, 88, 109
Hall, Richard, 220
Hamilton, Alexander, 55
Hamilton, Lee H., 222
Hanafi Muslims, 220–221
Hannay, 167

Hardening, target: efficacy of, 73, 74; initial assessment, 96–97; intelligence, 106; protective detail, 98–100; technical security, 100–106
Harrod's, car bombing of, 41
Harvard Draft Convention, 163–164
Hegel, George, 154
Henry, Emily, 122
Hesbollah terrorists, 6–7, 17, 74–75, 110
Hijacking, aircraft. *See* Aircraft hijacking
Holmes, Oliver Wendell, Jr., 130, 162, 222
Hostage: crisis (Iran), 14–15, 93, 223; U.N. Convention on taking, 54; U.S. relations with Syria and Iran and, 22–23
Hot pursuit, theory of, 151–152
Human rights, 118, 159, 168, 172–173
Humint (human intelligence), 111, 138, 232
Humint magazine, 133
Hussein, Saddam, 17

Ice pick, 26
IG/T, 55
Immunity, diplomatic, 116
In re Castioni, 165–166
In re Extradition of Desmond Mackin, 166
In re Extradition of Eain, 166
In re the Extradition of McMullen, 166
Incendiaries, 29
Individual, threatened, rules of engagement for, 186–187
Infiltration, 1386139, 232
Inspection, electronic, 103
Installations, U.S.: bombings of, 19–22; security of, 111–112, 233–235. *See also* Embassies, U.S.; Marine barracks bombing (1983)
Insurgency, 193
Intelligence: 1970's reforms effect on, 111; agent networks, 232–233; for executive protection, 106; human, 111, 138, 232; infiltration, 138–139, 232; limitations of, 66–67, 129–130; need for, 91; police-like requirements of, 232; preemption and, 124–125; sharing, 89; target

hardening and, 106; training, 91–92; Vietnam legacy and, 232–233; warfare and, 66–67. *See also* Covert responses
Intelligence Oversight Board, 137
Inter-American Convention on Terrorism, 90
Interdepartmental Group on Terrorism (IG/T), 55
International Law Association, 195
International Law Commission, 87
International law, gaps in, 147–148
Intrusion detection systems, 101–102
IRA, 13, 40–41, 45, 231
Iran: attacks on Kuwait, 15–16; hostage crisis, 22–23, 93, 223; -Iraq war, 17; Lebanon and, 1–2, 15–16, 18–19; Marine barracks bombing and, 15; safe havens, 241; sponsorship of terrorism by, 1–2, 3, 14–17, 22–23; -Syria partnership, 18–19; U.S. warning to, 119
Iraq, 17, 20
Irish Republican Army (IRA), 13, 40–41, 45, 231
Islamic Jihad, 15, 17, 19, 43–45, 110, 232
Israel, 121–122, 148, 203, 205
Italian Red Brigades, 13

Jackson, Andrew, 150
Jacobsen, Dave, 155 n.2
Jeahnig, Walter, 222–223
Jefferson, Thomas, 208
Jenco, Lawrence, 17, 155 n.2
Jenkins, Brian, 195, 216
John Paul II, Pope, assassination attempt on, 21
Joint Chiefs of Staff, 77
Judgment, political, morality and, 196–198
Just grievance, 204
Justice Department, 51

Kelley, Paul, 197
Kentucky coal mine strike, 26
Kevlar, 106
Khmer Rouge, 193
Khomeini, Ayatollah, 17, 19, 110
Kidnappings, 16, 17
Kilburn, Peter, 155 n.2

Kiritsis, Anthony, 220
Kissinger, Henry, 46, 159, 231
Koch, Noel, 112, 113, 114
Kroesen, Frederick J., 88
KTW bullets, 27
Ku Klux Klan, 139–141
Kuwait Airline hijacking (1984), 16,
    21–22
Kuwait, Iranian attacks on, 15–16

Laqueur, Walter, 14, 215
Latin America, Soviet sponsorship in,
    61
Law: constitutional, 161–162;
    development of, 157–158;
    international, 147–148; intrinsic
    moral value in, 208 n.6; of
    proportionality, 123
Law enforcement officers, training of,
    91–92
Lead agency responsibility, 51, 187,
    190 n.15
Lebanese Armed Revolutionary
    Faction, 241
Lebanon: diplomacy in, 93; Iranian
    attacks on, 15–16; multinational
    peacekeeping force (NMF) in, 22,
    222; Syrian-Iranian partnership in,
    18–19. See also Embassies, U.S.;
    Marine barracks bombing (1983)
Legal issues, 128–130
Legal recourse, 157–174; covert
    responses and, 134–137; definitions
    of terrorism and, 160–163;
    economic summits and, 157–158;
    extradition, 163–167; force, 167–
    171; obstacles to, 242–244;
    preemption, 163. See also Force, use
    of
Lenin, Vladimir, 65
Letelier, Orlando, 39
Levi, Edward H., 141
Levin, Jeremy, 16, 19, 155 n.2
Levy guidelines, 141
Liberation, wars of, 63–66, 86–87,
    158–159, 170
Libya: diplomats from, 18; safe havens,
    241; sanctions against, 93, 239–
    240; sponsorship of terrorism, 1, 3,
    14, 17–18, 23; training camps

operated by, 18; U.S. warning to,
    119
Libyan People's Bureau (London)
    incident, 18
Limpet mines, 39
Lippman, Walter, 213
Liuzzo, Viola, 140
Locke, John, 153
Lod Airport massacre, 50
London Declaration, 89–90
London Economic Summit Conference
    (1984), 54, 157–158
Long commission report. See Report of
    the DOD Commission on the Beirut
    International Airport Terrorist Act
Long, Robert L., 177
Los Angeles Olympics, 111–112, 236

Macheteros, 2
Madison, James, 55
Marine barracks bombing (1983):
    aftermath of, 110; debate over
    response to, 67; events leading to,
    22; Iranian financing of, 15;
    Mayaguez crisis and, 176–177, 184;
    political consequences of, 62; rules
    of engagement and, 176, 177–179;
    suicide vehicle used for, 44;
    transient bureaucratic interest in, 61
Martyrs' Mausoleum bombing, 11–12
Marx, Karl, 65
May 15 group, 20
Mayaguez crisis, 175–177, 184
Mayer, Norman, 43
McCamant, John F., 210 n.24
McFarlane, Robert C., ix–x, 117–118,
    146, 168, 180
McGlinchey v. Wren, 166–167
McLuhan, Marshall, 226
Mechanics of violence, 25–33;
    chemical, biological and toxin
    agents, 4, 31–32, 191–192,
    208 nn.3, 5; explosives, 28–29,
    104–105; incendiaries, 29;
    mechanical devices, 25–26; nuclear
    devices, 32–33; small arms, 26–28;
    standoff weapons, 29–31
Media, the, 213–227; accessing, 215–
    218; censorship of, 222; excesses of,
    223–225; manipulating, 219–220;
    mobilizing, 223–226; morality, 218–

219; portrayal of policy by, 6–7; public's rights to know and, 220–223; technological advances and, 213–214, 224–225

Meir, Golda, 126

Meyer, Armin H., 50

Mhaydali, Sana, 214

Middle East, Soviet sponsorship in, 61. *See also* specific countries

Military action, 71–77; advantages of, 76–77; arguments against, 74–75; human rights issue and, 118; preemptive and preventive, 82 n.40; Shultz-Weinberger debate over, 114–118; tests for, 75–76, 114. *See also* Engagement, rules of; Force, use of; Proactive responses; War(fare)

Military, U.S.: competence of, 78–79; as target, 68–71

Missiles, wire-guided, 30–31

Mivtzan, Elohim ("Wrath of God"), 126–127

MNF, 22, 222

Monroe, James, 151

Montesquieu, Baron de, 153

Montreal Convention concerning aircraft hijacking, 54, 136

Morality, 191–211; acceptance of convention and, 192–193; classes of terrorism and, 199–201; of covert responses, 133–144; criminal act vs. warfare view of terrorism and, 201–207; definitions of terrorism and, 194–196; exhaustion of alternatives criterion and, 205–206; just grievance criterion and, 204; law and, 208 n.6; likelihood of success criterion and, 206; media, 218–219; national authority criterion and, 202–204; new weapons and, 191–192, 207; political judgements and, 196–198; proactive responses and, 128–129, 203–204; reprisals and, 205–206; of using force, 152–155

Moro National Liberation Front, 18

Mortar systems, 30

Mousavi, Mir Hossein, 72

Multinational peacekeeping force (MNF), 22, 222

Munich Olympics massacre, 50, 126

Munitions, protection from, 104–105

National Security Agency (NSA), 112

National Security Council, 51

National Security Decision Directive 138, 67, 112–113

National sovereignty, 89

NATO, 13, 88–89

Naulilaa, skirmish at, 120–121

NBC-TV, 221

Neale, William, D., 79 n.2

NEST, 52

Networks, agent, 232–233

New York Times, 221

Nicaragua, sponsorship of terrorism by, 20

Nicholson, Harold, 115

Nimeiri opponents, 183

Nixon, Richard, 50, 52

North Atlantic Treaty Organization (NATO), 13, 88–89

Nuclear devices, 32–33

Nuclear Emergency Search Team (NEST), 52

Nuclear waste dispersal, 32–33

Oakley, Robert B., 51, 146, 148

OAS, 90

Oberdorfer, Don, 224

Office for Combating Terrorism, 50

Office of Safeguards and Security, 52–53

Olympics, 50, 111–112, 126

Opaque bullet-resistant materials, 106

Organization of American States (OAS), 90

Organized crime, 37

Palestine, 2

Palestine Liberation Organization (PLO): Black September group of, 126; credibility of, 215; Israel's nonrecognition of, 203; Soviet Union and, 12–13; Syrian control of, 19–20; use of multiple bomb car tactic, 45

Panic alarms, 102

Party of God, 81 n.22

Pentagon, 114

Personnel self-protection training, 235–236

Philadelphia Inquirer, 115

Physical security, 101–102, 110, 233–235, 245 n.1. *See also* Target hardening
Poison gas, 31–32
Police matter, terrorism as, 88–89
Police rules of engagement, 188
Police training, 91–92
Policy(ies): competing influences on, 55–57; deterrence, 53–54; impact on, 4; media and, 6–7; moderate vs. aggressive, 6–7; patience, 244; for use of force, 171–172; Vietnam legacy and, 146. *See also* Strategic responses
Polisario Liberation Front, 18
Political exiles, 240–242
Political sanctions, 239
Polycarbonates, 106
Postal conventions, 136
Pouch, diplomatic, 18, 87
Powell, Jody, 219
Preemption: diplomacy and, 91–92; efficacy of, 91–92; intelligence and, 124–125; legal provision for, 163; military, 82 n.40; morality and, 203–204; problems of, 124–126
Premeditated attacks, 68–69
Press, the. *See* Media, the
Pressure, diplomatic, 238–239
Prevention, 82 n.40
Private security industry, 5
Proactive responses, 109–131; Article 51 of U.N. Charter and, 119–120; diplomacy and, 115–117; morality and, 128–129; NSDD 138 and, 112–113; Reagan administration discord and, 112–119; reprisals, 120–124, 148, 205–206; retribution, 126–128. *See also* Executive protection; Military action; Preemption
Projectiles, 27–28
Proportionality, law of, 123
Protection, executive. *See* Executive protection
Protective detail, 98–100
Public attitudes: toward antiterrorist policies, 49; toward collective responsibility, 122; toward covert acts, 143, 144; toward terrorism, 210 n.24; transiency of, 71–72; toward using force, 181
Public transportation as bombing sites, 45–46
Public's right to know, 220–223
Puerto Rican separatists, 2
Pyongyang government, 11–12

Qaddafi, Muammar, 1, 17–18, 119, 239–240
Quainton, Anthony, 50–51
Quinn v. Robinson, 166

Radio. *See* Media, the
Rand Chronology of International Terrorism, 68
Randolph, Eleanor, 224
Random targets, 69
Rapid energy transfer projectiles, 27–28
Ray, Charles, 241
Readiness, ensuring, 185
Reagan administration, 53, 109–110, 112–119, 236
Reagan, Ronald, 4, 6, 67, 73, 74, 91–92, 118, 146, 178, 235
Red Army Faction, 1
Reflectometers, time domain, 103
Refugees, 165
Regier, Frank, 17
Report of the DOD Commission on the Beirut International Airport Terrorist Act, 77, 79 n.3, 177, 178–179, 197–198
Reprisals, 120–124, 148, 205–206
Responsibility: collective, 122; lead agency, 51, 187, 190 n.15
Retribution, 126–128
Revel, Jean-François, 7–8
Revolutionary Guard, 18–19
Rightist groups, 2. *See also* specific groups
Rights, human, 118, 159, 168, 172–173
Rockets, 30–31, 42
Rogers, William, 50
Roosevelt, Franklin Delano, 125
Rosenthal, A.M., 221
Rowe case, 139–141

Safe havens, elimination of, 240–242
Salameh, Ali Hassan, 127

Sanctions, 74, 93, 239–240
Sandinista government, 20
Sayer, Robert, 51
Scalfaro, Oscar Luigi, 63
SCC, 51
Scenarios, formulation of, 97
Schaufelberger, Albert, 20
Schenck v. United States, 162
Schiavone, Louise, 218
Schlesinger, James, 71
Scramblers, 104
Searches: bomb, 105; physical, 103
Second Lateran Council (1139), 191
Secret Service, 52
Security: for diplomats and dignitaries, 236–237; efficacy of, 73; physical, 101–102, 110, 233–235, 245 n.1; private, 5; rules of, 184–185; technical, 100–106; of U.S. installations, 111–112, 233–235
Security personnel: common modes of attack on, 189; for executive protection, 98–100; at U.S. embassies, 186
Selection, target, 95–96
Self-defense: as rationale for using force, 169, 172; training, 235–236; U.N. Charter on, 147–148, 150. *See also* Executive protection
Seminole Indians, 150–151
Shiite Moslems, nature of, 110
Shultz, George, 53–54, 66, 67, 75, 82 n.35, 110, 114–118, 123, 134, 142, 143, 159–160, 163, 169, 170–171, 180, 188–189, 205, 231
Sikhs, 45
SLAP rounds, 27
Small arms, 27–28
Small, William, 221
Soap dish bombs, 39
Solzhenitsyn, Aleksandr, 199, 210 n.18
South African blacks, 201
South Korea, 11–12
Sovereignty, national, 89
Soviet Union: definition of terrorism, 86; Export Administration Act amendment and, 21; infrastructure of world terrorism from, 12–13, 21, 60–61, 64–66; paramilitary power projection, 80 n.17; sponsorship in Middle East, 12–13, 61; support of

"wars of liberation", 63–66, 158–159; United Nations and, 86–87
Spadolini, Giovanni, 1
Special Coordination Committee (SCC), 51
Special Security Group (SSG), 55
Special Situation Group, 53
Speciality, principle of, 165
Spectrum analyzer, 103
Speech, freedom of, 222
SSG. *See* Special Security Group
Standoff weapons, 29–31
State Department, 20–21, 50–51, 57, 235–236
State-sponsored terrorism, 11–24; Aung San bombing and, 11–12; consequences for U.S., 61–62; current strategic responses to, 134; defined, 79 n.2; evolution of, 12–14; growth of, 21–23; increase in, 60; Iran, 1–2, 3, 14–17, 22–23; Libya, 1, 3, 14, 17–18, 23; London Declaration and, 89–90; nature of, 73–74, 77–78; Nicaragua, 20; other countries, 20–21; Palestine, 2; Reagan on, 119; reprisals against, 123; resources provided by, 62; Soviet role in, 12–13, 21, 60–61, 64–66; State Department list of, 20–21; support and sophistication of, 73; Syria, 3, 18–20, 22–23; Western values as target of, 62–63
Steel armor, 106
Stockman, David, 117
Strategic responses, 229–247; components of, 229–230; current, 134; diplomats and dignitaries, security for, 236–237; economic, diplomatic and political pressure, 93, 238–240; intergovernmental cooperation, 88–89, 237–238; personnel self-protection training, 235–236; physical security, 101–102, 110, 233–235, 245 n.1; safe havens, elimination of, 240–242. *See also* Force, use of; Intelligence; Legal recourse
Strike teams, 183–184, 238
Success, likelihood of, criterion of, 206
Sudan, 183

Suicide bomb attacks, 43–45, 47, 61, 72, 74
Summers, Harry G., Jr., 8
Summit Seven nations, 9, 54, 89–90, 157–158, 243
Surveillance, audio, 102–104
Sutherland, Thomas, 155 n.2
Syria, 3, 18–20, 22–23

Target hardening: efficacy of, 73, 74; initial assessment, 96–97; intelligence, 106; protective detail, 98–100; technical security, 100–106
Target selection, 95–96
Target study, 96–97
Technical security, 100–106; audio surveillance countermeasures, 102–104; bullet-resistant materials, 105–106; communication, 100–101; explosives and munitions protection, 104–105; physical security, 101–102, 110, 233–235, 245 n.1
Technological advances, media and, 213–214, 224–225
Teflon-coated bullets, 27
Tehran, hostage crisis in, 14–15, 93, 223
Telephone analyzer, 103
Television terrorism, 216–217, 225–226
Tennessee v. *Garner*, 152, 163, 190 n.16
Terrorism, definitions of, 79 n.2, 135, 160–163, 194–196
Thatcher, Margaret, 231
Threat modeling, 96
Threat response, 104–105
Threatened individual, rules for, 186–187
THV round, 27–28
Time domain reflectometers, 103
Title 18, 135–136
Title 28, 137
Tokyo convention (1963), 136
Tovar, Hugh, 119, 120, 129–130
Toxin agents, 31–32
Training, 91–92, 146–147
Training camps, Libyan-operated, 18
Transmitters, drop, 104
Transnational terrorism, defined, 160
Transparent armor, 105

Transportation Department, 52, 57
Transportation, public, as targets, 45–46
Treasury Department, 52
Tupamaros, 215–216
Turkey, response to terrorism, 5
Turkish terrorists, 13
TWA flight 847 hijacking, 22, 223–224, 241
Tylenol scare, 31

U.K.-U.S. extradition treaty, 166–167
Ulster Catholics, 201
United Nations: Charter, 119–120, 147–150; contributions of, 85–86; diplomacy and, 85–87; efficacy of, 9, 149; hostage taking convention, 54; inability to condemn terrorism, 210 n.18; Soviet bloc in, 86–87
United States v. *Toscanino*, 165

Values, 62–63, 142, 143, 144
Vehicle bombs, 35–47, 245 n.1; in Beirut, 41; booby trapped, 46–47; checking for, 38; construction of, 36–37; defenses against, 44–45; evolution of, 47; for killing occupants, 37–40; with large quantities of explosives, 42–45; methods of, 35–36; with multiple bombs, 45–46; with munition launching system, 42; popularity of, 35; proxy, 40–42; remotely controlled, 40; uses of, 28–29
Video equipment availability, 213–214
Vienna Declaration on the protection of diplomats, 9
Vietnam legacy, 146, 180–181, 232–233
Villa, Francisco, 151
Violence, mechanics of. *See* Mechanics of violence
von Clausewitz, Carl, 177–178
von Moltke, Helmuth, 229
Vriesman, Wayne, 225
Vulnerability study, 97

Walzer, Michael, 123
War(fare), 58–83; against democracy, 2–3; against U.S. military targets, 68–71; chemical, 4, 31–32, 191–

192, 208 nn.3, 5; guerilla, 193; intelligence community and, 66–7; of liberation, 63–66, 86–87, 158–159, 170; realities of, 60–63, 67–68; rules of, 153–155, 169–170; Soviet revolutionary process and, 63–66; terrorism as, 201–207; validity of premise of, 59. *See also* Engagement, rules of; Force, use of; Military action

Washington Conference, 191

Washington Monument, threatened bombing of, 43

Washington Post, 6, 12, 146, 219, 221, 224

Watkins, James D., 109, 114, 129, 143, 198

Watts riots, 223

Weapons, 29–31, 191–192, 207. *See also* Mechanics of violence

Weathermen, 201

Webster, Daniel, 150, 169

Webster, William, 112

Weinberger, Caspar, 75–76, 82 n.35, 114–118, 169, 171, 177, 180–181

Weir, Benjamin, 17, 155 n.2

West Virginia coal mine strike, 26

Western alliance, erosion of, 5

Western Europe, 64, 88–90

Western nations, cooperation between, 74, 81 n.34, 88–89, 237–238

Wilson, Woodrow, 151

Wisconsin, University of, bombing in, 43

Working shift, protective detail's, 98–99

World War III, 2–3. *See also* War(fare)

"Wrath of God", 126–127

Yoder, Edwin M., Jr., 224

Young, Andrew, 222

About the Editors and Contributors

Terrell E. Arnold is presently a consultant to the Department of State on terrorism and crisis management, as well as a consultant to several private firms. He also serves as executive director of the Institute on Terrorism and Subnational Conflict. During 1983–1984, he served as principal deputy director, Office of Counterterrorism and Emergency Planning, Department of State. He is a former senior foreign service officer of the United States Department of State with wide background in the foreign relations of the United States, particularly with countries of the Middle East, Latin America and East Asia. He served in the U.S. Navy during World War II and again during the Korean War. He is a graduate of Stanford University, holds a masters degree from San Jose State College, and is a graduate of the National War College.

Neil C. Livingstone is an international businessman, lecturer, and consultant on terrorism and national security affairs. He currently serves as president of the Institute on Terrorism and Subnational Conflict and as adjunct professor in the Georgetown University National Security Studies Program.

At the present time, Mr. Livingstone also serves as a consultant to Jaycor and SRI International; a member of the boards of directors of the National Center for Export-Import Studies (Georgetown University), the International Strategic Studies Association, and the Institute for Public Safety; a member of the advisory boards of the Canadian Business Roundtable and the Boyd and Grace Martin Institute of Human Behavior (University of Idaho); and is a founding member and member of the board of directors of the Solidarity Endowment, an organization established in the U.S. to promote the goals and purposes of Polish solidarity.

Mr. Livingstone has advised many top government and business leaders on terrorism and low-intensity conflict and is a frequent media guest on the subject of terrorism and defense policy. He is the author of numerous articles and monographs on terrorism and foreign-policy topics, and his book *The War against Terrorism* was published by Lexington Books in 1982. Mr. Livingstone holds degrees from the College of William and Mary, the University of Montana, and Tuft's Fletcher School of Law and Diplomacy, where he completed his Ph.D. dissertation in 1982.

Harry H. Almond, Jr. is professor of international law at the National Defense University and adjunct professor in the national securities studies program at Georgetown University. He was formerly senior attorney advisor, international law, in the Office of the Secretary of Defense. Mr. Almond has a Ph.D. in international law from the London School of Economics, a J.D. from Harvard Law School, and undergraduate degrees from Cornell and Yale. He is a member of the bar in New York state and of the U.S. Supreme Court, and is widely published in the areas of international law, arms control and disarmament, deterrence, and terrorism.

Father James Burtchaell has earned degrees in theology from the Gregorian University in Rome, the Catholic University in Washington, and Cambridge University in England, from which he holds a Ph.D. in divinity. He is a professor of theology on the regular faculty at Notre Dame and has been elected president of the American Academy of Religion. He has served as a consultant and committee member for the Danforth Foundation, the American Council of Learned Societies, the Fulbright Commission, the National Endowment of the Humanities, the Indiana Conference of Higher Education, and the Association of American Colleges. He was the founding chairman of the Council on the Study of Religion and the Center for Constitutional Studies. Father Burtchaell is the author of seven books, including *For Better, For Worse*, on marriage, and *Rachel Weeping, and Other Essays on Abortion*.

William R. Farrell, is a lieutenant colonel in the U.S. Air Force and a member of the faculty of the Naval War College. He holds a doctorate in political science from the University of Michigan. His military experiences have centered on counterintelligence and security matters both domestically and overseas. Dr. Farrell has written numerous papers and articles concerning policy development in light of the threat posed by terrorism. His book, *The U.S. Government's Response to Terrorism* is published by Westview Press. Dr. Farrell has provided assistance to the Office of the Joint Chiefs of Staff, the National Security Council, Office of the Chief of Naval Operations and the Department of Energy on the formulation of counterterrorism policy.

Christine C. Ketcham, as general manager of the Public Safety Group, guides the daily operations of its several divisions. Through her professional associations, Ms. Ketcham has gained first-hand experience with a variety of small arms and explosive devices, and she has studied and evaluated origins and methodologies of violence and terrorism. Holder of a B.A. from Upsala

College and an M.A. in education from Rutgers University, she has co-authored numerous articles on security, ordnance, and terrorism.

William D. Livingstone currently serves as press secretary to Senator Pete Wilson of California. He was previously press secretary to Senator James McClure, and before that he was deputy media director for the Senate G.O.P. Conference. He received his B.S. from Montana State University, and completed his graduate studies at the University of Southern California and the Fletcher School of Law and Diplomacy.

Harvey J. McGeorge II, CPP, is president of the Public Safety Group, a diverse technical security firm. He previously served with the U.S. Secret Service at the White House and as their technical representative on the Nuclear Emergency Search Team. Mr. McGeorge also served as an explosive ordnance (bomb) disposal specialist in the U.S. Marine Corps. A frequent lecturer on national security topics and veteran of many media appearances, Mr. McGeorge has written numerous articles dealing with terrorism, ordnance, and technical security topics.

James B. Motley is director of national security studies for Defense Systems, Inc. In addition to his primary interest in the area of low-intensity conflict, Dr. Motley also specializes in Soviet Studies, NATO affairs, and arms control. He has over twenty years experience in the government and academic sectors relating to political-military affairs. He has served as country director in the Office of the Secretary of Defense, a senior fellow at the National Defense University, political-military analyst in the Organization of the Joint Chiefs of Staff and on the Department of Army General Staff. Prior to joining the National Institute, Dr. Motley was a senior fellow at The Atlantic Council of the United States, where he was extensively involved in research analysis and assessment of a wide range of national security studies. He is a widely published author and has participated in numerous interagency defense and foreign policy symposiums.

Guy Roberts is currently a major in the U.S. Marine Corps serving as the international law legal advisor at Judge Advocate Division, Headquarters, Marine Corps, Washington, D.C. He is the legal advisor to the Marine Corps' Working Group on Combatting Terrorism and he is a member of the Department of Defense's Law of War Working Group. He received his B.A. (magna cum laude) from Arizona State University in 1972 and his J.D. from the University of Denver in 1975. He also holds degrees from the University of Southern California (A.M. International Relations, 1983), and Georgetown University (LLM International and Comparative Law, 1985). He is licensed to practice in Colorado, California, Arizona, Tenth Circuit Court of Appeals, Court of Military Appeals, and the U.S. Supreme Court.

Beth A. Salamanca is the director of security advisory services for McGeorge and Associates, Inc., an ordnance and technical security consulting firm. Before joining the firm, Ms. Salamanca served as a bomb disposal (EOD) officer for the U.S. Marine Corps. Her assignments included commanding a bomb disposal unit responsible for neutralizing live explosive ordance, and serving as an instructor and bomb security expert to the U.S. Department of State.

During her tenure with the State Department, Ms. Salamanca directed bomb security operations for numerous events including the United Nations General Assembly, Nato Ministerial and the 1984 Olympics. She has participated in training missions for U.S. ambassadorial protective personnel at high-threat embassies worldwide, served as a focal point for inter-agency liaison for explosives countermeasures, conducted post-blast investigations following the bombings of American embassies in Lebanon and Kuwait, and served as a member of a special delegation providing technical security to the British prime minister following the Brighton bombing. She has lectured on numerous occasions on bomb security topics, and has recently published a bomb security guidelines manual.

Robert M. Sayre is a senior career foreign service officer who has served as U.S. ambassador to Uruguay, Panama, and Brazil. Spending most of his thirty-five year foreign service career on Latin America, he served in Lima and Havana, and in Washington as director of Mexican affairs, as a senior member of the White House Staff, as principal deputy assistant secretary and acting assistant secretary for Latin American affairs. During 1981–84 he was director of counterterrorism and emergency planning for the Department of State.

Victoria Toensing is deputy assistant attorney general for the Criminal Division, Department of Justice. She has supervision for the fraud, appellate, and general litigation sections. The last has terrorism jurisdiction. She has also served as chief counsel for the Senate Select Committee on Intelligence and as an assistant U.S. attorney in the Eastern District of Michigan for five years. She has lectured and taught on national security and criminal law issues.

Charles F. Vance, as president of Vance International, heads a dynamic, full-service international security firm. During his fourteen years with the U.S. Secret Service, spanning four administrations, he coordinated the security arrangements for presidents, vice presidents, and numerous visiting heads of state. Mr. Vance is frequently called upon by the broadcast media for his expert commentary regarding incidents of terrorist violence. Additionally, he has presented expert testimony before the U.S. Senate. He has authored several articles and a monograph on related subjects.